W9-BRT-470

Praise for *When Prayers Aren't Answered*

"*When Prayers Aren't Answered* is a masterfully written appeal to recognize our intuitive understanding of life and God. With a deeply insightful sensitivity to the human condition, John Welshons asks us all to thoughtfully consider the assumptions under which we live much of our lives. Readers will experience a deep, long breath of spiritual fresh air. If the book resonates with your philosophy, you're on the right track. If it doesn't, reconsider the road you're on."

— Michael Adamse, PhD, author of *God's Shrink*

"John Welshons's strong, clear message brings us to the altar of the living God within. As clear as the work of Alan Watts and as strong as the devotional leanings of the heart, this book holds initiations for the true seeker."

— Stephen Levine, author of
A Year to Live and *Turning Toward the Mystery*

"This perceptive and insightful book looks into how our faith quivers when our prayers are unanswered. John gently entices us, through personal experience and engaging stories, to rejoice in each moment, reacquainting us with the eternal grace of wholehearted prayer."

— Nischala Joy Devi, author of
The Healing Path of Yoga and *The Secret Power of Yoga*

"Sometime in your life you have probably asked why your prayers hadn't been answered. And, most likely, you didn't get an answer to that question either. Now, in this compassionate and beautifully written book, John E. Welshons will help you find those answers."

— Allen Klein, author of *The Courage to Laugh:
Humor, Hope, and Healing in the Face of Death and Dying*

"John Welshons addresses some of life's most challenging spiritual questions with loving compassion and deep wisdom. *When Prayers Aren't Answered* will touch your heart and soul in a profound way, and it will leave you feeling peaceful and free."

— Mike Robbins, author of *Focus on the Good Stuff*

"John Welshons's insight and intuitive understanding of the human predicament gives one hope — hope that we will all learn to be happy in the face of 'unanswered prayers' in an unpredictable world. Simply put, John truly speaks from his heart, and for that we should all be grateful."

— Steve Adubato, PhD, Emmy Award–winning PBS broadcaster and author of *Speak from the Heart* and *Make the Connection*

"This is an eclectic, moving, poetic book of great wisdom. While reading it, I felt I was in a gentle, loving, peaceful place — a place in which I could understand what it means to be closer to God and closer to being the person that God wants me to be."

— Kent M. Keith, PhD, author of *Anyway: The Paradoxical Commandments*

When Prayers Aren't Answered

When Prayers Aren't Answered

John E. Welshons

New World Library
Novato, California

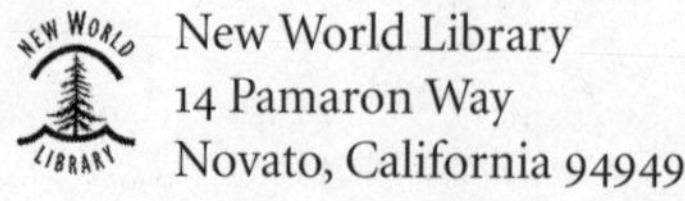

New World Library
14 Pamaron Way
Novato, California 94949

The experiences and stories used as examples throughout this book are true, although identifying details such as name and location have been changed to protect the privacy of others.

Text design and typography by Tona Pearce Myers

Library of Congress Cataloging-in-Publication Data
Welshons, John E.
When prayers aren't answered / by John E. Welshons.
p. cm.
Includes bibliographical references and index.
ISBN 978-1-57731-587-2 (hardcover : alk. paper)
1. Prayer. 2. Good and evil. 3. Suffering—Religious life. I. Title.
BL560.W47 2007
202'.118—dc22 2007025579

First printing, September 2007
ISBN-10: 1-57731-587-1
ISBN-13: 978-1-57731-587-2
Printed in Canada on 100% postconsumer-waste recycled paper

g New World Library is a proud member of the Green Press Initiative.

10 9 8 7 6 5 4 3 2 1

This book is dedicated to

Richard Carlson
(1961–2006)

a beloved friend and spiritual brother,
who, through his shining example,
taught us not to sweat the small stuff,
to acknowledge and embrace the big stuff,
to love everyone, without exception,
and to be happy, no matter what.

Let us not pray
to be sheltered
from dangers,
but to be fearless
when facing them.

RABINDRANATH TAGORE

Contents

Foreword

One day in the summer of 1999, when *Don't Sweat the Small Stuff* was just hitting its peak of success, I received a package in the mail containing the manuscript for a book entitled *Awakening from Grief*. The author, John Welshons, was a longtime friend and associate of two people I greatly admired, Ram Dass and Stephen Levine. I get many, many manuscripts from people asking for comments and endorsements, but there was just something very special about this one.

For one thing, grief had already touched my life profoundly. My dearest friend was killed in a car crash just two days prior to my wedding in 1981. My world was shattered. Shortly after that, I had the good fortune to spend a day with Stephen Levine in San Francisco.

What Stephen shared with me that day about grief and about life and death completely altered my perspective. I'm not sure what would have happened to me otherwise, but this close confrontation with death and loss became a major turning point in my life. In one brief moment of overwhelming sadness, my friend showed me how fleeting, uncertain, and precious life really is, and this single event inspired my speaking, writing, and teaching career. Because of this, I was intrigued to read this new book from a longtime friend and associate of Stephen's.

I absolutely loved *Awakening from Grief*! It contained some of the most beautiful writing I had ever encountered — unusual in the field of self-help books. I began talking about John and about his book in my lectures and seminars. And I resolved that he and I would become friends.

When we met a few months later, we quickly became much more than just friends. John is like a brother to me. He also has become one of my teachers. His words and his presence have comforted many, many thousands of people on this earth — and they have comforted me. I have never met anyone who walks his talk as much as John. I can't begin to tell you what a blessing it has been to have him in my life.

So when John first told me about this wonderful new book, *When Prayers Aren't Answered*, I offered to write this foreword without hesitation. I am quite certain that this book will help millions of people. With wisdom and compassion, John shows readers what to do when prayers aren't answered the way we want them to be. The teaching and writing the book contains are like a warm, comforting bath for the weary soul who may feel overtired and exhausted by life itself at times.

In it you will find timeless wisdom beautifully expressed. As he did in *Awakening from Grief*, John takes us into the heart of some of the most difficult experiences we human beings can have and then holds our hand and accompanies us through the darkness and back out into the Light of our own Soul. He can do this so skillfully because he has had so many encounters with loss, sadness, and pain in his own life, and he is very familiar with the paths that lead us back into the one true realm of healing — our own compassionate heart.

John is one of the rare "true" spiritual teachers. He is one of the most centered people I know, peaceful, and calm — seemingly in every circumstance. He does what he does not to get wealthy or famous but simply to help others. And his true gift is in making it all sound so doable. He deals with the most challenging aspects of life and yet makes it all seem like a natural part of being human. With John at our side, we feel like we can weather any storm life may send our way.

There is also something special about John that you might not pick up from reading his books. He is one of the funniest people I know! John has this amazing way of combining humor and wisdom, and I've never before known anyone who does that so effectively. Nevertheless, I have never once seen him use humor inappropriately. When the moment calls for seriousness and loving presence, John's heart is always open and his compassionate wisdom is always available. Over time, his sense of humor has really begun to sink in to my being. He has helped me immeasurably to see life differently, to be lighter and more spontaneous. Whenever I am with him or we talk on the phone or I get one of his wonderful emails, I just naturally feel peaceful, calm, and joyful. I feel a sense of trust and comfort that is far beyond what I feel with almost anyone else I know. I find myself smiling and relaxing, because John just naturally radiates those very precious qualities. What you will find in this wonderful book is reassurance — reassurance that through all of your trials and tribulations, through all of your confusion and doubt, through all of the sadness and difficulty that life has sent your way, you, too, have a dear and treasured friend accompanying you through the highs and the lows, holding your hand, never leaving your side. You will gain a new and refreshing perspective on life's difficulties and hardships, and on the spiritual opportunities that are present in virtually any circumstance.

This book will help you to see, and to know, that you are never alone. It will gently remind you that the most healing solution — to any problem — is more love.

To the amazing love that John helps us all experience, let me add my own, along with my deep gratitude for this opportunity to share my dear friend, and his incredibly beautiful new book, with you. May you be blessed to know the beauty and wisdom of your own soul!

Richard Carlson, PhD
Walnut Creek, California
December 2006

Editor's note: Richard passed away shortly after writing this foreword. He is deeply missed, but his work in the world lives on.

Acknowledgments

Special heartfelt, eternal thanks to my dear friend Scott Chesney for suggesting, over lunch one day, that I should write this book. He is an inspiration, and a beautiful living example of so many of the principles this book seeks to teach.

I thank Richard Carlson for having been one of the most treasured friends a human being could ever have. I thank him for his amazingly warm heart, his radiantly beautiful smile, his unfailingly loving friendship, his unflagging enthusiasm, and our many hilarious — sometimes poignant — conversations and emails.

I thank my beloved sister Judy for her effervescent love, cheerfulness, and humor, and for providing such a beautifully serene, sacred space in which to write this book.

I thank my dear friend Tom Decker for providing a beautiful "southern" sacred space where I could go to write when winter became inhospitable. And I thank him for so many wonderful conversations, and so many delicious cups of tea.

I thank my beloved sister Carole for being one of the greatest living examples of how to love God, love life, and find happiness, even when our human heart gets repeatedly broken.

I thank Georgia Hughes for her enthusiastic embrace of this project, for her keen eye, for her wise editorial instincts, and for being such a dear friend. I thank Paula Dragosh and Kristen Cashman for doing such a fine job of putting the final polish on the manuscript. And I thank Marc Allen, Munro Magruder, Kim Corbin, and the entire staff at New World Library for creating such a nurturing publishing environment.

I thank our Creator for the many prayers that have been answered.

And I thank my teachers for helping me to know what to do when prayers appeared to be unanswered.

I thank Meher Baba for being Love.

I thank Neem Karoli Baba for being Love merged with humor.

I thank Ram Dass for being my greatest spiritual friend and brother, for showing — by example — how to transmute spirit into form, and how to understand "fierce grace."

I thank Stephen and Ondrea Levine for showing how beautifully and sweetly Divine Love can manifest through human forms.

And I thank my beloved Maureen Murray… "Mozey"… "Ananda Mozey Ma" for her penetrating wisdom, her crystal-clear insight, her awesome love, and her tiny, powerful hands that send abundant, measureless warmth and healing out into the universe.

Introduction

Prayer and love are really learned
in the hour when prayer becomes impossible
and your heart turns to stone.

THOMAS MERTON

This is a book about communicating with our Creator, with God, with the Divine, with whatever you wish to call the One Light that underlies all of creation.

At some point in our lives, most of us have struggled to understand just how we do that, why we do it, and whether or not it works. And if we are honest, most of us will have to admit that there have been times when we have questioned whether there actually is a "Creator," whether He hears us, and whether or not He cares.

This book is rooted in the conviction that talking with God is absolutely possible and immeasurably helpful. Human history has been filled with amazing, awe-inspiring stories of lives dramatically changed by "miraculous" events, events that often seem to have occurred in response to prayer.

But there are also moments when, despite impassioned prayer, miracles have not been forthcoming. In these pages you will find unique, practical insights and methods for understanding those frustrating, life-changing moments. This book offers help with those times when you, or someone you love, have begged the Creator for protection, reassurance, or relief from suffering, and have heard no answer, found no miracle, and seen no mystic rainbow to wash away your woes or to reassure you that God is in control and that He cares about you and your loved ones.

It is not the intent of this book to change your religious beliefs. It does not seek to examine, refute, or undermine any religious tradition or philosophical perspective. Nor does it contain any theological or philosophical perspective it seeks to convert you to.

The intent is, rather, to explore those moments in life when our belief system fails us, when it fails to help us understand or make sense of the events of our lives and our world, especially those that are confusing, frightening, infuriating, or heartbreaking.

No matter what tradition we practice, many of us, at one time or another, will have a "crisis in faith." That crisis often comes when our understanding of God does not match up with the events around us, when it seems that a God who is all-loving could not possibly allow things to happen the way they are happening.

Every great religious tradition has the wisdom and the knowledge to help us in these moments of confusion and despair. But over the course of centuries, that wisdom has often become lost or obscured. Sometimes the teachers we have been exposed to have a limited understanding of their own tradition and a limited ability to help in times of crisis. They may be well-meaning, well-intended people, but they may not know exactly what to do or say in every situation.

You are probably reading this book to gain insight about something your belief system hasn't explained to your satisfaction. Approaching these issues is challenging, because personal religious beliefs can be so strong. As a writer I sometimes feel I am walking on eggs. My hope is that these words will be accessible to as many readers as possible, no matter what your religious or philosophical perspective is.

Many of the stories, insights, and practices contained here have been gathered over the course of forty years of studying world religions. I have learned a great deal from other cultures and traditions, which has helped illuminate areas of my own tradition where explanation and understanding seemed limited. It is my hope that this opportunity to look at life and at the "spiritual path" a little differently will not undermine your faith but will enhance it.

To some, what is offered may seem radically new. To others, it may just be slightly different. What we are looking at are areas of human life where we often get stuck, areas where our religious and cultural training has offered us limited tools for dealing with life's uncertainty.

It is my sincere hope that this book will help lighten your burdens and give you a fresh, inspiring new approach to your own spiritual path. It is up to you, the reader, to trust your own sense of what works and what doesn't. It is up to you to use these insights or to conclude that they don't fit with the way you experience Truth.

Recently, in a discussion about this book, one of my friends said, "There is no such thing as unanswered prayer. If we think our prayers aren't being answered, it means we aren't listening carefully enough to hear the answers."

Her statement seemed a little cold, especially considering the depth of despair many of us experience when our prayers appear to be unanswered. But there is also some truth to what she said. It is entirely possible that our prayers haven't been left unanswered but that we don't like the answer we've gotten.

Many of us have grown up in religious traditions that have given us a very simplistic notion about God and prayer. We sometimes tend to think of our Creator as a kind of cosmic vending machine: put in a prayer and get what you want.

But, obviously, that doesn't always work. And when it doesn't, we often find ourselves thrown headlong into some of the most difficult experiences of our lives. Not only are we facing hardships, challenges, and heartache, but the hardships, challenges, and heartache get multiplied when we fear that perhaps there is no God or that God doesn't care.

In the course of this exploration we will make the assumption that our Creator has given — and is giving us — everything we need to find love, happiness, and peace of mind, no matter what the circumstances of our lives are, no matter what is happening to our bodies, our lives, and our world.

It is my sincere hope that the journey we are embarking on will help each of us understand how to feel connected to our Creator... to God... in every moment... in every circumstance... no matter what.

My prayer is that you will come away from it with tools that help you know and experience without a doubt that you are *eternally loved, eternally cared for, and eternally safe.*

Honor the Light within you!

Author's Note

To simplify one aspect of this book, when I refer to the "Creator" or "God," I generally use masculine pronouns. This is in no way intended to ignore the sensibilities of those who don't feel comfortable with the notion that God is exclusively male. The use of male pronouns in referring to our Creator is not intended to define or imbue that Creator with any form of gender bias.

My own sense is that the Creator is beyond gender. It has no gender.

But we are human beings with human minds, and at times it can be useful to ascribe some human qualities to our Creator to help us find a familiar way to relate to Him, Her, or It. So for the purposes of convenience, I will refer to the Creator as "He" or "Him." I will also, at times, use concepts like "the loving arms of God." God — in Its formless state — has no arms. But since nothing is separate from God, we might also say that all arms are God's arms. Sometimes we need God to manifest in a form that has human characteristics, and God can certainly do that. Sometimes we will use the imagery of romantic love to characterize the relationship between human and Creator as one of lover and beloved.

One friend of mine used to say, "I am perfectly comfortable using the word *God* because I have no idea what it means." That is, roughly, our predicament. Whenever we talk about God, we are attempting to explain the unexplainable. We are attempting to give form and structure to that which has neither form nor structure.

But we have inquiring minds, and our minds want to know. In the course of our journey together we will come to understand that the *real* knowledge we seek is ever present and everlasting . . . deep within our own hearts . . . right under our own noses.

PART ONE

When the World Turns Upside Down

For the pleasures that come from the world
bear in them sorrows to come.
They come and they go,
they are transient:
Not in them do the wise find joy.

LORD KRISHNA, BHAGAVAD GITA

CHAPTER 1

A Look at Our Human Predicament

God, grant me the serenity
To accept the things I cannot change
The courage to change the things I can,
And the wisdom to know the difference.

REINHOLD NIEBUHR, "THE SERENITY PRAYER"

There are moments in life when we feel there is nowhere to turn. It seems God has forsaken us, that all hope for happiness and peace of mind is lost. We have offered impassioned prayers. We have begged, pleaded, cajoled.

We have bargained with God. We have promised that if only this one deeply longed-for desire is fulfilled, we will change our ways, become more spiritual, give up our self-centeredness and unkindness, renounce our addictive and unhealthy behaviors. We have prayed to have some desperate wish fulfilled, to have what we feel we *need* to be happy. Sometimes we are asking for something mundane and simple. Other times we are asking for a "miracle" to occur.

We ask for some healing. The disease gets worse.

We ask for a loved one to be healed and protected. They die.

We ask for our financial life to improve. We go bankrupt.

We ask for a beloved partner to help us heal a damaged relationship. They file for divorce.

We ask for the hurricane on the horizon to be diverted out to sea. Our community gets hit head-on.

We ask for a war to end. It becomes even more violent.

Sometimes we ask to *feel* the presence of God, of the Divine, in our lives. We want to know that God is here with us. Yet all we feel is a blank, empty, meaningless void.

At other times we use prayer as a means of discovering the power of the Divine. We ask God to prove His existence to us, to affirm His love for us, to demonstrate His power and dominion over everything.

In circumstances where we already feel *connected* to that power and presence, we sometimes ask the Divine to affirm that our prayers are heard, that our devotion is rewarded, that what we long for is in harmony with what God has planned for us.

Surely an all-good God wouldn't allow evil, disease, and suffering to exist. Surely an all-loving God would want us to be happy. Surely an all-powerful God can protect us from illness, misfortune, and danger. Yet there are times when our most impassioned, fervent, deeply felt prayers seem to be ignored.

We ask, and get rebuffed. Without explanation or comfort. We have identified the door we wish our Creator to open for us, and it is slammed in our face with a seemingly heartless indifference.

How do we go on? How do we find our faith?

How do we find our faith . . . *again*?

~

There are many perspectives we can take at these moments. We can conclude that God is not all-good, all-loving, all-powerful. We can conclude that God does not love us. We can conclude that we are being punished for something.

We can even conclude that there is *no* God.

But what if our "unanswered" prayer is not a demonstration that God is imperfect, or that God is not all-powerful, or that our relationship to God is imperfect?

What if our unanswered prayer is not meant to punish us or torture us? What if our unanswered prayer is not a demonstration that there is no God? What if our unanswered prayer is, rather, an invitation for us to discover God by looking deeper?

What if our unanswered prayer is showing us that it is our understanding of God that is imperfect?

Surveys, polls, and research studies consistently show that most human beings believe in God. And most people who believe in God offer prayers to God.

To determine whether the act of praying causes any scientifically measurable effect in peoples' lives, a number of recent research studies have focused specifically on the effects of prayer. These studies have questioned whether prayer makes any verifiable positive change in the life and health of those who pray, and those who are recipients of prayer.

One of the foremost spokespersons for this research is Dr. Larry Dossey. His books *Prayer Is Good Medicine* and *Healing Words* have explored clinical evidence that seems to demonstrate that prayer can have both measurable and verifiable positive effects. Many studies appear to show a correlation between positive change in people's lives and health when they pray, and when prayers are offered on their behalf.

What is most striking about this research is that it has also shown that, in certain circumstances, an individual need not be a believer and need not even know that prayers have been offered for him or her. It is still possible, at times, for such individuals to receive the benefit.

In many spiritual communities, there is a basic underlying belief that answered prayers offer positive proof of the existence of God, the power of God, and the all-merciful nature of God. Answered prayers are interpreted as demonstrations of the existence of that which is beyond human understanding... an all-powerful Supreme Being who can — at will — supersede the fundamental laws of science and can orchestrate "miraculous" events.

Furthermore, answered prayers are often interpreted as implicit confirmation that the person who prays and the recipient of the prayer have won God's favor, have somehow pleased the Creator, causing Him to bless them with healing, happiness, success, and relief from suffering.

If we acknowledge all of the evidence that miracles can and do occur, and we accept the scientific data that indicates a demonstrable correlation between prayer and positive change in the world of form, how do we begin to understand what it means when our prayers appear to go unanswered?

At the outset, let's set aside the belief that having our prayers answered *the way we want them to be* is a measure of our worthiness in the eyes of God. Let us assume that we *are* worthy in the eyes of God. Let us assume that God does hear our prayers. And let us assume that there is no such thing as an unanswered prayer. Let us assume that our Creator is benevolent. Let us assume that our Creator — God — is Love itself. And let us assume that God does not want us to suffer.

Let us assume, also, when we are suffering, that God has already offered us some means of alleviating our suffering, which we have been ignoring or which we have yet to discover.

God's love does not always come in the form of giving us what we want. It does, however, always come in a form that is enduring, ever present, and eternally available... no matter what is going on in our lives.

Consider for a moment the possibility that what we are being given, when our prayers aren't answered the way we want them to be, is the opportunity to develop a *deeper* relationship with God, a *deeper* sense of inner peace. Perhaps our insistence that God give us everything we want when we want it and run the universe the way we think it should be run is actually standing in the way of our ability to *know* God. Our desire for things to be different than they are is what keeps us out of sync with the world we are living in and keeps us disconnected from the experience of love and contentment that is available to us in this moment.

This book is a journey of discovery of that which is always available to us to lighten our load... to bring us back into our natural state of joy and connection with our Creator, even when our lives are difficult and even when our lives have been filled with loss, sadness, and disappointment.

There are two primary methods available to us for establishing an inner dialogue with God. They are prayer and meditation.

Prayer can be defined as "talking to God."

Meditation can be defined as "listening to God."

It is a simple but profound distinction.

For more than thirty-five years I have focused on meditation as the primary path to God. But recently I began to reflect on how the two routes to connection with the Divine can work in harmony. I realized that I do pray, I often pray, and sometimes my prayers aren't answered *the way I want them to be.*

Since the mid-1970s, one of the primary outward forms of spiritual practice in my life has been working with people who have experienced some profound life change that has left them heartbroken and devastated. I have worked with people going through divorce, people who have lost their fortunes, people recovering from addiction, people who have had spinal cord injuries, people who have been diagnosed with some difficult and frightening disease, people who are dying, and people who are grieving the loss of a beloved partner, child, parent, or friend. Through all of these experiences I have come to recognize that the prayers of many good, kind, decent, loving people aren't necessarily answered the way they want them to be.

A couple of years ago, at the Pacific Church of Religious Science in San Diego, I gave the first public presentation I have ever given on the subject of prayer. When the minister called to invite me to speak, I asked, "What would you like me to speak about?" She said, "How about some aspect of prayer? The month that you will be here is our month to focus on the power of prayer."

Given the nature of the work I do, somewhat jokingly I said, "How would you feel about a presentation called 'What to do when prayers aren't answered . . . the way we want them to be'?"

She loved it!

And when I spoke that Sunday morning, the congregation gave me an extraordinarily warm welcome before I had even said a word! It was an embracing wave of enthusiastic applause mixed with a deep spirit of gratitude.

I sensed that their enthusiasm arose because unanswered prayer is seldom discussed. To even address the issue is sometimes felt to be an expression of negativity that might actually undercut the power of prayer. In many circles, the thinking is, "Don't consider that your prayer might not work. Don't discuss the times it doesn't. Just keep praying and affirming."

But that doesn't offer solace to the millions and millions of us who have prayed for something that we didn't get or that didn't happen. And as a result of that unanswered prayer, many of us have had life-changing experiences that, for some, have undermined belief in God, in the benevolent nature of the universe, and in the power of prayer.

In many cases, when that happens, we don't return to church or to our spiritual community. We may become disappointed, cynical, and angry. We may spend years — perhaps the rest of our life — angry at God and alienated from our spiritual community. Those of us whose faith was already a little shaky may have asked that a prayer be answered to establish a stronger faith. Even those whose faith was strong may lose it entirely in the wake of an unanswered prayer. In these cases, many of us are left without support from our spiritual community and with no context for understanding the experiences that have left us so devastated.

Even if our reaction isn't that extreme, we are often left a little disoriented, a little distrusting. Our confusion can be amplified if we have previously experienced a profound answer to prayer or if someone we know has had some miraculous intervention in his or her life.

But now there is no answer, and all we feel is a damp, dark, heartless, empty void. We begin to wonder if our previous experience was an aberration — perhaps not really an answered prayer but just a coincidence. We doubt our faith. We wonder if God is really in control or if God really cares. We may even doubt the existence of God.

There is a pervasive sense in many of our religious and spiritual traditions that if our lives are touched by difficulty and sadness, we are not praying "correctly" or God is punishing us for something.

One minister spoke with me recently about how happy he is to see his tradition "maturing."

He said, "When I first joined my church it seemed like most of the members and most of the clergy were primarily concerned with 'princes, palaces, and parking spaces'! They only seemed to be interested in using their faith to procure the people and things they wanted in their lives. It was considered inappropriate to even talk about the difficult moments in life. And if a person wasn't able to use prayer and visualization to immediately manifest the partner of their dreams, the home of their dreams, the income of their dreams, and a parking space every time they needed one, they began to feel shame. They felt unworthy. They felt less spiritual than the people whose lives were going well. And since the church offered them no guidance for dealing with those difficult times in life, they would eventually stop coming to church."

He went on to say, "I am happy to see that changing now. Now we are better able to see the hand of Divinity... of the Creator... in every moment of life."

Every lecture and workshop I give in some way reflects on the inevitability of change in our life and in our world. Every one of us will have to deal with changes we don't like. The way we react to unwanted, unexpected loss in our lives, and to anything in our universe that we don't like, is the foundation of our grief. In essence, it is the resistance to change — so firmly entrenched in our minds — that creates our grief.

We can rail against the seeming injustice of this sometimes random, chaotic, unfair world. We can complain, feel victimized, and believe that God, or the universe, has somehow screwed up, has somehow conspired to single us out for punishment and misery.

Or we can look for the deeper truth in our life and in the universe. We can look for that which is eternal and unchanging. We can ask how this unwanted change in our lives might somehow make it easier to find God, to find the Divine, to connect with our Creator. Even if it doesn't seem to make that process easier at the moment, what it can do is give us the fuel and motivation for our spiritual journey.

When I speak in churches, I often ask the congregation to reflect for a moment on what prompted their search for God.

"You might think that suffering is evidence of some mistake that God has made," I say. "So let me just ask how many of you are here because your lives were always just *filled* with happiness? How many of you joined this church because you had so much love, so much joy, so much health, and so much financial abundance in your life that you just had to come to church to thank God?"

I ask for a show of hands. Usually, none rise.

The congregation gets what I am saying. The vast majority of us embark on our spiritual quest, our search for God, our pursuit of Truth, our search for meaning because we are confused, frightened, and often in either physical or emotional pain.

This is not to say that we should seek pain and suffering but merely to suggest that when suffering comes into our lives we should allow for the possibility that it might have something to teach us.

Moments of unanswered prayer and profound disappointment offer us a unique, if somewhat unwanted, opportunity to embark on a more focused search for God. Often what loss and disappointment do is strip away things in our lives that have been diverting our attention away from God. At this moment, that may be a difficult concept to grasp, but stay tuned. In the pages of this book we will begin to explore the many ways in which God, Truth, happiness, and inner peace are always available to us, no matter what happens in our lives.

Many of us have been raised in spiritual traditions that seem to suffer from a certain incompleteness, a limited understanding of what God and spirituality encompass, and an inability to comprehend and respond effectively to matters of human experience that fall outside the boundaries of the officially sanctioned dogma or story line.

One extraordinary example I will never forget came shortly after the publication of my first book, *Awakening from Grief*. I was on tour around the country doing lectures, workshops, and book-signing events. I was going to be in California, so I contacted a church in one of the towns I was visiting and offered to do a presentation.

The minister responded with disdain. She said, "Your material would have *no* place in our church. We never present programs that don't deal with the positive side of life."

I was a little stunned. But I couldn't help myself, I had to ask, "Does that mean that no one in your church dies? Does that mean that no one in your church has loved ones who die? And does that mean that no one in your church grieves when someone they love dies, or when they experience loss, sadness, fear, and disappointment?"

I could feel that my questions irritated her. She wouldn't answer them. And the response she did give was rather terse.

"I'm sorry, there's just no place for grief in our church. We talk about good health, happiness, and prosperity. We don't want to depress people."

I really couldn't believe what I was hearing. And I couldn't believe how shortsighted and unrealistic her perspective was. But it is certainly not unique in our culture or in our culture's religious institutions. Many of us find a great deal of solace, comfort, and support in our religious communities when we face serious life challenges. But, unfortunately, far too many of us don't.

In more than thirty years of doing this work, I have consistently seen how difficult it is for people to find meaningful understanding, open-hearted acceptance, and loving support when challenges and tragedies enter their lives. And the most devastating damage I have seen done in the lives of these individuals has come in situations where their spiritual community *shamed* them for experiencing grief.

I have seen that shaming done in so many ways. In general, it is done by communicating that if one is truly faithful, one would never grieve . . . one would always know that the tragedy is God's will and that God knows best, *or* that their loved one "is in a better place." Grief and sadness are viewed as selfish, self-indulgent, and even antithetical to faith.

In some spiritual communities, tragedies are seen as punishment from a wrathful God, leaving those who experience them to wonder how they could have done something so unforgivable, so reprehensible that God, who has been defined as all-loving, would single them out for misery, would feel that they deserve to have such an awful experience, to have their life shattered, to have their fragile, tender human heart crushed so violently.

If our Creator *is* Love itself, the belief that we might cause Him to lash out with seemingly wanton wrath and destruction, to act in what would appear to be a decidedly unloving manner, can do little else but make us feel like despicable wretches, unworthy of being connected to the Love that *is* our Creator.

One young woman I counseled had been married less than three years when her twenty-five-year-old husband was brutally murdered in a grisly random killing in Hartford, Connecticut. He was shot by an absolute stranger — for no apparent reason — in broad daylight.

As soon as the news of her husband's death reached their church, members of the spiritual community rushed to the grieving widow's side. But rather than comfort her in her time of incomprehensible, overwhelming grief, they chose instead to conduct an inquisition aimed at uncovering "where the sin was" in her household. So the message she received from her spiritual community — in the deepest, darkest hours of her grief — was not one of compassion and empathy but a heartless diatribe on how only sinners would be the recipients of such cruel punishment from God. The obvious implication was that this random, senseless murder was God's wrath raining down upon a sinful couple... or, perhaps, a sinful wife. The message she received was that her husband's random killing must have been *her* fault.

The response of this young woman's spiritual community was one of the most glaring examples of human cruelty I have ever witnessed. But it is not unusual. And the most heartbreaking thing was that the young widow actually believed their finger-pointing accusations. In subsequent months and years this wonderful young woman began acting out a course of astonishing self-destruction in her life. Only years later did she realize the toll that her spiritual community's self-righteous judgment had taken on her. After extensive counseling, she finally realized that at some level she had come to believe that she deserved to be abused. She finally began to see that the perverse theology that led her to be guilt-ridden and shamed — a theology she had been told was absolute truth — was actually a perversely twisted distortion of the love, compassion, and forgiveness Jesus taught.

So many religious teachings in all traditions do not take into account the fact that we are human beings with human emotions. We may strive to evolve and grow spiritually, but we do not discard our human emotions at the drop of a hat.

I'm not even sure we are supposed to discard our human emotions. One great spiritual teacher was asked what it means to be spiritual. His answer was that it meant to be 100 percent human *and* 100 percent Divine.

There is a wonderful story about a great Buddhist teacher who had spent years teaching his students about the impermanent nature of life in form. A fundamental tenet of Buddhist philosophy is the recognition that everything in form changes. The attachment to any form and the resistance to change are the causes of our suffering. The same principle is expressed in the biblical phrase, "Lay not up treasures where moth and rust doth corrupt."[1]

One day, the Buddhist teacher's teenage son died suddenly in a tragic accident. The teacher was devastated. His students found him weeping and wailing, obviously in excruciating emotional pain about the loss of his beloved son.

The students were perplexed and disappointed. They felt compelled to confront their teacher with what they saw as a contradiction in his being.

"Master," they said, "why are you weeping? Haven't you been teaching us for years about the illusory, impermanent nature of all things in form? Haven't you been teaching us that clinging and attachment are the causes of suffering? Now here you are carrying on about this death. Aren't *you* experiencing clinging and attachment? Isn't it *all* an illusion?"

"Yes," said the master, "it is *all* an illusion. And the death of a child is the most *painful* illusion of all."

Spiritual paths that are truly effective, and truly useful to their adherents, offer practices and perspectives that encompass all of life's potential experiences. They offer practices and perspectives that deal with the inescapable fact that we are human beings with human emotions. Truly helpful spiritual teachings also acknowledge that we live in a physical universe where change is inevitable, often unpredictable, and not always something we are happy about.

Unfortunately, many spiritual traditions are somewhat limited in their ability to meet the intensity of human experience and human emotion with genuinely helpful guidance and wisdom. In the more than thirty years that I have worked with people going through extremely difficult life transitions and losses, I have too often heard that when people looked to their spiritual community or their religious teachings for help, it wasn't there.

One wonderful woman named Chris shared some interesting insights. Her beloved twelve-year-old son, Teddy, died after a long, painful struggle with Hodgkin's disease. From the moment he was diagnosed, she prayed incessantly for him to be healed. After his death, Chris went through nearly two years of seemingly unrelenting emotional agony and despair. She was deeply wounded and angry at God. She said, "I felt like my mind, my heart, my life, and my faith were all just shattered. I was so angry at God that I couldn't bear to set foot in my synagogue."

Just before I met her, she had begun to feel some glimmers of lightness and joy returning to her life. I asked, "What has been helpful to you in finding joy again?"

Chris thought for a moment. Then she spoke. "I went into therapy for a while. But I don't think the therapist could really comprehend the depths of my despair. He seemed confused by it, and somewhat clueless about how to help. So therapy wasn't very useful.

"And my rabbi would come over to my house from time to time. He's a wonderful, loving person. I think my grief made him feel awkward and uncomfortable. He would usually wind up offering a few spiritual platitudes and then would abruptly leave. And frankly, I don't think he really believed what he was saying."

She was silent for a moment. Then she spoke again. "The greatest help came from my two dear friends, Mary and Shirley. They are neighbors of mine. I've known them for years. Our children grew up together. For months after Teddy died, Mary and Shirley would come over to my house every afternoon and cry with me. That was helpful."

Isn't that ironic? Our culture has so often treated tears as a sign of weakness. Many people avoid being in the presence of a friend or relative who is going through a difficult time because they are afraid they might say or do something that will cause that person to cry. Yet in truth the people who handle life's difficulties most effectively and in the healthiest manner are those who feel free to cry and to freely share their tears with others.

Again and again I have heard people say that when life becomes overwhelmingly difficult and frightening, when events happen that undermine our faith, our trust, and our happiness, when our hearts are broken and there seems to be no way to understand, explain, or comprehend what we are going through, the things that are *truly* helpful and *truly* healing are love and community — the feeling that we are not alone . . . that we have friends whose hearts are big enough to hold our pain without judgment or aversion.

There really isn't very much the human mind can do, with intellectual explanations, psychological theories, philosophical discourses, scriptural passages, or ancient story lines, that can heal our hearts when they are broken.

But a sense of loving community can.

~

Let us make one fundamental assumption: that God *is* Love. And that love is within us. We can never lose it. When we feel love, we are feeling God. The more love we feel, the closer we are to God. And when we lose ourselves in love we become truly connected with God. We become pure expressions of God's love in this world. Love is where happiness lies. Love is the only achievement that can bring real and lasting fulfillment.

In the Bible, we are told, "Whenever two or more are gathered in my name, there I am."[2] We could also say, "Whenever two or more are gathered in the name of Love, we are experiencing God."

In his wonderful book *Connect: Twelve Vital Ties That Open Your Heart, Lengthen Your Life, and Deepen Your Soul*, Dr. Edward M. Hallowell writes that in nearly thirty years of practicing psychiatry, he has consistently observed one fascinating truth: what really seems to help his clients — more than his expertise in psychiatric treatment — is their ability to cultivate the sense of connection to other people, to their community, to something larger than themselves.

> As a psychiatrist, I can always tell when my patients are starting to get better, because they start to increase their connections. They see more of their friends, or they deepen their relationships at work, or they rediscover an old interest like gardening or sailing, or they start going to religious services, or they get closer to their extended family, or they start having more fun with their immediate family. Far more telling than financial gains or other kinds of trophies, increased connection reflects improved emotional health. It also creates it.[3]

When we have problems, when our hopes are frustrated, when our hearts are "broken," many of us tend to *close* our hearts. We withdraw and disconnect. We make the assumption that our problem or our loss has disconnected us from love and from our ability to be happy. We decide that it is just too painful to allow ourselves to feel love. We react with fear. We get angry and depressed. We disconnect from the love within us. We say, "I won't let myself be so vulnerable. I won't let myself get hurt again."

We close our hearts at exactly the moment we most need them to be *open*.

When we feel disconnected from love, the world we live in inevitably looks threatening and dangerous. As long as our hearts stay closed, we have no real opportunity for healing.

The simple formula is:

The more we love, the closer we are to God.

The opposite is also true:

When we are fearful, angry, and disconnected, we have drifted away from God.

The more fearful we are, the more angry we are, the more disconnected we are, the further we are from God. Not separate from God. It would be impossible for us to ever be separate from God. But we can spend much of our life disconnected from our awareness of God. In some sense, God might be compared with the sun. It is always shining. And God is always loving, always offering us peace, always offering joy.

When we become enmeshed in life's fears, frustrations, difficulties, and heartbreak, all of those dark emotions block our ability to feel the presence of God within us, just like dark storm clouds block the light of the sun.

But the sun is always shining. And God's Light is always shining. No matter how severe the storms are, it never stops shining. On any cloudy, dreary, stormy, frightening day, if we can rise above the clouds in an airplane, we see that beyond all of the temporary darkness, the Light is always shining.

Getting back into that Light, the Light of God, is the path to healing. It is often most readily accomplished by connecting with other human beings.

When asked about prayer, the great Indian spiritual teacher Meher Baba would remind the questioner that we are all inextricably connected with our Creator, at all times. There is simply no way to be separate from our Creator. Our sense of separation from our Creator — and from each other — stems from a fundamental misunderstanding about our existence.

So our Creator, he said, has no choice but to listen to our prayers and to grant us whatever we ask for. But Meher Baba would also point out that our prayers may not be answered when we want them to be, or even how we want them to be. Sometimes, in certain circumstances, we might find that when our prayer *is* answered, we may no longer really want what we were asking for. What at one time seemed like a blessing and a relief might later be seen as a burden.

Meher Baba suggested that the highest form of prayer is merely asking for the love of God. He suggested that we ask to feel God's love, no matter what; to give love, no matter what; to forgive others, and ourselves, no matter what; to learn how to be kind, generous, honest, and sincere, no matter what.[4]

Ultimately, perhaps the greatest challenge of all is to ask that we might learn how to be happy in this world of unpredictable, unexpected, unwanted change.

This book is offered to all of us as a beginner's manual for exploring just how we do that.

CHAPTER 2

The Treasure Once Found . . .

The student gains by daily increment.
The Way is gained by daily loss.

TAO TE CHING

A few years ago I was going through what was without a doubt the most difficult time of my life. It was a period characterized by heartbreaking losses and seemingly endless disappointments. I had spent many years doing something I never wanted to do — running a business my sisters and I inherited when our father died. I never liked the business, but shortly after our father's death, my sisters turned to me and asked me to run it. I thought about it, prayed about it, meditated about it, and eventually agreed to do it part-time for six months. It wound up being full-time for twelve years.

After many attempts, we finally sold the business. That freed me to do what I *really* wanted to do, what I felt called to do, what I intuitively sensed God was asking me to do. I used the money from the sale to invest in a new business that focused on enhancing spiritual education and awareness in our culture through lectures, workshops, and publications.

It was a great blessing to have what seemed like a comfortable nest egg to invest in the new business, to have the opportunity to hire the best people available, and to produce all of our products and services with a high level of quality and care. At the time it seemed like God had rewarded the service to my family by giving me financial security to do work that was closer to my heart, work that emerged from an intuitive sense of my life's purpose and what I was supposed to be doing.

I began each day with a prayer of gratitude. I asked for Divine guidance. I visualized the successful completion of each day's tasks. I visualized each task contributing to the realization of the mission of the business. I ended each day with a prayer of thanksgiving and gratitude.

But after several years of hard work, extensive travel, and many sixteen-hour days, the nest egg that had originally funded the business had dwindled dramatically. While I had poured every ounce of creativity and energy I could muster into making the business a success, there were moments when it seemed like everything that could possibly go wrong was going wrong. My biggest corporate customer — a company that was responsible for about 80 percent of my income — went bankrupt. That caused a ripple of panic and unrest throughout the entire industry I served. Then 9/11 happened, and businesspeople became understandably skittish about air travel. Conventions and corporate meetings, the bread and butter of public speakers, were drastically curtailed.

I felt like a pilot whose aircraft was roaring down a runway, who suddenly realized that the plane was too heavy to take off in the atmospheric conditions that were present, yet it was too late to stop without crashing into the trees at the end of the runway. So the only thing to do was to keep going, keep giving it every bit of energy and thrust I could muster, to try to get it into the air.

Just before I realized that the new business was in trouble, my wife and I had become enmeshed in some heartbreaking, perplexing marital discord.

We tried, and tried, and tried to heal our relationship. We saw a total of seven different counselors, individually and as a couple. We prayed. We meditated. Still, we separated.

Eventually I found myself alone, in the apartment I moved into following the separation. Every week I was struggling to put together enough money to pay the bills and keep the business afloat. One very lonely Friday afternoon, I received a call telling me that a program I had been scheduled to present the following week with a large number of people registered — something that would have produced enough income to cover expenses for several months — had to be canceled because the facility where it was taking place had experienced a boiler explosion and fire, and was going to have to be closed indefinitely!

Now, even income that seemed assured had suddenly, unpredictably, evaporated. That Friday afternoon, I reached my breaking point. I fell to my knees and sobbed... hot, fevered, steaming tears pouring down my cheeks... overcome with despair, frustration, and humiliation. For several years, *all* of my energy had been going into trying to make my marriage and my business successful. It was what I understood God *wanted* me to do. Everything in my intuition told me that this was the correct course of action.

But despite my best efforts, my marriage to a wonderful woman had failed. And my business seemed to be failing. Rather than being able to look toward retirement, I was facing financial difficulties *and* divorce court. After nearly twenty years of hard work, I felt like everything I had worked for was falling apart. I was completely exhausted from all of the travel and long hours. I even felt that my physical health was in jeopardy. I was exasperated, devastated, and totally humiliated.

From my knees, I looked up at the altar in my living room. Then

I looked up higher, and shouted out to God, *"I really could have used some help here!"*

I sat back on my haunches, wiped away the tears, hung my head, and took a breath. I closed my eyes.

In the ensuing silence, somewhere inside me, I heard a soft yet powerful voice. It was a velvetlike voice of strength and compassion tempered with... *sweetness.* It whispered gently. And it roared with certainty.

"I *am* helping you!"

~

In the intensity of the moment, I was too emotionally overwrought to appreciate an unmistakable experience of Grace. Rather than being awed by this Divine visitation, I was actually *irritated.*

"Helping me to do *what*?!" I shot back defiantly. "I see precious little evidence of *any* help!"

I paused, assuming that my impudence would cause this benevolent voice of Grace to withdraw. I was *so* irritated that I'm not sure I wanted to hear anything further.

But the voice returned with a reassuringly compassionate certainty and conviction. "I am helping you to find the treasure which — once found — is *never* lost."

~

Tears poured from my eyes. My chest heaved. My body shook.

But this time the tears were not tears of frustration and self-pity. Now they were tears of gratitude and awe. Now they were tears that sprang from the incredibly transformative, reassuring feeling of being reminded — as I have been reminded at many critical moments in my life — that we are never alone and that no matter how confusing and chaotic life sometimes seems, there is always order and lawfulness behind it.

For the next few hours I just sat in meditation and reflected on the meaning of that phrase.

"The treasure which — once found — is *never* lost."

Those hours turned into days, the days into weeks. Each morning and each evening when I sat in meditation, I would reflect on the meaning of those words.

"The treasure which — once found — is *never* lost."

In the years that have followed, I have continued to reflect on that simple phrase. It has become the centerpiece of my life.

That phrase — offered to me in the depths of some of the greatest despair and confusion I have ever known — has given me the ability to perceive the events of my life differently. It has given me the recognition that what is being offered, in the midst of sometimes devastating loss and seemingly endless frustrations, might be something much greater than what was being asked for.

"Never lost."

In other words, *eternal*.

I was being offered the opportunity to find something... *eternal*.

~

I thought back on one of my teachers in India. He used to like to play a game with his students called "Seven Tiles." This teacher had "invented" the game. He would explain it to the participants. But each time he and his students played, the rules were different. No matter what happened, the teacher always won. When the students lost, they had to get down on their knees and rub their noses on the ground.

After a while, they would become irritated.

"This isn't fair!" they would say.

"What do you mean?" the teacher would ask.

"Well, we *always* lose! And *you* always win!"

The teacher smiled. "What you don't yet understand is that the loser *is* the winner."

~

What could that statement possibly mean?

"The loser *is* the winner."

In the mystical branches of the world's great religious traditions, paradox and contradiction are the fundamental tools of spiritual teaching. They are used to diminish the power of the rational mind. The spiritual traditions based in meditation and inner work have always seen the rational mind as the biggest obstacle standing in the way of direct experience of Truth... direct awareness of God. Simply stated, we cannot experience God by thinking. To "know" God, we need to cultivate levels of awareness beyond thought.

The problem is, our "rational" mind desperately wants to understand God's purpose in our life and in our world. It looks at our life and our world with judgment, defining much of what it sees as unacceptable. When our life and our world are defined as unacceptable, we are forced either to doubt God's existence or His compassion, or to construct some completely irrational story line to explain and justify God's actions. In either case, we are relying on our rational mind to chart the course of our salvation.

We find God not in thought but in experience... in the unfolding experience of love. The only thing that can block our awareness of love is a discordant thought. An unacceptable event can't block our awareness of love, but our thoughts about that event can. Since we are constantly judging the acceptability or unacceptability of our lives and the world we live in, our minds are constantly full of discordant thoughts.

In and of themselves, our minds are not rational. We *think* they are, but in their core they are not. Human beings have to be taught to think rationally. On their own, our minds are full of chaos. They are full of fearful, angry, judgmental, greedy, desirous, violent, dissatisfied, bizarre thoughts.

Swami Vivekananda described our predicament this way: "The human mind," he said, "left to its own devices, carries on like a drunken monkey with St. Vitus Dance, that has been stung by a scorpion."[1] In other words, our thinking minds are generally filled with totally random, erratic, chaotic, agitated motion.

The problem is, we seek to make sense of the events of our lives and our world with those erratic, chaotic minds. In the midst of all of the chaos and discord our minds embody, we want our life and our life story to follow some reasonably comprehensible story line. We want it all to make sense. And we want to understand how it all makes sense. We want to see God's actions in tangible, visible ways, and we want to know that He is acting in a loving, fair, and just fashion.

Perhaps what we really want to know is that the Supreme Being is not encumbered with a mind that is as disordered as ours is.

But perhaps we are trying to understand something that is not understandable. Perhaps we are attempting to apply rules and structures to a system that operates beyond the rules and structures our human intellects can understand. We have been seduced into thinking that this universe, which is so vast and so incomprehensible, should operate according to simple, easily understood rules and values that exist only in fairy tales.

The physical universe operates in incredibly complex yet eminently predictable ways. But our human world is a world of uncertainty and unpredictable change. While we may be able to precisely calculate the exact position of the moon on August 22, 2054, at 3:43 P.M., we have no way of knowing, with any degree of certainty, our own status or location ten minutes from now. In our world, anything can happen. We may know when and where we were born, but we have no way of knowing when we will die or what will happen to us in the years before we die.

The path to happiness, peace, and security lies somewhere other than our world of form. The traditions that use paradox and contradiction as teaching devices also suggest that the "spiritual path," the "journey to God," is about discovering God within our own beings. Most of us have been looking for happiness, security, fulfillment, and God outside ourselves. We want other people, external circumstances, and events to make us feel secure and happy. But perhaps that is not where we find security and happiness.

We don't find God with our minds. We find God in our own hearts. As Jesus said, "The Kingdom of Heaven is within you." The Eternal Realm of Infinite Love, Infinite Peace, and Abiding Joy is within us. There is no place else to look, and no place else to find it.

To find heaven, we merely have to *give up* our attachment to having things work out the way we want them to work out. Our preconceived notions about how things should be is what stands in the way of our happiness. It is our anger at God, and our conviction that He isn't running the universe properly, that stands in the way of our actually knowing Him. If we didn't want the circumstances of our lives and our world to be different than they are, we could be happy right now!

We are caught in a trap, a trap created by our own minds. And that trap says, "Here is how I want my life to go. Here is how I think the world should operate. And, dear God, take notice, if things don't go the way I want them to, I'm going to be really angry at you!"

At times that anger is entirely understandable, absolutely inevitable, and eminently forgivable. But that anger is also the primary impediment to feeling really connected with God, and really happy.

In her wonderful book *Loving What Is: Four Questions That Can Change Your Life*, Byron Katie examined her own life, which had involved decades of deep, chronic depression, seething anger, and uncontrollable rage. After much inner work, she concluded that there is a simple formula for understanding human happiness and human suffering: "The only time we suffer," she says, "is when we believe a thought that argues with what is... that argues with reality"[2]

We need not conclude that suffering is good for us, or that God wants us to suffer, or that God causes our suffering. We need only conclude that there are moments in life when things don't go the way we wanted them to, or hoped they would go. In those moments, things are just the way they are. We have come face-to-face with what is.

Wanting the universe to be fair creates a major roadblock on the road to happiness. This universe of form isn't fair. At least, it isn't fair in the sense that our limited human minds understand fairness. Whenever our minds say, "Things shouldn't be this way!" we are setting up the conditions of our own unhappiness.

The path to God is about discovering that which is "real" and "unchanging," words that might be considered synonymous with "eternal." From the mystical point of view, whatever changes isn't considered to be real. Conversely, that which is real never changes.

We are, obviously, looking at a different definition of the word *real.* Generally, whatever we observe and experience in our limited human condition is defined as real. A bad headache seems real. Our body seems real. A storm seems real. Winning the big game seems real.

But the spiritual definition of *reality* is quite different. In the spiritual sense, *real* implies unchanging. Headaches and storms pass. Bodies age, decay, and die. The joy of winning passes. And everything else in our universe of form changes. Every moment is different and unique. Our bodies change. Our minds change. Our moods change. Our beliefs change. The weather changes. Our environment changes. Every *thing* in some manner takes form, exists for a period of time, changes, decays, and dies.

Every *thing* changes.

If we begin to look at our spiritual path as a quest to discover that which is eternal and *unchanging*... we begin to understand that the highest Truth, the clearest manifestation of God is something that never changes. As *A Course in Miracles* states, "Nothing real can be threatened. Nothing unreal exists. Herein lies the peace of God."[3]

If what we are in search of is eternal, then it is always available to us. Once we find it, we cannot lose it.

It is "the treasure which — once found — is *never* lost."

Over the course of my life, especially during the past thirty years when much of my work has been focused on people who are dealing with unwanted, unexpected change, I have seen that there is *no* loss, *no* change, *no* disappointment that can arise in our lives that in and of itself can undermine or erase our inherent ability to be happy.

I have seen people working with debilitating diseases, spinal cord injuries, the loss of a job or profession, the loss of a business, the loss of a dream, a life decimated by addiction... the loss of a beloved spouse, partner, friend, brother, sister, mother, or father, even the loss of a child. While these losses usually bring in their wake a tremendously challenging period of sadness and disorientation, I have consistently seen that it is possible for us to eventually move through that sadness and disorientation into a period of profound transformation.

While the loss becomes a part of us, while we are changed forever by each loss, I am still awed by the miraculous resiliency of the human heart, the human soul, the human consciousness, the human spirit. It is almost as if loss can at times pave the way for a miraculous spiritual healing, a magnificent unfolding of the soul.

We often expect that if we are good — if we pray, meditate, give money to charity, go to church or to temple regularly — if we pay our taxes, show some kindness to others, and generally act as good and responsible citizens, that God will protect us from anything bad or unpleasant ever happening to us. So when bad or unpleasant things *do* happen, we feel victimized and betrayed. We feel that God has forgotten us, or is punishing us for something, or has simply screwed up.

But there is a deeper level at which we can look at all of this: God protects us not by prohibiting anything bad from happening in our lives but by giving each and every one of us — as standard equipment when we are born — *everything* we need to handle *anything* that happens to us.

What God gives us is the opportunity to connect directly with Him, to taste the Eternal, to become a vessel for Divine Love, to literally *know* God, to experience the indescribable bliss of connecting with the very Being, the very Light, the very Love that created us. God manifests in this world of form, through every molecule and every atom. Everything in this universe is intimately connected with God. But God also exists beyond all forms. It is this eternal, omnipresent, formless, all-merciful Being of Pure Love we are really seeking. It is the source of all of our happiness and every moment of inner peace we have ever experienced.

No matter what happens in our lives, we can never lose our ability to connect with love, peace, and joy. Those qualities are the essence of our beings. They are the essence of God. They are the ways in which we consciously experience and express God. They are the source of everything.

When we touch love, peace, and joy, we are touching our true nature. We are touching God.

~

When I first heard the phrase "The loser *is* the winner" some thirty-five years ago, I didn't understand it.

But, over the course of those thirty-five years, my life has involved many losses. It has also involved many triumphs, many moments of happiness, and many successes. But the triumphs, moments of happiness, and successes would not have been sufficient to counteract all of the loss and sadness, unless I had had tools to look at it all differently... to work with it all as a means of spiritual awakening, to recognize that losing sometimes paves the way for a greater win than we had ever imagined.

Despite the fact that my life has been filled with loss, I am happier than I have ever been. And I feel more connected to God, to the Divine, to our Creator, than I ever have.

Has God always given me what I wanted? Often not.

But God *has* given me what I *really* want, which is a route to experience pure, unbounded, unconditional Love, enduring happiness, and a constant method for connecting with our Source, with the One... *consciously*.

Together, in the coming pages, we will explore how that happiness and connection has come into my life despite many unanswered prayers, and how it can come into yours.

CHAPTER 3

Understanding That Which Is beyond Understanding

All that the imagination can imagine
and the reason can conceive
is not, and can not be,
a proximate means of union with God.

SAINT JOHN OF THE CROSS

What is our understanding of God? What does the word *God* mean? How does God manifest in our lives? How does God manifest in the lives of others? How does God manifest in this confusing, seemingly chaotic world?

These are crucially important questions. Our understanding of God forms much of the basis for our faith — for how we worship, how we attempt to connect with God, how we attempt to feel God's presence in our lives, how we live our lives, what values we hold, what we feel is important, what we feel is possible . . . how we pray, why we pray, and what we pray for.

Philosophers and theologians have struggled for centuries to come up with a workable, comprehensive definition for *God*.

Who or what is . . . He . . . She . . . It?

Saint Anselm concluded that the only possible definition for God would be a *non*-definition. He said that God is "that than which nothing greater can be thought."[1]

God has been defined as the Prime Mover, the Mysterium Tremendum (Tremendous Mystery), the Supreme Being, the Almighty, the Creator, the Heavenly Father, the Father-Mother, the Absolute, the One, the One in the Many, the Ancient One, and the Highest of the High.

But all of these names and definitions of God can leave us a little perplexed and empty. So we seek to understand what the qualities of God might be.

What is He? She? It? . . . *like*?

The descriptions that most clearly encompass the concept of God are omnipotent (all-powerful), omniscient (all-knowing), and omnipresent (existing everywhere). The qualities most often attributed to God as He functions in His creation are all-loving and all-merciful.

Our concept of God, and our questions about the presence of these qualities of God's Being, form the basis for most of the conflicts, contradictions, and questions that underlie our explorations in this book.

Many of us have been moved to ask how it could be possible for God to allow monumental natural disasters like Hurricanes Katrina, Rita, and Wilma in the fall of 2005, which killed over 2,000 people, destroyed over 350,000 homes and 70,000 businesses, damaged millions of other homes and businesses, nearly destroyed the entire city of New Orleans and countless smaller communities along the coast of the Gulf of Mexico, and Florida, and displaced millions of people. How could God allow the Asian tsunami in December 2004, which killed over 250,000 people? Or violent earthquakes like those in Iran that have killed more than 50,000 people in a matter of seconds and displaced hundreds of thousands of others. How could God allow human-made disasters like the terrorist acts of September 11, 2001, and school shootings like the ones at Columbine and Virginia Tech?

For many of us, the "problem" stems from our view of God. Most of us have a belief system that philosophers and theologians refer to as anthropomorphic. That is, we perceive God *essentially* as a large and complex human being — a Divine manager, a cosmic orchestra conductor... a being who looks like us, who thinks like us, who has a rational plan for His creation, who feels the way we feel, and who acts in ways that we would act.

To hold that view of God, we have to see Him in essence as a grand puppeteer, seated somewhere high in the sky, like the image of God on the ceiling of the Sistine Chapel, miraculously pulling the strings of our lives and actions, and pulling the strings of the lives and actions of everyone on earth, consciously causing everything that happens to happen, deciding to allow great storms to sweep away millions of people, deciding to trigger earthquakes, avalanches, and floods, deciding to allow nineteen hijackers to take control of four airliners and wreak havoc on the very foundations of Western civilization, deciding to create some illness in our body or in our loved one's body.

If we assume that God is consciously and calculatingly making such decisions, we might easily conclude that God is cold and cruel and takes some pleasure in torturing us. Or we might conclude that God is angry, and we are — either individually or collectively — being punished for our sinfulness. Either alternative seems to contradict the idea that God is all-loving.

On the other hand, when things go well, we tend to believe that God decided to allow us to have what we want, that somehow we were able to curry the favor of our Creator, that we are being rewarded for being good.

In addition to attempting to define God, religious leaders and theologians have sought to identify some mechanism for determining how we are perceived in the eyes of God. Since it is all a mystery, how do we know whether we are traversing the spiritual path successfully? Just how pious, holy, and righteous are we? Have we pleased our Creator? Or have we angered Him?

The proposed answers to these questions are as numerous and varied as the multitudinous religious denominations on earth. John Calvin, founder of what has become the modern-day Presbyterian Church, concluded back in the 1500s that the most clear-cut evidence of God's favor is affluence. According to Calvin, if we are wealthy, we can assume that we have pleased God, that God loves us, and that — in Christian terms — we are saved. It was a rather contradictory belief, given the fact that the Bible says, "It is easier for a camel to pass through the eye of a needle than for a rich man to enter the Kingdom of Heaven."[2]

Many religious denominations and "spiritual" teachings popular today are rooted in the same equation of wealth with happiness and salvation, the belief that God is the source of abundance . . . an infinite, eternal reservoir of wealth that can and will fill every material and economic void, if only our faith is strong enough. If we are experiencing any lack in our lives, it is simply the product of erroneous thinking.

Another approach to evaluating where we stand in the eyes of God is to perceive physical health and longevity as the most accurate measuring sticks. A number of religious traditions have favored this approach. Christian Science, founded by Mary Baker Eddy, perhaps the most prominent of these, bases its teaching on the biblical statement that "man" is created in the image and likeness of God.

"God," said Mrs. Eddy, "is perfect." If God is perfect, then disease, illness, and imperfection have no essential reality. If "man" is created in the image and likeness of God, then "man" must — by virtue of his essential identity with God — also be perfect. According to Mrs. Eddy, illness does not exist. Its apparent existence is only possible to the extent that we believe it exists. And that belief in illness is a product of erroneous thinking.[3]

These forms of belief and their prescribed practices can in many circumstances be extremely useful. There is a significant benefit to training one's consciousness to be more focused and more positive. Cultivating higher, clearer thought patterns to counteract all of the negativity in our minds and our environment can only have positive results in terms of heightening our happiness and enjoyment of life . . . and sometimes our health.

But the truth is that prosperity and physical healing come only to some people some of the time. If we focus on healing and prosperity as the only acceptable evidence that we are in harmony with our Creator, our spiritual path can become very limited. It can constrict our consciousness rather than enhance our awareness of God's Light and Presence. Narrowly defining the success of our spiritual pursuits can actually magnify our suffering rather than alleviate it. We can become embarrassed and estranged from our spiritual community. We can experience greater disconnection from God because we feel less worthy than those who appear to be successful in their quest for positive results from prayer.

When our prayers appear to be unanswered we often assume that we have not prayed properly. Or we assume that God does not perceive us as worthy to regain our health or to have our prayer answered.

But neither of these assumptions is particularly useful. Neither helps clarify the significance of unanswered prayer in our relationship with God. Neither helps us understand that there might be some immensely significant message, or lesson to be learned, from being denied whatever it is we have been asking God for.

So let us return to our original quest to understand who and what God is, how we can connect with God in our daily lives, and how to understand and work with the results of prayers that seem to be unanswered.

CHAPTER 4

Toward a New Understanding

The purpose of prayer... is not to influence God to grant you special favors, but rather to remind yourself that you are always connected to God.

DR. WAYNE W. DYER

In a recent conversation with my friend Rabbi Earl Grollman, author of *Living When a Loved One Has Died*, I asked for his thoughts about unanswered prayer.

"Well," Earl said, "I have three thoughts about unanswered prayer. First of all, it may be that the *highest* form of prayer is not a prayer of supplication but a prayer of praise and thanksgiving. In the Jewish tradition it is believed that in the world to come, *all* prayers will be prayers of praise and thanksgiving, not asking God for anything — just thanking God for *everything*."

Earl went on, "Secondly, I think we should realize that we have no way of knowing whether what we are asking for is really the best thing for us. Perhaps God knows something we *don't* know.

"And finally," Earl said, "God can say no. That's something we don't like to hear, but I do think God can say no."

Earl's clear, concise perspective is extremely helpful. But some important questions remain unanswered. For instance, how do we learn to be thankful when our life is full of suffering? How could it be that healing, health, prosperity, happiness, and safety for us and for our loved ones might not be the best things for us . . . or for them? If God loves us, how can He say no to something that might relieve our suffering?

A couple months later, I was visiting Ram Dass at his home in Hawaii. One morning as we were finishing breakfast, I mentioned this book and asked if he had any thoughts he'd like to share. As is his habit, he closed his eyes and became intensely quiet. He was listening to hear his deepest intuition. I closed my eyes and joined him in a moment of reflective meditation.

As we sat together in silence, I began to notice how much Hawaii reminds me of a heavenly realm. A pervasive, mystical heart energy gently guides the sweet, healing hands of nature to calm and awaken all of the senses. Hawaii is a generous, attentive, welcoming hostess who gracefully lulls her visitors into a blissful, naturally tranquil state. The environment itself makes one feel safe, healed, and whole.

Soft, fragrant trade winds were gently wafting through the open windows of Ram Dass's house . . . serene, mellifluous currents carrying fresh floral scents of orchids and jasmine. It's easy to feel close to God there — easy to feel the benevolent, healing caress of Nature.

After a few moments, Ram Dass opened his eyes and spoke. "When most people ask God for something," he said, "they are asking from ego rather than from the depths of their soul. They are asking that their ego's desires be satisfied. They're not usually asking to know their souls. They are asking for worldly rewards rather than spiritual awakening."

Since Ram Dass and I have both many times worked with parents who have lost children, I asked — on their behalf — how a parent's prayer that a beloved child be protected from danger, or healed from an illness, might be considered a worldly reward and might be ascribed to the ego rather than the soul.

"Well, it's the ego that wants 'my child' to be safe and healthy," he said. "It's the parent's ego wanting to perpetuate the child's ego. And that's natural. But that's coming from a place of attachment to the world of form. In the world of form, the physical body and the personality are believed to be the totality of a person's being.

"But at the level of the soul, there is no sickness, no death, and no separation. Only at the level of the soul can we understand these things, because the ego can never make sense of them."

His answer seemed to arise from an exalted realm of consciousness that most parents whose children have died might have difficulty experiencing. To bring our discussion back to a more earthly level, I asked, "How can a grieving parent understand the agonizing pain they feel as anything other than punishment from a cruel, uncaring God?"

"They have to let the pain do its work," Ram Dass replied. "In an odd way, the pain is their child's legacy to them — their child's 'gift' to them. They can't push the pain away. The pain has to be allowed to tear their heart open. The healing begins when they can start to feel more gratitude that the child came into their life than despair and outrage that the child died. The gratitude is what heals the despair.

"It can be a long, painful process. It involves understanding — ultimately — that the child's work on earth was finished. No matter how short their life seemed, their soul had completed its work. They couldn't have died if their work wasn't finished. It just wouldn't have happened. In most of these circumstances a large part of the child's work was to open their parents' hearts in a very dramatic way by dying the way they did."

The healing of grief and loss often comes when we begin to look at our life from our soul's point of view rather than from the point of view of our personality and our intellect. That is, rather than look at how our intellect and ego are being frustrated and disappointed, we begin to look at how our soul might be using these experiences to flourish, to aspire toward its own greatness, to fully unveil itself to us.

In essence, Ram Dass's responses are not that far removed from Rabbi Grollman's. Both imply that not getting what we want can offer us a spiritual opportunity we might have missed had we gotten what we wanted. We generally consider the loss of a child to be among the most painful experiences a human being can have. But even such an incomprehensible loss can be a catalyst for profound spiritual growth. In such cases, most of us would gladly choose not to have that spiritual growth if it meant we could avoid the suffering that paves the way for it. But sometimes we don't have a choice. Every parent who has lost a child would gladly give up any amount of potential spiritual growth if by doing so they could bring their child back to life. When that choice is not available, the only choice we do have is the choice between living the rest of our days consumed by bitterness and victimization, or learning to let go of how we think life should have been in order to move into an acceptance of the way life is. Letting go of what we wanted and opening our hearts to what is, is a major turning point on the path to joy. It is not easily accomplished, but it is the unerring route to happiness and peace of mind.

Love and happiness, as generally understood in this culture, are dim, watered-down reflections of their true spiritual radiance. Love, in our society, most often refers to a powerful emotional experience that involves attraction, possessiveness, and control. We love others when they fulfill our desires and make us feel good about ourselves. We equate happiness with satisfied desire. If those we love stop fulfilling our desires, our love can quickly turn into hate. If circumstances don't align themselves to satisfy our desires, our happiness quickly turns into anger and despair.

As we evolve spiritually, we begin to experience deeper levels of love and happiness that have little to do with what we achieve, whom we are with, what we own, or how the world is behaving around us. As love grows, it eventually becomes unconditional. When we let go of wanting, we experience love as pure inner joy, unaffected by external circumstances. From the soul's point of view, that essential, unending joy is the culmination of all of our spiritual striving.

Nevertheless, we have to honor the fact that when we are denied something we deeply yearn for or we lose someone we dearly love, we often experience paralyzing emotional distress. In those moments, love feels excruciatingly painful. Joy seems absolutely unattainable. Our understanding of these issues is further complicated because sometimes when we pray we get what we desire, and sometimes we don't. Sometimes we experience the healing, but sometimes we don't.

~

My own life has been an interesting laboratory in which to observe these polarities. The very fact that I am alive is a direct result of the power of prayer. In 1953, just before my third birthday, I contracted one of the last cases of polio in the United States. It was diagnosed as bulbar polio, the most deadly and debilitating form of the disease. While I lay for weeks in an isolation hospital, paralyzed and comatose, with fevers in excess of 105 degrees, the doctors told my parents that my case was hopeless.

"You need to prepare for the worst," they said. "There is a 95 percent chance that your son will die. And if he lives, there is a 99 percent chance that he will be severely handicapped. He will probably have to spend the rest of his life in an iron lung."

My father said, "What can we do?"

The doctors said, "Pray."

My parents were already strong believers in the power of prayer. In fact, their marriage ceremony eight years earlier had been performed by Dr. Norman Vincent Peale, author of *The Power of Positive*

Thinking. They left the hospital where I lay dying, went home, and called our minister. Then they called all our relatives. Then they called their friends and acquaintances. In a short time, prayers were being offered by hundreds of people in dozens of churches and synagogues.

One evening our minister came to our house to pray with my parents. Sometime after midnight he went home. My mother went to bed. My father felt no urge to sleep, so he went to my room. He lay down on my bed and continued to pray. At about 2:00 A.M., just as he was beginning to drift off to sleep, he had an amazing, spontaneous vision. In an unfamiliar, beautiful realm of consciousness, he saw my hospital room. Since I was in isolation, he had never been allowed to visit. But he saw an image that never faded from his memory. He saw Jesus standing next to my hospital bed, smiling softly, one healing hand placed lovingly and reassuringly on my forehead.

My father awoke, jumped up, and ran across the hall into the room where my mother was sleeping. He gently, firmly awakened her. Through laughter and tears he said, "Don't worry, John is going to be all right."

Twenty minutes later, my parents' telephone rang. It was the head nurse on the isolation ward. "There has been a miracle!" she said. "For no apparent reason, your son's fever has broken. He is awake and alert. There is no sign of significant paralysis. And he is demanding pancakes!"

Fifty-four years later, I still love pancakes. And the spiritual healing that came to me through prayer at the age of three eventually formed the foundation for my entire life. Even as a child I realized that God had spared my life and that I owed my life to God.

I also realized something most people in our culture don't want to think about — that children can get sick and can die. While most parents do their best to shield themselves and their children from that knowledge, it has always been quite vivid for me. I understood three important things at an early age: that there are no guarantees in this life, that I am on borrowed time, and that every moment is precious.

But being miraculously healed did not presage a life of perpetual ease and wonder. Like everyone else on earth, I have been through many periods of difficulty and many challenges. I have gone through seemingly magical periods when all of my prayers seemed to be answered as soon as they were offered. But I have also experienced many times when it appeared — for long periods — as if none of my prayers were being answered.

Early childhood was difficult, involving many years of recuperation and rehabilitation that made most "normal" childhood activities impossible. Later, when I was eleven, my parents fell back into a deranged pattern of alcoholic behavior that had haunted them in the years prior to my birth. It nearly destroyed our family. From that point on, throughout my teenage years, it seemed that no prayer was answered. I begged and pleaded with God, wailing and crying out through a nightly flood of tears, imploring God to answer my prayers, begging Him to return happiness, peace, and sanity to our home. Nothing worked. No answers came. For years, each day brought only more discord and misery.

Eventually I learned to hate my father and hate God. I developed a kind of agnostic view of life. I still believed that there must be some amazing creative force behind the evolution of this extraordinary universe, but I no longer trusted in the benevolent nature of that force. Life looked absolutely bleak and barren to me. I would often say, "If there is a God, I certainly wouldn't want to be in His shoes. I certainly wouldn't want to be responsible for this mess."

The years of intense emotional and psychological suffering eventually resulted in some amazingly transformative effects. The isolation and convalescence in early childhood taught me how to function in solitude, an ability that became useful years later when I pursued spiritual disciplines that involved extended periods of meditation and silence. The sadness, confusion, and despair connected with my parents' drinking vividly demonstrated to me the suffering inherent in a life consumed by addictive and compulsive behaviors. Through my parents' lives, I learned what I didn't want my own life to become. The deep depression those years engendered eventually led me into psychoanalysis with an exceptionally gifted psychiatrist. Our work together was another major turning point in my life. To this day, I think of him as my first guru. His guidance helped me understand the many levels, complexities, and largely unrecognized powers of our human minds.

One night about six months after beginning therapy, while lying in bed, I experienced an extraordinary spontaneous mystical awakening into the state of consciousness that Tibetan Buddhists call "Clear Light." It was a conscious "meeting" with the formless, infinite Light that infuses, suffuses, and connects all creation. It gave me an unassailable recognition that the creative force we call life, the essential energy that keeps my heart beating and your heart beating, is exactly the same force that supports every form of life on earth: the flowers, the trees, the grass, the fish, the birds and animals, all one, all connected by one primordial energy. In one moment of spiritual certainty, I recognized that all life is yearning to know its true nature, to return to its source, to consciously experience oneness with our Creator and with each other.

In the wake of that experience, I was never the same. My life became a quest to return again and again to that indescribably blissful transcendental awareness, a journey back to the beginning... of time ... of form... back to eternity.

But despite the enormously transformative effects of that extraordinary awakening, the losses, disappointments, and sadness have still come. I have experienced the deaths of both of my parents, all of my grandparents, a beloved nephew, and many, many beloved friends. I found the partner of my dreams, only to experience several years of heartbreaking marital discord that eventually ended in divorce. I have also had many business and financial challenges.

Yet, through it all, I keep feeling closer to God.

How do we understand these dramatic swings? How do we understand that sometimes we seem to be living in a state of benevolent Grace and sometimes we feel like we are totally disconnected from God? How do we understand why difficulties sometimes lead to spiritual experience? How do we understand why sometimes, when we lose people, things, and dreams we are attached to, we wind up actually feeling closer to God?

Simply stated, if there really is a God, and if prayer really works, how can we understand why sometimes we get what we ask for and sometimes we don't?

It is possible that the answer involves the search for *balance* our universe is always engaged in — an essential balance that is neither benevolent nor malevolent. It just is. It is the state of balance that most clearly mirrors the One Light, the Clear Light underlying all creation. Our souls constantly yearn to reattune themselves with that primordial balance, through the harmony generated by opposing energies and opposite experience.

A story about a great Buddhist teacher may offer some insight. The teacher was challenged by one of his students because he appeared to be giving contradictory teachings.

"Master," the student said, "I don't understand. You tell one student one thing and another student exactly the opposite thing. Why aren't you consistent?"

The master smiled and fell silent for a few moments.

Finally he said, "It's very simple. In my role as a teacher, I am — metaphorically speaking — following my students down a path that I know very well but they are not familiar with. Even in the dark, I know where the edges of the road are, but they can't see them. Whenever I see a student drifting off to the left and in danger of falling into a ditch, I call out, 'Uh-oh, go right!' And whenever I see them drifting off to the right and about to fall into a ditch, I call out, 'Uh-oh, go left!' You see? That's really all there is to it. It isn't contradictory. It's just about keeping them on the path, going in the right direction. I am trying to help them avoid the pitfalls they can't see. I try to help them avoid getting stuck in a ditch."

This teacher's perspective offers great help in understanding some of the moments when the experiences of life just seem incomprehensible. Still, we can't ignore the fact that we sometimes have to deal with experiences so heartbreaking, and so mind shattering, that clever, entertaining stories don't easily soothe the resultant emotional turmoil.

For example, in the late 1970s, a young couple named Steve and Anita experienced something that remains among the most heart-wrenching stories I have ever heard. They lived in Oregon, where they had recently moved in search of a more peaceful life. One serene, uneventful afternoon, their beautiful eleven-year-old daughter, Rachel, was abducted, raped, and brutally beaten to death.

What kind of "balance" might God, or the universe, be seeking to offer Rachel — or her heartbroken parents — through such an experience? How can we perceive any good in such an event? How could her parents *ever* recover, ever trust in God again?

Steve was asked to come to the crime scene to identify Rachel's body. I can scarcely imagine the chaotic cacophony of thoughts and emotions he must have experienced. He and Anita were devastated. Their beautiful Rachel's precious young life was snuffed out in one brief instant of random, heartless violence.

A few weeks later, Ram Dass wrote a letter of condolence to Steve and Anita. Even now, some thirty years later, it stands as one of the most powerful statements of love, compassion, and insight I have ever read. As you read it, try to put yourself inside the hearts and minds of two grieving parents whose entire psychological, emotional, and spiritual universe has just been shattered. Imagine the depth of their grief, the immensity of their outrage, the incomprehensible struggle to maintain even a shred of spiritual awareness in the face of such devastating emotional agony. Then listen to the wise, compassionate words offered in this letter:

Steve and Anita,

Rachel finished her brief work on earth and left the stage in a manner that leaves those of us left behind with a cry of agony in our hearts as the fragile thread of our faith is dealt with so violently. Is anyone strong enough to stay conscious through such teachings as you are receiving? Probably very few. And even they would only have a whisper of equanimity and spacious peace amidst the screaming trumpets of their rage, grief, horror, and desolation.

I cannot assuage your pain with any words. Nor should I. For your pain is Rachel's legacy to you. Not that she or I would inflict such pain by choice. But . . . there it is . . . and it must burn its purifying way to completion. You may emerge from this ordeal more dead than alive . . . and then you can understand why the greatest saints, for whom every human being is their child, shoulder the unbearable pain, and are called the living dead. For something within you dies when you bear the unbearable . . . and it is only in that dark night of the soul that you are prepared to see as God sees, and to love as God loves.

Now is the time to let your grief find expression. No false strength. Now is the time to sit quietly and speak to Rachel and thank her for being with you these few years and encourage her to go on with her work, knowing that you will grow in compassion and wisdom from the experience.

In my heart I know that you and she will meet again and again and recognize the many ways in which you have known each other. And when you meet you will, in a flash, know what now it is not given to you to know . . . why this had to be the way it was.

Your rational minds can never "understand" what has happened. But your hearts, if you can keep them open to God, will find their own intuitive way.

> Rachel came through you to do her brief work on earth (which included her manner of death). Now her soul is free and the love that you can share with her is invulnerable to the winds of changing time and space.
>
> In that deep love, include me too.
>
> So much love,
> Ram Dass

Nearly thirty years later, Steve and Anita still well up with tears when they revisit their grief about Rachel's death. But something deep inside them has allowed them to live, to love, and to move forward in their lives. Some tiny, all but imperceptible thread of consciousness and connection was touched by Ram Dass's words. Eventually they were able to use their grief to deepen their spiritual work. Recently Anita said, "For six months after we received that letter, we worked with the wisdom it contained. We heard the truth in it. It was the light at the end of our tunnel. We thought, if we can work with this, if we can work with some of these ideas, we can go on."

~

In 1996 I spent about six months visiting with a thirty-eight-year-old woman named Marjorie. When we met, she was already in the fifth stage of breast cancer. She was a beautiful woman, a glorious soul, and a dedicated yoga teacher. She had practiced meditation for many years.

Marjorie had an extraordinary softness, openness, and clarity. She was also amazingly lighthearted, given the gravity of the situation she was dealing with. She was one of those rare beings who even before the onset of her disease had actually done some intense inner work to prepare for her own death.

One day while I was visiting with her, she said, "I am so grateful to have had nearly twenty years of meditation practice. Watching how each breath arises, exists, and passes away, arises, exists, and passes away... into the next breath... and the next breath... and the next breath. I realize that for twenty years now I've been practicing dying into each moment, watching each breath take birth, live out its life cycle, and die. I am no different from my breath. I took birth, I am living out my life cycle, and soon I will die. Eventually I will take a breath that will be my last. I just don't know which one it will be." At that moment, she actually started giggling.

Marjorie had tried many different healing modalities, both conventional and alternative. She had gone through surgery, radiation, and chemotherapy. She had done Chinese herbal treatments, homeopathic remedies, megavitamin regimes, acupuncture, craniosacral therapy, and sound and vibrational healing. She had also turned to spiritual healing work with pranic healers, shamanic healers, a Reiki master, and a Christian Science practitioner.

Her disease continued to progress. Finally, she decided to make one great effort at encouraging her body to turn back toward health. She said, "I'm going to have a healing event at my house. I'm going to take an entire weekend and have dozens of people I love come over to meditate, and pray, and sing, and chant, and perform healing rituals. We'll keep the spiritual energy and the Light flowing all weekend. I just want to see what will happen. I want to see if my body will respond. Perhaps we can create a healing atmosphere by just focusing completely on Light, Love, and God."

Marjorie held the weekend healing ceremony. Immediately afterward, those who were present agreed that there had been a powerful and palpable feeling of spirit, Grace, and Presence in Marjorie's home that weekend.

"It was immensely joyous," said one friend. "I've never experienced anything like it. There was such healing power, and such love suffusing the entire house, and surrounding Marjorie. I am sure that she will be healed."

Despite those sentiments, a few days later Marjorie's doctors informed her that her disease had worsened. Her primary tumor was larger, and they now detected metastases to her liver and the bones of her rib cage and spine.

I sat with her just after she got the news. "How do you understand this, Marjorie? In the light of this most recent disappointing diagnosis, how do you understand the unmistakable feelings of healing and Grace you and your friends experienced the other day?"

She thought for a few moments. Finally she said, "I think the worsening of my disease *is* my healing. The one thing I don't want is to die. It's the one thing I don't want to accept from God. It's the one way I don't fully trust the universe. I'm going to have to let that aversion and distrust go. I'm going to have to trust in the wisdom and benevolence of what is. I'm going to have to surrender into the natural course of the universe rather than continuing to fight against what I don't want. I'm going to have to learn to fully connect with God, and fully trust in the universe as I journey into the unknown on this trip I don't want to take. That's the *real* healing... learning to trust in God and just *allow*."

~

Even those who are blessed to spend time in the company of great saints sometimes experience healing, and sometimes don't. For instance Neem Karoli Baba — known to his devotees as "Maharaji" — was a great Hindu saint who lived in India in the twentieth century. He was an extraordinary being with extraordinary powers. Miraculous healings happened around him regularly. People dying of cancer spontaneously healed. Blind people regained their sight. A soldier who had gone off to fight in a war was miraculously protected in a fierce battle. Maharaji always denied having done anything, but these miracles usually followed shortly on the heels of one of his devotees' asking for his help.

But he didn't heal everyone. He seemed to have a sense that there were times when healing was appropriate and times when it wasn't. At one time, the children of a devotee came to say that their father was near death. They asked if Maharaji could do something. He picked up a banana, blessed it, and sent it home with the children. He said, "Give this to your father."

The father ate it and shortly thereafter regained his health.

Another time, members of a different family came exhorting Maharaji to heal a sick relative. He again took a banana, blessed it, and gave it to the family, saying, "Give him this. He'll be fine." The man ate the banana and died.

I asked one of Neem Karoli Baba's closest disciples, "What do you make of all that?"

The devotee said, "Well, I make of it that there are certain circumstances where healing is possible, and other circumstances where it isn't. Ultimately the real issue is, what is in the best interests of the soul? What work did that soul come to earth to do? And what will best facilitate the work the soul came to do?"

In truth, from the spiritual point of view, dying is neither a punishment nor necessarily a tragedy. Religious traditions pay lip service to the belief in a glorious afterlife, but then they turn around and act as if God has made a mistake or is punishing anyone who dies. It is completely contradictory.

If someone we love dies, we understandably experience profound emotional pain. And if something happens to our body that might lead to our own death, our belief systems and emotional stability are often seriously challenged. In either case, death isn't a punishment. It isn't the end of our existence. And it isn't the end of the world. Working through the emotional and spiritual challenges these events give rise to can result in some of the most profound spiritual growth of our lifetime.

~

In India there is a story about another great saint named Sombari Maharaj. One day Sombari Maharaj was giving his devotees *prasad* — food that has been blessed by the Master. To one particularly devout young follower, Sombari Maharaj handed two potatoes. He said, "Here. Go down by the river and eat *both* of these potatoes."

Now, in India, one is generally expected to pay scrupulous attention to the instructions of one's guru and to methodically and meticulously carry out those instructions. So the young devotee went down to the river. He was about to eat the first potato when a feeble, frail old beggar came along and meekly said, "Baba, give me one of your potatoes. I'm *very* hungry. You have two potatoes, I don't have anything to eat."

The young man's heart was touched. Of course . . . how could he keep both potatoes and deny this elderly gentleman some food? Ignoring the explicit instructions of his guru, he gave the second potato to the old man.

When the young devotee got back to the ashram, Sombari Maharaj already knew what had happened. He screamed at the devotee, "You fool! You idiot! I told you to eat *both* potatoes!"

Eventually, Sombari Maharaj calmed down. Finally he sighed and said with resignation, "Oh well, I guess it wasn't your destiny."

Within a few years, that young devotee became a very successful attorney. Then he was elected to be a high-ranking judge. He became both prominent and highly respected. He also became very prosperous. He married well and had a number of children who also married well and lived extremely successful lives.

Still seated at the breakfast table in his home on Maui, Ram Dass and I continued our discussion about unanswered prayer. We reflected on the potato story.

"All of that worldly success was understood to be the first potato," Ram Dass said.

"I know," I said. "So what do you think the second potato was?"

Without hesitation, Ram Dass said, "God. The second potato was God. The devotee was given the opportunity to become enlightened, to know God consciously, in this life. But he didn't take it. Still, he had an excellent life — in worldly terms. But he missed the chance to merge with God."

I thought for a moment. "Maybe there is a kind of hierarchy of blessings that are available," I said. "Perhaps we have to examine what it is we are *really* asking for. If we are *really* asking for health, wealth, a happy family, and safety, that's one thing. But if we are *really* asking for God, if we are *really* longing to *know* God, if our deepest and most fervent desire has been to *experience* God fully in this life, it just may be that losing our health, losing our wealth, and losing our sense of safety are — at times — greater teachings than keeping them."

"That's right," Ram Dass agreed. "Once you ask for God, He isn't going to let you have anything that doesn't bring you closer to Him. It just can't happen. He'll prevent it, no matter how much you protest."

CHAPTER 5

When Expectations Turn Upside Down

To penetrate into the essence of all being and significance and to release the fragrance of that inner attainment for the guidance and benefit of others — by expressing, in the world of forms, truth, love, purity, and beauty — this is the sole game that has intrinsic and absolute worth. All other happenings, incidents, and attainments in themselves can have no lasting importance.

MEHER BABA, *DISCOURSES*

The stories in the previous chapter may seem a little perplexing in light of the events or questions that prompted you to read this book. You may say, "I wasn't asking for some mystical union with God. I was just living my life, minding my own business." Or, "I was merely asking for health, financial security, a happy family, and safety. And I didn't *get* those. All I got was disappointment and misery. It isn't fair."

But perhaps another, deeper part of you has been longing for a deeper experience of life and of God. This is a theme we will examine again and again in the course of our reflections.

From our soul's point of view we are always searching for God. Our pursuit of love, peace, happiness, and satisfaction is our soul's yearning for God, our soul's longing to return to its source. These experiences can come only from a meaningful engagement with our source... with God. Whenever we have experienced love, peace, and happiness, we can be certain that — for a moment, at least — we have somehow touched God. We have touched the essence of our souls. We have gotten a glimpse of who we truly are.

But our culture offers so little support for such a lofty, mystical, and transcendent impulse that many of us learn to deny it, even though it remains in our subconscious mind as the preeminent yearning of our being, subtly infusing every effort we make to find happiness.

The existential questions that arise over and over for us, the ones that are really expressions of our soul's yearning, are:

Who am I?

Why am I here?

What is this universe, and this life, all about?

Isn't there something deeper and more meaningful? Can I experience it?

Or, as one rock group sang in an impassioned musical prayer about twenty-five years ago, "I want to know what love is!"

A friend of mine named Michael has had some extraordinary, and unexpected, success in business. Fifteen years ago, he and his wife and their three young children were living pretty much hand to mouth in an extremely modest home. He was an intelligent, creative human being who had become bored and frustrated by the limitations of his finances.

For several years he prayed to become successful. He learned creative visualization. He learned affirmative prayer. He did daily positive affirmations.

Now Michael and his wife own four magnificent homes, each

surrounded with a sizable amount of acreage. They have five magnificent cars and a mind-boggling investment portfolio valued at nearly 100 million dollars. Michael has achieved an impressive amount of fame in his profession. He has succeeded far beyond his wildest dreams.

Recently, we met for lunch. When I saw him, he looked exhausted and sad, dazed and emotionally flat. His eyes were glassy and a little empty — that look people get when they've been numbed by life's confusion and complexity. His head and shoulders were askew, distorted by weeks of acclimating to chronic neck pain.

I said, "Michael, you don't look well."

I was serious. But Michael made a pitiful attempt at playfulness. He smiled weakly, contorted his face, and said, "Thanks a *lot*!"

But he was clearly in no mood for comic banter. His countenance became intense and businesslike. With an air of urgency, he said, "John, how do you stay so happy and calm?"

I quieted for a moment. "Meditation and surrender," I said.

"Right. I should have known you would say that."

But I had the sense that he wasn't really hearing my answer.

He said, "I'm really very unhappy and anxious in the lifestyle I live now. I have no free time... no time to be quiet and meditate. Practically every moment of every day is taken up with some form of business or family commitment. I have little time to do the things I love. And when I do have the time, I can't do most of it because my neck is in such pain.

"I wanted success so much that I have many times ignored my intuition and made business deals that really didn't feel right, that didn't feel harmonious with who I am and what I believe. I got greedy, and now I'm paying the price.

"When I think about it, I realize that I was happiest when my life was much more simple, when I had time to meditate, when I felt like I had a spiritual life, when my marriage was more like a true partnership. Now, it's like my wife and I are executives running a huge empire. I look in our office at home and I see mountains of bills. And I feel like we're drifting apart, like our values are no longer in sync. My children are all becoming snobs. Two of them are suffering from chronic depression, and acting out badly. They are always in trouble at school, and sometimes in trouble with the police. One of my daughters has dyed her hair black and wears black nail polish and black eye makeup. She attempted suicide last year. My son was recently arrested for drug possession. I'm being sued by three different people, investigated by the SEC, and audited by the IRS. We have a staggering amount of cash outflow each month, and the pressure to keep bringing in the money needed to keep it all flowing is really getting to me.

"I know that feeling connected to God — the way I used to feel — is the only thing that will save me, and yet I just don't seem to have the time or space in my life to make that happen."

~

The very next day I was having tea with another old friend named Susan. She was telling me about Robert, a man she has been in a relationship with for more than ten years.

"Robert keeps making more and more money and becoming less and less happy. He's filthy rich, and yet he complains constantly. He gets infuriated at the drop of a hat. He owns several beautiful homes, but he doesn't take the time to enjoy any of them. Most of them sit empty most of the time. He is chronically depressed, and he worries that he will commit suicide someday. He has so much to be thankful for, and all he experiences is emptiness and frustration.

"It's actually come to the point that I can barely stand to be with him. He is such a troubled soul. He has no spiritual life. He's cynical, angry, and depressed. And his body is starting to break down. He has high blood pressure, diabetes, and chronic stomach problems. It's really sad. He doesn't enjoy his life and he doesn't enjoy his success."

~

Over the years as I have watched Michael and Robert become more and more successful — in worldly terms — as I have seen their prayers for worldly success answered, I have also seen their health and happiness deteriorate. In such circumstances, I remember Meher Baba's statement that sometimes, when we get what we pray for, we find that it really doesn't bring the happiness and contentment we were hoping for. I also wonder just how bad the physical problems will become before Michael and Robert will listen, before they will turn inward and seek happiness in the only place it can be found... in their own hearts.

Most esoteric healing traditions have known for centuries that there is an inviolable correlation between our state of happiness and our physical health. In recent years, even practitioners of traditional Western medicine have come to understand this correlation. We know that stress, anger, and depression change our body chemistry in ways that can undermine our overall state of health.

Often, chronic pain and other ailments can be a means for our body to get our attention when we're not listening to our inner self... our intuition... the voice of our soul. Sometimes our body will start by manifesting a little discomfort and will gradually keep "turning up the heat" until eventually we are bedridden with some pain or illness that can't be cured until we change the conditions causing our unhappiness. This correlation is not true of every physical illness or condition, but it is true far more often than many of us realize.

In general, either we have to find a way to change the aspects of our lives we don't love or we have to find a way to love those aspects.

Love is the greatest healer.

Over the course of my life, I have known many, many wealthy people. And very few of them are truly happy. They often purport to be happy, but in truth many are edgy and embittered, anxious and aloof, judgmental of others, frightened of losing their fortunes, frightened of not having as much as their neighbors or the other wealthy people they associate with, constantly desperate to make more money, and always feeling the reason they are not fully happy is that they still don't have quite enough. Their "happiness" often derives from a sense of entitlement and superiority, from the fleeting exhilaration of multi-million-dollar business deals and the short-lived excitement of an expensive new car or an enormous new state-of-the-art home.

But the sense of entitlement and superiority is divisive and isolating. It engenders a sense of separateness rather than connection.

There are, however, a few wealthy people I know who are truly happy. Ironically, they are the ones who are doing something that might seem outlandish, something that seldom occurs to those who are busy amassing their fortunes.

The happy ones are giving their money away! Not *all* of it, usually, but significant amounts. And when I have noticed their unusual state of happiness and have asked them what it is in their lives that makes them most happy, they never say, "Well, it's my beautiful mansions, and my beautiful jewels, and my beautiful cars." They never say, "It's my huge investment portfolio." They always say, "It's giving my money away and helping other people. That makes life meaningful. The other stuff is pretty empty."

In the words of Mahatma Gandhi:

> We are born to serve our fellow man. We cannot properly do so unless we are wide awake. There is an eternal struggle raging in man's breast between the powers of darkness and of light, and he who has not the sheet-anchor of prayer to rely upon will be a victim to the powers of darkness. The man of prayer will be at peace with himself and with the whole world. The man who goes about the affairs of the world without a prayerful heart will be miserable, and will make the world also miserable.[1]

CHAPTER 6

When Fear Inhibits Love

The opposite of love is fear,
but what is all-encompassing can have no opposite.

A COURSE IN MIRACLES

When we ask God for something, our prayers of petition are offered in two primary ways: 1) we ask to have something we want or to achieve something we want to possess; or 2) we ask to not have things and experiences we don't want.

We ask God to give us health, financial security, peace of mind, harmonious relationships, success, and protection from danger. Or we ask God to take away illness, financial difficulties, sadness, and exposure to peril.

Sometimes we pray for our loved ones.

And sometimes we pray for things on a larger scale: we pray for world peace, we pray for entire nations, we pray that our environment be healed, we pray that the political candidates we favor are elected, we pray to be protected from things like storms, earthquakes, floods, and wars.

If we examine our motives honestly, we will usually find that there is some form of fear inspiring our prayers. We are *afraid* of something. And we are asking to be protected from whatever we are afraid of.

The fear that inspires us to pray actually gives us the most significant clue in our efforts to understand unanswered prayer. When our prayers aren't answered the way we want them to be, we often have to experience the things of which we are afraid. We are forced to confront our fear.

All fear arises from lack of trust in the universe. There are many experiences we just don't want. We are afraid that if we experience them, happiness will become impossible. We won't be safe. We may be emotionally shattered. Our life will be incomplete, unfulfilling, or more difficult than we are prepared for.

A line in the Bible says, "Perfect love casts out Fear."[1] *A Course in Miracles* reduces our predicament to a simple formula: there are only two states of being . . . love and fear. Either we are in love, or we are in fear. Every moment we are not loving is a moment of fear. Fear is what separates us from God. It is the *only* thing that separates us from God. When we are fully in love, we are fully in God.

So the "separation" we experience when we are fearful is only apparent separation. There is simply no way to be separate from God. At worst, all we can have is a perception of separateness, and that perception is generated by fear. When our perception is clear, and our mind is free of fear, our consciousness becomes like a pristine, unclouded window through which the light of the sun, the Light of God, can shine unobstructed. That pristine clarity is Love.

But when our perception is cloudy, our window becomes opaque, sometimes a little dusty, sometimes completely occluded with dust.

The dust is fear. When fear predominates, the sun is no longer visible. Though just beyond the window it shines in all its radiance, inside — if our window is covered with dust — all we can see is darkness.

So confronting our fear offers us a profound spiritual opportunity. When the Tibetan master Chogyam Trungpa Rinpoche was asked what *enlightenment* meant, he replied, "absolute fearlessness." Fear is generated by powerful discordant mental formations. It arises from forgetting that we are spiritual beings and thinking instead that we are physical beings. In the world of form there is no enduring safety. We can only *really* feel safe by aligning with our spiritual identity — our soul. Unless we do that, we are always plagued by the sense that we are not safe, although, in the realm of the spirit — of soul — we are eternally safe.

Fear also arises from the sense that the universe — God — is capable of making mistakes. From the spiritual point of view, everything in the universe is perfect. This can be a difficult principle to accept, especially when we are enmeshed in fear, sadness, and disappointment. But, ultimately, it is our judging minds — our "arguments with reality" — that constantly define the world as imperfect. Ironically, owing to its inability to offer any meaningful long-term solutions to our quest for happiness, this world is perfectly designed to guide us back to God.

Our greatest fear is that we are separate. But in the realm of spirit, we are always connected to God. We are all one.

Every one of these discordant perceptions is erroneous. We all have them. But it is useful to bear in mind that they are all forms of fear. A large part of our spiritual work lies in becoming aware of them and working to eliminate them from our consciousness.

Our problem is not that the universe of form is filled with change and uncertainty. Our problem is that we have erroneous, discordant, inharmonious, and illusory perceptions. Change and uncertainty don't cause our unhappiness. Living in fear and resistance to change cause our unhappiness.

~

It is understandable, and reasonable, that those among us who believe in God ask for His help. At times, as a result of our asking, we perceive Divine Intervention. We sense that we have been protected from danger or that a great blessing has miraculously been bestowed on us. But if God's help doesn't come when we ask or how we ask, we are left to deal with whatever it was we didn't want to deal with. In those moments, we always have the opportunity to embark on the path of awakening.

We awaken by dealing consciously, openly, and honestly with the life circumstances we sought to avoid, by diving deeper into the depths of our own soul. That is where we find real safety, real perfection, and real connection. That is where God's love and assistance exist eternally. Within our own souls. In the core of our being. In the changeless *eternal now*.

Whatever we fear is showing us the parts of our minds that perceive the universe as dangerous, imperfect, and unacceptable. In other words, our fears are showing us the aspects of God's creation that we have placed outside "the One" — outside our hearts, outside our capacity to love. The people and things we fear, dislike, and find unacceptable are signposts pointing to the places in ourselves where we are stuck, where we need to focus our spiritual work.

In truth, nothing exists outside the One. Nothing exists outside God. When our minds perceive parts of the universe as dangerous, imperfect, and unacceptable, our minds are closing off our awareness of God.

Learning to love that which we fear, and that which we feel we cannot love, is the fundamental path to human happiness. It is not just some noble, impossible-to-attain spiritual exercise on the path to sainthood. It is the foundation of spiritual life. It is the way we heal the sense of separation that forms the foundation of our suffering. No matter how hard we try, there is no way to fully ignore the things we dislike. The best strategy is to acknowledge them, embrace them . . . and learn to love them.

For instance, even when we have spent a lifetime trying to ignore the inevitability of death, there is no way to fully remove it from our consciousness. We may be clever enough to keep it buried beneath the surface of awareness, so that we seldom think about it. But it is still there. In moments of uncertainty or danger, or in moments when we find ourselves in the presence of someone else's death, it is nearly impossible to keep our own awareness, our own fear, completely subdued. It may burst forth in a sudden flood of tears or in an overarching sense of anxiety and emotional discomfort.

We learn of a child who died. Suddenly we feel a flash of terror about the vulnerability of our own children. We learn that the spouse of a friend has died, and adrenaline and sadness pour through us. We can't help but reflect on the vulnerability of our own partner. A friend who is roughly our age or younger suddenly dies, and we can't help but think about how vulnerable we are.

The fear we experience in these moments arises from a devious and destructive trick our minds tend to play on us. Our minds tell us that we need to worry in order to be safe. They trick us into being frightened, anxious, contracted, and hypervigilant.

Let me invite you to ask yourself two questions: "When, during the entire course of my life, has worrying *ever* made me safe?" and "When has worrying ever led me to happiness?" As you ask those questions, try to distinguish between worry and cautiousness, worry and prudence, worry and preparation.

Cautiousness, prudence, and preparation are generally the result of rational thought patterns. They are words that characterize sensible, fruitful actions. They give rise to actions intended to protect and care for ourselves and our loved ones. They emerge from experience, learning, and wisdom.

Distinguish also between worry and intuition. Intuition is a more visceral sense. It can manifest as a sometimes vague, other times palpable, feeling of discomfort, a discomfort that prompts you to change course in some way. You aren't fearing a potential danger... you simply know, intuitively, that you need to move in a different direction.

There are also positive intuitions. You feel mystically drawn in a certain direction; you have palpable feelings of well-being and safety; you "know" what is the right thing to do.

This discussion about worry is not meant to suggest that we should ignore danger, or act irresponsibly, or turn a blind eye toward injustice. It is merely intended to point out that there is no benefit to be gained from worry. None.

In fact, worrying just dissipates the energy that we would otherwise have available to respond to danger. It clouds our perception. It inhibits our ability to access our intuition. When we are living in love rather than fear, our intuition naturally becomes more clear and present. When we are living in love, we are in harmony with the universe. The heightened intuition that arises from a harmonious connection with the universe allows us to recognize real danger much more quickly than when we are worried.

Since worry, fear, and anger are so intimately tied together, it's interesting to note that in the highest forms of martial arts, like karate and aikido, the student is taught not to respond to attack with fear or anger. The masters of consciousness who evolved and transmitted these traditions have long understood that anger and fear cloud the mind and dissipate our strength. We simply cannot respond to danger or attack as quickly or as effectively if our minds are filled with fear and anger.

Nevertheless, our minds keep telling us that we need to be in these very palpable, very uncomfortable mental and emotional states in order to be safe.

When we don't fear anything, we no longer need to exclude anything from our fields of vision, from our awareness, or from our hearts. We can look at it all — everything in the world, with all the blemishes, dangers, horrors, and injustices — without having to turn away or close our hearts.

The effort to exclude any aspect of life, any aspect of the universe, from our consciousness is one of the greatest sources of individual human suffering. Each person, each event, each aspect of the universe we try to exclude from our heart causes a fracture in our being.

Our being, our soul, our consciousness are already one with God. Trying to exclude any aspect of God's creation is an attempt to deny an aspect of our self.

In simple, personal terms: if what we fear actually happens, or if what we are praying for doesn't happen, we are afraid that we will never again be happy, that we will never again feel love, joy, and peace of mind.

If someone we love dies, we fear we will never again experience that unique, precious ecstasy we felt in their presence. We fear we will never feel complete. If we lose our health, we fear that we will never be able to find happiness in a body that isn't "normal." If we lose our money, we fear that we will be embarrassed and humiliated, incapable of overcoming the worries and inconveniences involved in being economically diminished in the eyes of the culture. If we pray for a new job and we don't get it, we fear we will never find joy and fulfillment in our professional lives.

On and on the train of fear goes . . .

But fears don't just apply to our personal lives. We have profound and deep-rooted fears about our society, our country, and the world.

We fear the loss of civility and kindness in our society. We fear that if our government isn't run the way we think it should be run, we are doomed. We fear that if humanity doesn't wake up to the potential environmental disasters we are creating, eventually our planet will become uninhabitable.

Just examine, for a moment, the fear and anger generated in the realm of politics. Examine how religious belief tends to exacerbate that fear and anger. It doesn't matter whether we are talking about the conflict between Protestants and Catholics in Ireland, between Sunni Muslims and Shiite Muslims in the Middle East, between radical Islam and "the infidels," between Arabs and Jews, between Islam and Hinduism, or between fundamentalist Christianity and the more progressive secular elements of our own society; the result is essentially the same. Both sides in each conflict fear the other. And both sides tend to characterize the other as evil: at best, misguided; at worst, actual messengers of Satan.

No matter what one's political persuasion, few would argue that political campaigns in the United States have taken on an increasingly contentious, mean-spirited quality in recent years. In nearly every contest, both sides do their best to paint the other side as immoral. Candidates seldom make any clear, positive statements about the good they intend to do. Instead, they spend most of their time attempting to inflame the electorate's passions, to make voters fearful of opposing candidates and angry about those candidates' perceived wrongdoings, mistakes, and character flaws.

Why?

Because the people who manage political campaigns understand — as Adolf Hitler understood — that fear and anger are powerful motivators. They believe that the most effective campaign strategies are those that engender a response of fear and anger in the voters' minds.

The problem is, we human beings tend to be at our worst when we are motivated by fear and anger. We do irrational, heartless, violent things. Our fear and anger have formed the basis for every war, every injustice, every genocide, every human-made disaster in the history of the human race. Our fear and anger have caused every act of human cruelty, self-centeredness, excessive consumption, and environmental depletion.

People who use fear and anger to motivate other human beings, no matter what the hoped-for end result might be, are contributing not to the advancement or enlightenment of humanity but to the degradation and possible destruction of humanity.

When we fear others we tend to feel justified in directing hatred toward them. I vividly remember this happening in the 1960s during the Vietnam War. When I finished high school I was eligible to be drafted. But it was difficult — if not impossible — to discern a single coherent justification for the war. Vietnam was a tiny country in an essentially undeveloped region of Asia halfway around the world. It was clearly no threat to the United States. Yet we unleashed a horrific conflagration in a minuscule, impoverished country where life was difficult enough without the intrusion of our war. American soldiers were dying, and innocent Vietnamese people were dying. It was difficult to envision any good that might come from continuing the conflict.

The internal conflicts generated by the Vietnam War propelled me into the antiwar movement. But I soon observed something very curious. Many of the leaders of the antiwar movement were themselves seething with anger and resentment. In many circumstances, they were advocating violence. During a huge antiwar rally in Washington, D.C., in 1968, a riot broke out because a large contingent of demonstrators began hurling rocks and bottles at the police and National Guard, who were merely there to keep order in the streets of the nation's capital.

The demonstrators had already been hurling insults at the police, calling them pigs and berating them with obscenities. When they couldn't provoke the police and National Guard with verbal assaults, they resorted to inflicting physical injury.

The police and National Guard responded with tear gas canisters, an essentially benign response to a flagrant provocation. But that precipitated another, larger volley of rocks and bottles being thrown back at the police.

What struck me as I watched was that the police and National Guard were acting with a great deal more restraint and passivity than the antiwar demonstrators, and the antiwar demonstrators were acting much more warlike than the people they were protesting against.

As I stood on the corner that day, a question arose in my mind that has stayed with me ever since: How do we stop war with violence?

~

The answer is, we don't.

We don't right the wrongs of the world by spreading more anger and hatred. And we don't find happiness by excluding others — individuals, families, races, nations, and events — from our hearts.

The policemen and National Guardsmen were living, breathing, feeling human beings with mothers, and fathers, and wives, and children, and they were doing what they believed to be their duty, what they believed to be right. The vast majority of them weren't there because they wanted a confrontation with the youthful war protesters.

They were there simply because it was their job, their duty, to try to maintain order. The antiwar protesters were the ones who wanted a violent confrontation.

A few years later, I came across the following statement from one of humanity's most beloved messengers of love, peace, and forgiveness, Saint Francis of Assisi. He said, "While you are proclaiming peace with your lips, be careful to have it even more fully in your heart. Nobody should be roused to wrath or insult on your account. Everyone should rather be moved to peace, goodwill, and mercy as a result of your self-restraint."

CHAPTER 7

When the World Turns Upside Down

God cannot be explained.
He cannot be argued about.
He cannot be theorized,
nor can He be discussed and understood.
God can only be lived.

MEHER BABA, *GOD SPEAKS*

There are times in life when our confrontation with what we fear comes so suddenly, swiftly, and unexpectedly that it can take years to integrate the teachings offered by the experience. Some among us face difficulties that — in the warm, insulated cocoon of our cultural denial — we might never have imagined, experiences so *unimaginable* that we might not even have acknowledged the fact that we feared them. These events are often so far outside the realm of expectation that we couldn't even have imagined offering prayers to ask that we be protected from them.

Still, such circumstances can offer unparalleled opportunities for spiritual growth and for cultivating deep connection with God. In his landmark book *When Bad Things Happen to Good People*,

Rabbi Harold Kushner offers us a unique glimpse into his own personal journey, an intense analysis of many of the issues we are exploring here.

When his first child, a son named Aaron, was diagnosed at the age of three with an extremely rare congenital malady called progeria, or "rapid aging," Rabbi Kushner's universe was torn to shreds. The diagnosis was coupled with a devastating prognosis. Rabbi Kushner and his wife were told that their beloved son "would never grow much beyond three feet in height, would have no hair on his head or body, would look like a little old man when he was still a child, and would die in his early teens."

Rabbi Kushner was thrown into a desperate, anguished struggle to understand how God could allow such a thing. After all, Rabbi Kushner knew himself to be an essentially good man, doing good work... God's work. Why was he being punished when the world is so full of selfish, self-centered people of questionable character who have healthy children? And why would God allow, or cause, such suffering for an innocent child like Aaron?

These questions haunted him. As he began to honestly examine the world around him, he saw a vast amount of unfairness and seemingly undeserved suffering. Selfish, dishonest, ruthless people become wealthy, and good-hearted, generous people often wind up with financial difficulties and a myriad of seemingly undeserved problems.

The rabbi concluded that the best way to understand our predicament as human beings is to resolve that — perhaps — God is not all-powerful. Perhaps God is a just God and an all-loving God, but not an all-powerful God. He suggested that we let go of the notion that God causes or controls every event on earth.

> If God is a God of justice, and not of power, then He can still be on our side when bad things happen to us. He can know that we are good and honest people who deserve better. Our misfortunes are

> none of His doing, and we can turn to Him for help. Our question will not be Job's question, "God, why are You doing this to me?" but rather, "God, see what is happening to me. Can you help me?" We will turn to God, not to be judged or forgiven, not to be rewarded or punished, but to be strengthened and comforted.[1]

An extremely loving, caring, compassionate human being, Rabbi Kushner has obviously explored these issues with deep sincerity, unimpeachable integrity, and an impressive scholarly understanding of Old Testament theology. His thesis is both interesting and thoughtful. It has helped millions of people to deal with the complexities and contradictions of being human, the disappointments and inequities of life in the physical universe, and the concept of a Supreme Being and the challenges of relating to Him, or Her, or whatever It is.

In a sense, though, what Rabbi Kushner suggests is that we perceive God as a limited God, and therefore as a God who isn't really God. His eloquent, heartfelt, sincere articulation of his own inner struggle is still much encumbered by the limitations of human intellect. Throughout his book, Rabbi Kushner examines the issues solely in terms of rational human thought. His explorations and examinations are exclusively rooted in human concepts of good and evil, right and wrong, justice and injustice, fairness and unfairness, love and hate, reward and punishment. Through deductive reasoning, Rabbi Kushner uses all of these qualities to measure the extent and reach of God's power and presence. At the core of Rabbi Kushner's struggle is the quest to find a way to continue to understand God as the Supreme Paternalistic Being . . . the Benevolent Father, who protects, rewards, and loves, despite the evil and suffering in this world that He created.

In essence, Rabbi Kushner's conclusion is one that at its core is still rooted in an anthropomorphic definition of God. He applies human concepts and human values to the Creator, then tries to deduce which of those concepts and values might logically be embodied in God, given the empirical evidence available in the world of form. It is also a concept of God as something essentially separate from His creation, something one can theorize about but not something one can experience.

For many of us, Rabbi Kushner's thesis may not be satisfactory. The limitations he places on God's ability to participate in His creation and on our ability to somehow consciously connect with and experience God may leave us with a sense of discontinuity and incompleteness. Because if there is a God, then God by its very nature created everything, exists everywhere, and infuses everyone and everything with life.

So we are back to the starting point of our inquiry. How can we understand suffering and evil when we posit the existence of a God who is all-powerful *and* all-loving?

Compare Rabbi Kushner's concept of God with the classic expression "Not a leaf falls off a tree without the will of God." Our problem, as Rabbi Kushner outlined it so eloquently, is that if we understand and define God purely in terms of human values, then it is impossible to see God as all-powerful *and* just. He can be one or the other, says the rabbi, but not both. If God is all-powerful, if His will is being done on earth, then the rabbi concludes that God is clearly not just.

Perhaps what we need is some mechanism for stretching our concepts of God, God's will, God's love, and God's justice.

Perhaps God is nothing like a human being. Perhaps the will of God is nothing like human will. Perhaps God's love is vastly different from the needy, expectant love we often experience as humans. Perhaps God's values are nothing like human values.

And perhaps God's justice is different from human justice.

As humans, when we speak of will we are speaking of intent. We are speaking of a tenacious effort to control. When we say a child is willful we mean that the child is unruly, defiant, self-absorbed, and unaccepting of authority. We are saying, essentially, that the child cannot be controlled. We understand the concept of will to encompass intense desire coupled with a relentless, manipulative control of the external environment.

Perhaps God's will is more like the Taoist concept of *wu wei*, or effortless doing. Perhaps God's will is all of the accumulated tangible results of the forces set in motion by whatever impulse originally created the physical universe, like the lawful, predictable circular waves moving out in ever-expanding orbs from the point at which a stone is dropped in water.

Is it the stone's *will* to create the expanding spiral of waves? Perhaps not. Perhaps the stone doesn't care. But, in terms of the results, we might easily see the expanding spiral of waves as the stone's will. We might also call it "an unintended result." But it is an inviolable, unavoidable result of action taken. Whether intended or unintended, the result of the action or event is long lasting, affecting the surface of the water and the water beneath the surface for great distances.

Every action or event in the physical universe has effects that radiate far out from the originating point. In the physical universe, there is momentum and inertia. There is a relentless balancing of opposites. As Newton pointed out, every action has an equal and opposite reaction. And what from certain vantage points looks like chaos, from others looks extraordinarily orderly.

We need only observe the predictability of the planets and stars, and the incomprehensible fact that the physical universe itself appears to be infinite. For the most part, the multitudes of planets and stars move through that vast boundless space in orderly paths — all maintaining their spatial relationships with each other in patterns, motions, and orbits that can precisely be calculated and predicted over billions and billions of years.

What — other than an infinite being or force — could possibly have created an infinite universe with so many long-range, long-lasting, inviolable control mechanisms?

Perhaps what we are being called on to do, in order to move into a new phase of human evolution and gain a more comprehensive understanding of our Creator, is to finally let down the walls that have so long separated science and religion. Why would scientific discovery in any way undermine the belief in God?

It might very well undermine ancient, outmoded, mythological beliefs and story lines about God. It might very well undermine archaic notions about God. But I have never seen anything in the way of scientific evidence that has refuted or even challenged the existence of a single, primordial energy source.

In fact, just the opposite is the case. We know through quantum physics that there is only one energy in the universe... one light... one source of all that is. We now know — *scientifically* — that everything in the physical universe... *every thing*... is made up of that same one energy.

The notion that we are all one is no longer some sentimental New Age tagline espoused by starry-eyed, latter-day flower children.

It is literally true.

Albert Einstein, generally considered the greatest genius in human history and the preeminent pioneer in the field of quantum mechanics, suggested that he did not arrive at his understanding of the basic laws of the universe through his rational mind. Einstein recognized the limited ability of the rational human mind, and deductive reasoning, to fully discover "truth."[2] Even when the mind is fully engaged, the observations of quantum physicists often involve lawful processes that defy human logic.

Some of the greatest scientists of the twentieth century have reported that when they examine data gathered through the most advanced instrumentation and techniques available, much of it doesn't make any rational sense. For instance, when they observe the electron, one of the fundamental building blocks of form, they recognize that much of what they see is indefinable. It defies categorization. It both is and isn't. It is both large and small. It moves and remains stationary. It changes and remains static.

Amazing!

At the cutting edge of science there is a recognition that the traditional methods of scientific inquiry have important limitations. Science has long been rooted in the fundamental proposition that only what can be observed and measured is real or, at least, scientifically significant. But we now understand, through quantum physics, that the very act of observing phenomena can cause the phenomena being observed to change. And thus, gathering scientific data can become rather challenging. If observing phenomena can cause the phenomena to change, and what *can* be observed scientifically sometimes defies logic and clear definition, then the tools we have at our disposal for understanding the universe through intellectual and scientific means are indeed limited.

Nevertheless, it would appear that many scientific insights are closer to "truth" than many ancient religious fairy tales that discount, ignore, and express hostility toward science. Perhaps in the next phase of human evolution, science will merge with our religious beliefs. Perhaps someday science and religion will walk hand in hand to illuminate a new understanding of our existence, the universe in which we live, our Creator, and our role in this life.

For now, the perceived conflict between science and religion is just as heated as the conflicts between the religions themselves. Practically every religious tradition believes that it is the only way. And people who discount the existence of God often believe that "pure" science is the only way to perceive reality. Isn't it more likely that, though each has a different view of truth, they each have only a partial glimpse of truth? Every religious tradition and every path of scientific exploration has uncovered some elements of the Truth of our existence. Each has a few kernels of insight, a few pieces of the universal puzzle, but no religious or scientific tradition that I have encountered has been able to construct a total picture of who we are, where we came from, and what our lives are meant to be about.

Our predicament as human beings was exquisitely portrayed in that wonderful old story about three blind men. Encountering an elephant for the first time, one man touches the tail and says, "Aha! An elephant is like a snake." The second man touches the elephant's leg and says, "No! You're wrong! An elephant is like a tree!" The third man touches the elephant's side and says, "You're both wrong! An elephant is like a mountain!" They argue and argue and argue, each one convinced that his limited "view" of the elephant is the correct one.

Both religion and science suffer from the same predicament. The problem is, every religion and every scientific discipline may turn out to offer us nothing more than well-meaning attempts to explain the unexplainable. The very limitations of our ability to grasp or understand it all cause us confusion. And that confusion gives rise to an uncomfortable sense of insecurity. Our insecurity gets triggered when someone else's belief system appears to be in conflict with our own. We may not fully understand what it's all about. But we often fall into the trap of thinking that, despite our own fog of confusion, if we can convince other people that we are right and all the other explanations of reality are wrong, then at least we will feel a little more secure about our own belief system. We gain a certain form of security simply because other people agree with us. So, in reality, insecurity and fear — much more than any perceived mission — are at the root of both evangelism and intellectual arrogance.

~

For the moment, though, let us continue to look at some of the ways in which cutting-edge science helps us understand spiritual principles. Despite the fact that quantum physics recognizes that there is only one energy in the universe, we still seem to perceive multitudinous unique and distinct forms. But when we boil it all down to its essential ingredient, it is all made of the same one energy. And that energy is light.

So that means, again, that you and I are literally one. We are made up of the same substance. And there is only one of it. All of these unique and distinct forms we see — whether floor, wall, ceiling, chair, table, bed, sofa, car, tree, flower, bird, grass, planet, sun, human being, Christian, Muslim, Buddhist, Hindu, Jew — are made up of exactly the same one light. And all of the forms we perceive are just the result of that one light vibrating at different rates of speed. All physical phenomena are just patterns of slowed-down light.

In his 2005 Christmas Eve homily, Pope Benedict referred to the birth of Jesus as, "the breaking of God's light upon a world full of darkness and unsolved problems.... Wherever God's glory appears, light spreads throughout the world." He went on to quote John 1:5: "'God is light and in him is no darkness.' The light is a source of life. Wherever God's glory appears, light spreads throughout the world."[3] And quantum physics continually refers to "the one light," the source and substance of *all* matter.

In another astonishing discovery, we now understand that a powerful electron microscope can allow us to actually see that forms which appear solid and inert are neither solid nor inert. They are made up of molecules of the one light that are dancing in, out, and around each other, constantly moving, constantly changing. Even the most "solid" rock is made of dancing molecules of the one light.

So every form in the universe is connected because it is all made up of the same substance, and every form is vibrant, vital, and alive. Through science we know these truths. But we don't live, think, and act as if we know them. The result of ignoring these scientific truths, and their complementary spiritual truths, is selfishness, self-centeredness, and disconnection. And the result of selfishness, self-centeredness, and disconnection is loneliness, stress, disillusionment, and misery. When we think and act from selfishness and disconnection, we are negating our essential oneness, ignoring our connection with the one energy that binds us all. We are obscuring our true nature.

The two questions that lie at the core of our spiritual pursuits — our efforts to "awaken" — are "How do we get free of our loneliness, stress, disillusionment, and misery?" and "How do we actually see and feel the One Light we all share?"

One of the most interesting explanations of our universe and its purpose was offered by Meher Baba in his extraordinary book *God Speaks*. To simplify a relatively weighty treatise, Meher Baba essentially set forth the notion that in the beginning, God was all there was. And God, in "its" highest form, is neither good nor evil. "It" just is.[4]

A vast, formless, edgeless, immeasurable, infinite ocean of existence, God longs to know itself. That longing is the first form. That longing acts like a wind blowing across the previously still surface of the ocean, creating a seemingly infinite number of waves. The waves create bubbles. The bubbles experience themselves as separate from the ocean, but they are identical with it. They, too, are water. They contain every essential ingredient of the ocean itself. But they experience themselves as separate. They are only apparently separate, however. They experience that apparent separation through the thin outer skin of their form, which apparently separates them from their source. But, in essence, they and their source are one.

In the above analogy, the ocean represents God, and the bubble represents our individual soul. They are one. All that exists and all that happens in this universe of form is the expression of that one energy, that one light — God — seeking to know itself.

In India, in 1973, when I first encountered the teaching that God, in its original, formless form, is neither good nor evil, I felt strangely uneasy. Most of us have grown up attached to the notion that God is all-good. We derive a great deal of solace and comfort from it. Yet we are also attached to the notion that God is all-powerful. As we have seen, the two concepts are somewhat incongruent.

But if we begin to understand that God is the One, the only One, the One Light, then we can begin to understand that the route back to God — the route to enlightenment, the route to consciously experiencing that oneness — is a very clear path. It is the path of love.

Our greatest asset as human beings is that we have the capacity, by virtue of our fully developed consciousness, to actually experience God. It is possible that all of creation has been moving toward the evolution of some mechanism for that One Light to consciously know itself.

And though it knows itself through the totality of its creation, it can know itself most clearly through our human consciousness.

And through the ever-expanding bliss of love.

~

How do we begin to consciously experience that oneness?

By acting and thinking in ways that are expressions of that oneness — by loving — and by delving deeply into the depths of our consciousness through contemplative prayer and meditation.

When we look at the codes of conduct suggested by the great religions of the world, the behaviors that are considered good are behaviors that express unity, or oneness. Love, kindness, friendliness, generosity, honesty, compassion, and caring all express our inherent connectedness... our inherent oneness. They are behaviors that unify us.

In contrast, anger, hatred, hostility, dishonesty, thievery, violence, and callous indifference are all expressions of disconnectedness... or twoness. In overly simplistic terms, good behaviors unify and harmonize us, and bad behaviors divide and separate us.

There is another level to this good versus evil discussion. The good behaviors are what will make us happy. Since evil goes against our inherent oneness, our inherent connectedness, it can only bring suffering and misery. Every time we think or speak or act in a manner that expresses disconnection, we experience a subtle cry of agony in our soul.

The answer to the question "Did God create evil?" can only be yes because God created everything. There is nothing . . . no thing . . . that is separate from God. Not that God set out consciously to create evil and suffering; it is merely the inevitable result of the duality inherent in form. We can see it as a scientific principle rather than as a theological story line. But God is still the One . . . the *only* One. God remains completely unchanged and totally untainted by His entry into the world of form.

No matter how much evil we think exists in the world of form, love is still the expression of that oneness. It is the conscious recognition of our essential connection with other beings and with all that exists. So God created both good and evil in equal measure. Perhaps not consciously or intentionally, but as an inevitable result of the very act of creation. Every action in the physical universe has an equal and opposite reaction. If this entire universe exists in order for God to know itself, and if God is the One, the one energy that forms the substance of every thing in the universe, then acknowledging and expressing that oneness in our minds and in our lives is the route back to God.

The way to acknowledge and express that oneness is to increase the amount of love in our lives.

~

As a child I was often the recipient of that infamous wagging parental finger that accompanied the ominous warning "You had better be good!" As it was delivered, it didn't make being good sound like fun. Instead, being good sounded like punishment.

Many of us have grown up in religious traditions that communicated the same thing: that the codes of conduct and morality we are taught are given to us by a punitive God to punish our "sinfulness" and deprive us of enjoyment.

Ironically, just the opposite is the case. It is the good behaviors that actually bring us happiness. Not simply because they are good but because they are the avenues to becoming connected, to becoming rooted in our oneness, to becoming a vibrant, living expression of our true nature, leading us to the spiritual union and awakening to love we so long for.

The reason that selfishness, self-centeredness, and disconnection lead to loneliness, stress, disillusionment, and misery is that selfishness is a denial of our true nature. Selfishness runs both counter to who we truly are and against the grain of our essential oneness.

~

To apply these concepts to the nitty-gritty hurts, problems, and disappointments that have inspired you to read this book, let me say that in all my years of working with people who are suffering through loss and heartbreak, the turning point for them almost always came when they began to reconnect with others. That reconnection can take many forms. One of the most effective routes I know is to find some practice through which you begin to connect with others who have experienced a similar loss or problem. This strategy is at the core of every successful twelve-step program, as well as organizations like Compassionate Friends.

I have repeatedly seen that the most difficult aspect of the experience we call grief is the sense of aloneness, or isolation. What we have been looking at in this and the previous chapters are the religious, spiritual, and scientific underpinnings of our essential connectedness. So when we feel alone and disconnected, all our problems seem worse. In fact, disconnection not only exacerbates our problems... disconnection *is* the problem. It is the fundamental cause of all human suffering.

Since "connectedness" is the fundamental truth in the world of form, the sense of disconnection is the fundamental illusion. Connectedness is our true nature. Living with a sense of disconnectedness is experiencing ourselves to be disconnected from who we truly are. Just as disconnection, isolation, and aloneness create most of our suffering, they also prevent us from healing through periods of suffering. From that perspective, the tendency of many religious institutions to engender more disconnection and more isolation, rather than offer us methods for healing our sense of separateness, is both ironic and tragic.

We may have suffered loss, sadness, disappointment, and betrayal, but we are never disconnected from our Creator and never disconnected from love, peace, and joy. We need only find new ways to access that which is always within us.

PART TWO

Why We Might Think Our Prayers Aren't Answered

The mind is indeed restless,
Arjuna: it is indeed hard to train.
But by constant practice . . . the mind in truth
can be trained.
When the mind is not in harmony,
the divine communion is hard to attain,
but the man whose mind is in harmony attains it,
if he knows, and if he strives.

LORD KRISHNA, BHAGAVAD GITA

CHAPTER 8

"Why?" The Most Difficult Question

Mind wants to know that which is beyond mind.
To know that which is beyond mind, mind must go —
vanish, leaving no vestige of itself behind.
The humor of it is, the mind, which is finite,
wants to retain itself and yet know Truth, which is infinite.

MEHER BABA, *THE EVERYTHING AND THE NOTHING*

We have explored, from a variety of perspectives, the problems we face because our culture offers us so little guidance for dealing with life's inevitable difficulties. Instead of diving into the richness and depth of our spiritual traditions, we have often kept them quite superficial, allowing great traditions to be transformed into simple-minded structures more focused on supporting our cultural beliefs than guiding us toward spiritual transformation. We have selectively extracted the teachings we like and ignored those we don't. Our spiritual traditions have become so diluted that they no longer offer real opportunities for deep inner transformation.

In this section of the book, we will explore how prevalent assumptions, prejudices, and behavior patterns have created a difficult environment for spiritual transformation. This section is offered to help us see how our culture has lulled us to sleep and has engendered an atmosphere that is almost antithetical to spiritual growth. We are looking at the places where we habitually get stuck so that we might grow through them and get on with the joyous adventure of spiritual awakening.

~

Large spiritual problems grow from tiny seeds of thought. They may stem from misguided thought patterns or unenlightened belief systems. They get planted by our cultural training and take root in our consciousness, eventually growing into enormous, invasive, opportunistic weedlike plants whose root systems choke off our inner light and whose profuse branches obscure our ability to see the "outer" light.

In the work I have done with grief and loss, I have repeatedly seen that our mind tends to keep asking one question over and over. Unfortunately, it is a question that keeps us stuck in the endless loop of sadness and confusion. It is the question "Why?" "Why did this happen?" "Why did this happen to me?" "Why did this happen to someone I love?" "Why didn't God do something?"

The frustrating truth is that there are no answers to these questions.

Or, rather, there *are* answers, but none that will fully satisfy our human minds.

We can theorize, postulate, speculate... construct intricate cosmological, philosophical, and theological scenarios intended to imbue our desolation with some profound meaning. But the truth of the matter is, no intellectual explanation can truly mend a broken heart. No intellectual explanation is completely satisfactory, especially to our human minds, because our human minds endlessly question everything.

Many "faith" communities ask us to set aside our doubts and

questions. We are called upon simply to have faith. Sometimes we are told that having faith also requires us to set aside our human emotions, to blindly trust in God.

But that concept of faith requires a complete surrender of our questioning mind. It requires that we try to give up our human intellects and our human emotions. It requires that we replace them with a theory that we may not fully believe, a theory that supersedes intellectual understanding. We are asked to trust in God when, in a very profound and personal sense, it appears that God has violated our trust.

If we suppress our human emotions because we feel shame about them, if we have been taught that we shouldn't be experiencing what we are obviously experiencing, these emotions won't just magically go away. They wind up buried deep inside us, simmering, bubbling, and festering like molten lava.

If we think we have been successful in our efforts to suppress these emotions, we will very likely begin to experience a subtle but ever-growing emotional numbness. We will begin to feel and act like robotic automatons, stumbling through life in an emotionless stupor... drifting through each day on autopilot, feeling empty, frustrated, and depressed. We may become unusually tired. We may withdraw from the world. Even the most rudimentary social interactions may begin to seem unbearably demanding. We may sit at home alone in the dark, curtains drawn, ignoring the ringing of the phone, unable to respond even to friends and loved ones who call to offer their love and support. Our home, through neglect, may become dusty, dreary, and encrusted with mementos of the past we scarcely have time or energy to revisit.

We may also find ourselves inexplicably cranky and judgmental, intolerant of even the most benign people and events. Even when we think we have these powerful emotions buried, they will occasionally bubble up to the surface like a once dormant, now spontaneously active volcano. Sometimes the energy from these suppressed emotions can burst forth in wildly unpredictable, seemingly irrational eruptions of anger, hostility, even violence.

Then, through guilt and remorse, we may stifle ourselves, and our explosive despair turns inward once again, morphing back into dark, dreary depression and emotional numbness.

The truth of the matter is, we are human beings with human minds and human emotions. There is simply no way to deny our thoughts and feelings and still be happy and healthy. Yet we have to realize that neither intellect nor emotions, in and of themselves, can bring us to happiness. We need to learn how to deal openly and honestly with the fullness of who we are, our physical bodies, our emotions, our intellects . . . and our souls.

Those who have had the Grace to experience a direct connection with God, with Truth, know that such an experience can and often does supersede intellectual understanding. But even those among us who have had such a mystical awakening, a taste of "enlightenment," still have human hearts that hurt and human minds that question. We got a taste of Grace, of mystical Union, of the Spirit, that we thought would be absolutely transformational, that would change our lives forever. But a few days later a part of our mind is questioning its validity.

"Did that actually happen?"

"Was it real?"

"Maybe I just imagined it."

The quest for intellectual understanding is inherent in the human experience. But there is a point at which intellectual understanding is just not possible. Our relentless quest to achieve intellectual understanding can become the most formidable obstacle standing in the way of reclaiming happiness and peace of mind.

In one of the many ways Buddha diverged from most spiritual leaders, he never asked his followers to "have faith." He knew that what he experienced was available to all of us. Instead of offering spiritual platitudes and asking that people believe them, Buddha simply taught us how to have the same experience he had, so that we might know the Truth for ourselves. The essence of his path was meditation. Not theory, but experience. Not philosophical and theological story lines, but direct awareness of Truth.

It is nearly impossible to force the mind to stop questioning. But if we acknowledge that the deepest and most meaningful aspects of human existence may lie beyond our emotions and beyond the understanding of the intellect, it may be a little easier to allow ourselves to let go of the incessant questioning, doubting, and chattering of our minds. For most of us, the mind just has to burn itself out. We have to become totally frustrated and exhausted by the futility of searching for happiness through our thinking minds. Eventually, like a computer that has been fed an insoluble problem, our minds just give up. When that happens, *real* awakening can begin.

Becoming fully human, and fully Divine, requires that we transcend thought and move into experience. That is, we learn to stop thinking so much about our experiences and just *experience* them.

Our habitual tendency to ask why will never heal our grieving hearts. Thinking about experience always keeps us from fully experiencing it. When we live in our thinking minds, we are always at least one thought away from directly experiencing life. Allowing ourselves to fully experience our emotional pain, without attempting to couch it in mitigating thoughts and rational explanations, is the beginning of the healing of grief.

It is also the beginning of our awakening to real joy. Our efforts to suppress our sadness, through whatever means we employ, have the unfortunate side effect of also suppressing our joy. We simply can't turn off our emotions on only one side of the ledger. If we turn off our sadness, we inevitably turn off our happiness as well.

The real healing of grief, the real awakening into being fully alive, feeling fully engaged in our life experience, often begins when we are willing to open to the fullness of our human experience: the horror and the beauty, the sorrow and the joy, the darkness and the light.

From that point, we start to recognize how vast our hearts really are, how much more resilient than we ever imagined. We begin to see that our consciousness is without boundaries. We see that our capacity for compassion, for ourselves and for others, is unlimited.

After a great loss, people often ask me, "When will my grief go away?" The truthful answer is, "Never." But that doesn't mean that life will be forever miserable or that you will be forever sad. It simply means that every experience we have changes us and remains a part of us forever. That includes loss and disappointment.

It is quite possible to emerge from the cocoon of suffering that follows in the wake of loss with a heightened, more expansive appreciation for life, a deeper, more abiding joy, and a profoundly enhanced capacity for love and compassion. But that takes some work on our part. It takes a willingness to transcend the part of ourselves that revels in feeling victimized. We all have a tendency to feel victimized and to feel wronged. Until we resolve that we want to be happy more than we want to be right, we will remain stuck. So long as we are addicted to our tale of woe, we can never be happy and free.

When we start to recognize that much of our sadness and disappointment is a result of our peculiar and unrealistic cultural training, when we start to realize that we are by no means alone in our suffering, when we become willing to take charge of our own minds, our own consciousness, and our spiritual destiny, the path to freedom and joy opens before us.

Though the sadness of our losses and disappointments may forever remain a part of us, those very same experiences can also be catalysts that help us grow deeper in our awareness of the expansive nature of our consciousness and the unlimited nature of our hearts.

The challenge is to let go of our attachment to our questions, doubts, and outrage. We will still have all of those thoughts in our minds, but slowly we can begin to allow ourselves to not give so much importance to them.

When my dear friend Richard Carlson was preparing his wonderful book *For the Love of God: Handbook for the Spirit*, he interviewed the Dalai Lama. I asked Richard, "What was the most interesting thing His Holiness said?"

Richard said, "Well, I was amazed at how happy he seems to be all the time. So I asked him if he had any of the same thoughts that the rest of us have, you know, like anger, judgment, sadness, greed, lust, and confusion.

"He just laughed that wonderful, childlike laugh of his and said, 'Oh *yes*! I have *all* those thoughts. I am just a normal human being. The only difference is, I have learned not to pay any attention to those thoughts!' "

When we let go of the question "Why?" or, at least, when we learn not to pay so much attention to it, we can allow ourselves to just experience our experiences, and grow through them.

CHAPTER 9

We Have a Limited View of Life and of Ourselves

Prayer means learning to see the world from God's point of view.

ABRAHAM JOSHUA HESCHEL

One of the most popular philosophers of the twentieth century, Alan Watts illustrated the limitations in the way we view ourselves by telling the story of a young man who approached him one evening after a lecture. The smiling young man began proudly telling Watts about his girlfriend and how wonderful she was. Eventually, he pulled out his wallet and opened it to show Watts a photograph of his beloved. It was a standard, wallet-sized photo, $2\frac{1}{2}$ inches by $3\frac{1}{2}$ inches.

The young man smiled proudly and lovingly. "That looks just like her!" he said, pointing to the photo.

"Really?" said Watts. "Is she *that* small?"

The point is that we often see ourselves symbolically more readily than seeing who and what we *really* are. We do the same thing with the world around us. Think of how many times we have found ourselves in beautiful natural surroundings, looking directly — in absolute awe — at something like the Grand Canyon, Niagara Falls, or Mount Rainier.

Suddenly, someone nearby will say, "It looks just like a postcard!" We nod enthusiastically in agreement. We rarely notice, and hardly ever question, the bizarre, skewed manner in which our perceptions have become distorted. For many of us, a photograph is more familiar, more recognizable, than the real thing.

We are part of a whole. When we live in artificial, human-made, climate-controlled environments, we don't learn to tune to the flow of nature. We don't develop the capacity to understand our dependence on and interconnectedness with the natural world. In the absence of direct immersion in the natural world, we lose the awareness of our inherent connection with it.

In fact, modern Western culture, supported by sometimes questionable interpretations of biblical teaching, has long held the notion that humankind is destined to dominate nature. Certain forms of Christianity, in particular, have tended to see human beings as separate from the natural world, a belief that has engendered a profound arrogance, an indifference to the health and well-being of the environment, and an indifference to the overall health and well-being of humanity. At the same time this teaching gives us the false hope that every disease can be cured and every problem in the natural world can be corrected through human intervention. This attitude has put us on the path to destroying our planet through wanton pollution of our air and water and ceaseless depletion of the earth's natural resources. We have consistently believed that the problems we are creating, if there are any, are exaggerated. We believe we will have plenty of time to find solutions later.

Our culture has readily subscribed to the notion that every story can have a happy ending and that every individual is supposed to live happily ever after. We have become quite capable of blithely ignoring the inherent dangers and uncertainties in our physical universe, and the inherent dangers and negative consequences of our unwise actions.

Many philosophical materialists — including Sigmund Freud — have suggested that our fascination with the afterlife is but one more delusional projection of our "happily ever after" complex. The suggestion is that many people who embrace the notion of a glorious afterlife do so in the absence of clear and direct experience. Whether or not there actually is an afterlife is somewhat inconsequential for most people, who believe there is simply because it gives them comfort. Most people hold tenaciously to that belief without any corroborating evidence or experience.

There is an enormous difference between believing something simply because someone else has told us it is true and experiencing that it is true because we have direct, firsthand knowledge about it. It is the difference between the certainty of those who have had a near-death experience and those who believe in the afterlife simply because they have been told it exists. It is the difference between the certainty of those who have had a profound experience of mystical connection with God and those who believe in the potential of connection with God simply because they have been told about it.

Freud also asserted that it is impossible for the human ego to imagine its own extinction. That is, he believed our minds cannot comprehend the fact that we will inevitably die. He suggested, therefore, that our minds construct ideas about eternal afterlife primarily because of the fear engendered by our ego's inability to imagine its own death.

While Freud intimately grasped certain aspects of the human mind and was the first to map out many levels of the conscious and subconscious minds in an insightful manner, he failed to grasp the totality of who we are and how our minds function.

From the spiritual perspective, it is important to remember that our intuitive hearts literally know everything. We know Truth. No matter how often we ignore our intuition, no matter how much effort and energy we put into denying and ignoring the realities of life in the world of form, no matter how skilled we become at ignoring the part of ourself that is wise, there is still always a part of us that knows the truth. No matter how much we ignore the fact that we are all going to die, there is always a core awareness within us that knows we are. No matter how much we ignore the fact that our everyday thoughts and actions have far-reaching and long-lasting consequences, there is always a core awareness within us that knows these things.

And no matter how much we ignore the fact that we are all connected, that we are all one... there is always a core awareness within us that knows we are.

What we most often ignore is actually the most important dimension of our being — our identity as a soul. From the standpoint of our soul, we are infinite, eternal beings of Light. We are permanently connected to, and in all essential respects one and the same with, God. To see ourselves as anything less than this, to think that our finite bodies, minds, and personalities are the totality of our existence, can only lead to a sense of incompleteness and despair. Because there is always a subtle, quiet place within us that knows the Truth of our magnificence. To live and think and act as if we are less than we really are brings enormous dissatisfaction.

So much of our suffering in life is caused by the practice, fully supported by our culture, of ignoring these truths. So many of our problems arise from a fundamental disconnection with our own awareness, our own wisdom, and the natural world. Once we disconnect ourselves from what we know, and what is real, we are free to careen headlong into illusory beliefs and bizarre behaviors. None of those beliefs and behaviors, rooted in illusion, can ever bring lasting happiness.

Once we believe we are our body and our personality, we will continually pursue happiness where it can never be found. Once we believe that our happiness comes from wealth, possessions, fame, youth, power, sex, narcotics, or alcohol, we become capable of acting in extraordinarily ruthless and selfish ways to get what we think we want. And once we believe that it is actually possible or is our divinely ordained right to subdue and dominate the natural world, we become capable of thinking and acting in bizarre, disconnected ways.

But the very same mind that makes us miserable can also lead us to joy.

Buddhist teaching affirms that at our core all humans are kind, loving, and compassionate. This loving, compassionate kindness is sometimes referred to as our "true nature," or our "Buddha nature." Although there is usually some significant effort required as we strive to come into harmony with our true nature, the process involves unfolding — or unearthing — that which is already within us, not adding something we didn't already have. Buddha suggests that only the full awareness of our true nature and learning to live in harmony with it can bring us happiness.

A few years ago, a number of Western psychologists invited the Dalai Lama to join them for a conference on the similarities and differences between Western psychology and Buddhist psychology. At one point, one of the Western psychologists mentioned the term *low self-esteem*. He spoke the words in passing, almost with a sense that it was an inevitable characteristic of the human mind and therefore a given in human experience.

The Dalai Lama looked stunned. He said he didn't understand. He wasn't sure what the concept of low self-esteem meant. He asked that it be translated into his native language. His translator struggled for a few moments. Eventually, his translator concluded that there is just no way to translate *low self-esteem* into the Tibetan language. In Tibetan culture, there is no such concept. When the Dalai Lama began to grasp what the term meant, a strange look of compassion and wonder spread across his face. At that moment, his very sweet, deliciously expressive face seemed to say, "Oh my goodness, can Westerners ever come up with some extraordinary ways to suffer!"

Can you imagine living in a culture where low self-esteem doesn't exist?

In the Tibetan Buddhist culture, and in many other non-Western cultures, when a child is born, the entire community gathers to celebrate the birth of a celestial being, a being of Light who has come to earth to bless us. An angel, a divine being, has taken form to be among us, to help us, and to bring more Light into the world.

In our culture, a new birth is also greeted with great celebration. But while we enjoy the cuteness, beauty, and innocence of a newborn infant, much of our momentary joy is colored by anticipation and expectation. We say, "Oh, what a beautiful baby! Maybe she'll go to Harvard some day. Maybe he'll be President of the United States! Maybe she'll be a doctor! Maybe he'll be a famous movie star. Maybe she'll invent the drug that cures cancer!"

We are creating the sense that infants are not enough just as they are. They may be beautiful, and we may be joyful that they have been born, but the real meaning and importance of their life will come later. We begin telling our children — and thus ourselves — that our value as human beings will be measured by how much we can collect, achieve, and accomplish. The message is that our arrival on earth is not so much a gift as it is the beginning of a contest . . . a relentless quest to prove ourselves worthy of love.

Western culture has undeniably been affected by the peculiar Christian doctrine of original sin, which posits that as soon as we are born, we have already lost our connection with God. We therefore, as a culture, have a difficult time perceiving the essential spiritual purity of children, the fundamental completeness of their being. Most of us, from the moment of our birth and for the rest of our life, are constantly striving to be redeemed, to overcome our "sinfulness," to compensate for our fundamental lack of worthiness. We spend our lives striving to feel that we are acceptable in the eyes of our Creator and in the eyes of humanity.

We teach children that it is what they become that will determine their worthiness to be loved and to be happy. They must learn, and do, and produce. They must impress us. This is the essence of socialization and acculturation in modern Western culture. We become other-directed rather than inner-directed, looking outside ourselves for happiness, approval, and fulfillment. We look into the eyes of others — first our parents, then other adults, then our relatives, our friends, our community, and our peers — to see if we are okay. We spend much of our lives asking, "Am I enough? Do you love me? Do I look good? Have I done a good job? Am I complete yet?"

And for most of us, the culture keeps answering no.

Even when the answer is yes, our training is so ingrained that we can never seem to feel we have gotten *enough* approval.

No matter how good we become at achievement, there is almost always someone better than us. No matter how rich we become, there is usually someone wealthier. No matter how much power we amass, there is usually someone more powerful. No matter how beautiful we become, there is usually someone more beautiful.

The vast majority of us have not and will not achieve the pinnacle of success as defined by our culture... the pinnacle of beauty, strength, wealth, athletic prowess, intellectual achievement. Most of us are, in worldly terms, rather average.

And we are never at a loss for reminders of our shortcomings, at least in the eyes of the culture. Just look at any magazine for the messages being sent by the mainstream media. One of the first things that becomes clear is that, as a culture, we are obsessed with beautiful, slender, youthful, toned bodies and wrinkle-free faces. We are addicted to the notion that we can win the lottery, win the big game, remake ourselves into whatever we perceive the culture holds as an ideal. We believe that doing so will make us happy.

Through our media, we are also constantly surrounded by images of violence and images that depict violence as entertainment. We are fascinated by murder, brutality, and depravity. We encourage dishonesty, selfishness, greed, and anger. We think that the naked human body, as God created it, is not to be seen by children. But we bombard them with images of sexuality and images that equate sexuality with happiness and success.

Rarely do we offer our children magazines, television programming, advertising, and movies that promote kindness, generosity, compassion, and wisdom. Instead, they receive, each and every day, messages that tell them that they can be happy only if they look like this, wear this, drive this, put this on their hair, eat this, smell this way, invest their money here, have this dream home, take this drug, take this dream vacation, find the perfect mate, lose this much weight...

Our culture is so attached to youth that we will do almost anything to pursue the illusion of holding on to it. We have creams, dyes, pills, potions, and gels designed to help us erase the effects of aging. We can color our hair and erase our wrinkles. Cosmetic plastic surgery has become a widely accepted, mega-billion-dollar industry in our culture, constantly advertised and fully supported with widespread cultural approval. Medical statistics show that more than 10.2 million cosmetic surgery procedures were performed in the United States in the year 2005. And that number is expected to increase every year for the foreseeable future. We even have a number of television reality programs dedicated to following the lives, practices, and procedures of plastic surgeons and their patients.

In contrast, in many non-Western cultures it is the elders who are most appreciated because they have the greatest wisdom, knowledge, and experience. The elders are the ones who have lived long enough to know a great deal about life, about what is important, about the things that have real and lasting value.

~

Right now, as you are reading this, starvation continues to be one of the greatest causes of human suffering in nearly every corner of the globe. Every five seconds, somewhere in the world a child dies of starvation. Despite all of the extraordinary economic, agricultural, and medical resources we have at our disposal, despite all of the advanced technology and knowledge we have at our fingertips, and despite all of the abundant wealth we possess, there are still many cultures where two parents have to give birth to ten children in order to have one who reaches the age of twelve. Yet so much of what we have could so easily and gracefully be shared with others.

At this very moment, our own culture suffers from an abundance of overeating and obesity. The resultant health problems are enormous, creating an extraordinary burden on our health-care system. In our culture millions of people spend billions of dollars on products and programs designed to help them lose weight. And millions of people freely spend billions of dollars on plastic surgery they don't need.

Once when I was talking about all of this at a lecture, a woman approached me during the break and said, "One of our problems is we don't cultivate wise elders in this culture. When people are surrounded all their lives by the belief that old age is a time of misery, defeat, irrelevance and meaninglessness, they don't become wise as they age, they become anxious, fearful, and embittered."

She was absolutely right! We sometimes lose sight of the fact that our experience of life is a manifestation of the cumulative effects of culturally generated self-fulfilling prophecies. We hang on to youth because so many people have told us that youth is the best part of our life!

We shun aging because our lives feel so unfulfilled. We approach middle age in a panic, fearful that we have already missed the best years of our lives. We don't want to get old without ever having experienced the happiness, fulfillment, passion, and connection we expected, that were all supposed to have been a part of our youth.

Dr. Robert Kastenbaum, the great gerontologist, clearly understood many of the problems inherent in our culture's delusions about how to achieve happiness and fulfillment. In a 1978 article in the *Gerontologist*, Kastenbaum said that the "limitations and distortions of our core vision of what it means to be a person become starkly evident in old age... if to be an old person is to suffer abandonment, disappointment, and humiliation. This is not a 'geriatric problem.' It is the disproof of our whole shaky-pudding technology, science and all. If our old people are empty, our vision of life is empty."[1]

I don't know about you, but I can honestly say that my youth, especially my teenage years, was the worst time of my life. I didn't really even begin to be happy until I was in my late twenties.

I can also honestly say that throughout my life, some of the most interesting and delightful people I have ever known — many of whom I have regarded as my most treasured companions, friends, and teachers — have been people in their seventies, eighties, and nineties. They are the rare ones, the ones who haven't been seduced by our culture into thinking that they are useless or problematical simply because they are "old."

Despite our upside-down perceptions and the profusion of products and techniques designed to reverse or erase the aging process, the latest psychological and sociological studies show rather conclusively that the happiest time of life — even in our culture — occurs during the years after we reach the age of sixty. The same studies show that the unhappiest years are those from twenty to twenty-nine, exactly the years we most want to cling to.

Isn't it interesting that in recent decades we have come to understand that the cultures that haven't been affected by technological progress often possess a far deeper wisdom about human happiness and a far greater ability to live a meaningful life than we — in our modern, technology-obsessed, self-absorbed world — have?

We now look to yoga, meditation, Eastern philosophies, contemplative prayer, tai chi, qigong, acupuncture, Native American wisdom traditions, and a vast array of other philosophies, practices, and diets that hearken back, in some cases thousands of years, to earlier times when all the world was viewed as sacred; when the interconnection between human beings and the natural world was fully understood and appreciated; when the interconnection between human beings and the spiritual realms was fully recognized; when the interconnection between all human beings was instinctively known and honored; when health, healing, and happiness were seen to be intimately connected with one's diet, actions, and states of consciousness; and when it was understood that the primary route to happiness was to utilize one's life for spiritual awakening.

While our culture sees aging as a catastrophe and the time of retirement as a tragedy, in India it has traditionally been seen as the most important time of one's life. In India one can embrace aging because one is finally "free" to do the most important work a human being can do, the work of spiritual awakening.

When we are fully focused on God, we generally become wiser. For the younger members of the traditional Indian family, the grandparents become, literally, like gurus. They are the family's connection to the Divine, the wise ones who are there to offer advice, assistance, and insight. They are revered like great saints. Their children and grandchildren are honored to have them living in their homes so they can share in the benefits of their grandparents' evolving wisdom and enlightenment.

~

These principles have come into play with many of the elders I have worked with following the death of a beloved spouse. Initially, the survivor is heartbroken, heartsick, and disoriented. Our culture has offered grieving spouses little or no context to prepare for this experience and little or no context to find meaning in life following the death of their mate. Without their partner at their side, life becomes confusing and frightening, seemingly devoid of meaning.

As we work together, through various approaches, we begin to find ways for them to experience the eternal, undying love they always carry in their hearts for their physically departed spouse. We begin to explore the parts of them that might, even if only occasionally, have longed for more solitude. Now they have that solitude. We also begin to find ways for them to laugh again. In time, we begin to explore the Indian model of the senior years, how the elders in the society can become the true leaders of the society, the seers and sages.

Many of my most successful and dedicated meditation students have been widows and widowers in their sixties, seventies, and eighties who had never prepared for their new solitary lives. They had never thought of using the solitude, the inevitable physical restrictions, and the reduced social life brought on by the aging process as the most advantageous conditions for cultivating their spiritual life.

A number of years ago I began to see an interesting parallel between our spiritual pursuits and the process of aging. When we really want to nurture our spiritual awareness, we often remove ourselves — at least temporarily — from the outside world. We go off to an institution — a monastery, an ashram, a retreat center, or a meditation center. These centers are usually austere and institutional. We love the environment they create because it's so supportive of the inner work we want to do.

We want a private room so we're not distracted by the need to be social. We want quiet so that we're not distracted by sounds. We often do yoga so that we can sit in meditation for extended periods without having to move. When we sit in prayer and meditation, we generally close our eyes so we aren't distracted by visual stimuli. All this "frees" us to do our inner work.

Now look at what happens to us when we get old. We often wind up living alone in an institution. We lose most of our relatives and friends, so we have fewer opportunities, and fewer obligations, to be social. Our bodies get a little problematical, so we can't move around as much. We lose our hearing and our eyesight, so we're no longer distracted by sounds and sights.

Isn't that remarkable? Just when we are at the point in our lives when we really should start preparing to go to God, nature — naturally — gives us the optimum ingredients for a life of prayer, meditation, contemplation, and inner growth.

But our society is so upside down, we never consider that there might be some immensely positive effects to these natural by-products of the aging process. We're far too absorbed in thinking that it's all a catastrophe . . . a mistake. We think that God has screwed up because our loved ones have died, our bodies are falling apart, and we're losing our physical abilities. We think that God has abandoned us, when in fact He has given us all of the conditions we need to come to know Him. We often miss that opportunity because we're so consumed with being a victim, with being depressed and outraged because we're not young anymore and things aren't like they were when we were young.

So we hang on to the illusion of a youth that wasn't really all that fulfilling. And we shun the period in our lives when we might achieve real happiness. The truth of the matter is, the only widely accepted lifestyle offered to our elders in this culture is to do everything they can to pretend they're still young!

We tenaciously cling to all of the things we simply can't take with us when we die rather than cultivate our inner beings in preparation for going into "the formless." We miss the opportunity to cultivate the qualities of being that we can take with us, the qualities that might make old age and dying the greatest trip of our lifetime.

With just a slight change in perception, just a slight adjustment, we always have the opportunity to see life differently. What is required is learning how to let go of the neurotic, shortsighted, culturally bound notions of who we are and what our lives are about. When we can do that, a vast new universe of possibilities — for happiness and fulfillment — opens up before us.

There is one helpful principle to keep in mind as we begin to evolve toward recognizing the awesome nature of who and what we truly are: "Just because a lot of people believe something doesn't make it true."

There was a time when nearly everyone on earth believed that the earth was flat. It took a few courageous, unintimidated explorers to help us all know the truth. A handful of special people had an intuitive sense that things were not the way most people believed them to be. The explorers were willing to take great risks to advance our understanding.

For the past five hundred years, as a result of their uncertain and perilous journey, the rest of the human race has benefited from a much more accurate knowledge of ourselves, our planet, our universe . . . and our place in the cosmos. And in the years and decades to come, the human race can benefit from the inner exploration you are embarking on.

~

Each of us is a soul. Our soul possesses a natural transcendent capacity for eternal joy, right at the core of our being. That place of transcendent joy endures through anything and everything that happens to us. There is a part of us, an abiding realm of consciousness, that has never changed, not even slightly, since before we were born.

It doesn't change as we get old.

And it doesn't change when we die.

The only true happiness in life, the only true security, comes from growing into a full awareness of this formless, infinite, eternal soul. Anything we have identified as who and what we are — a male, a female, a husband, a wife, a widow, a widower, a father, a mother, an old person, a child, an American, an intellectual, an athlete, a beautiful person, an unattractive person, a success, a failure, wealthy, poor, ambitious, lazy — is just an illusion. These identities are illusions because they are all transitory. They are subject to change, decay, and death. Collectively, they form the incredibly limited, culturally defined, hopelessly distorted lens through which we view ourselves. But these distorted perceptions have nothing to do with who we truly are.

CHAPTER 10

We Rarely Prepare for Difficulties

Remember, friends, as you pass by,
As you are now, so once was I,
As I am now, so you must be,
Prepare yourself to follow me.

EPITAPH ON AN EIGHTEENTH-CENTURY TOMBSTONE IN ASHBY, MASSACHUSETTS

At one time in my life, I lived next door to a wonderful man named Jack. When I first met him, he was eighty-six years old. He was small in build, no more than five feet four, and seemed slightly frail. But he was energetic, proud, and active. I would watch him mowing his lawn in the summer and shoveling snow from his driveway in the winter. I marveled at his enthusiasm for life. Early in our relationship, I learned that he felt no need or desire for anyone to help him in any way. He was very comfortable financially, and he could easily have hired someone to do these jobs for him, but he didn't.

I sometimes became concerned for him, especially on hot days in the summer and cold days in the winter. I would look out the window and see Jack chugging around his yard or up and down his driveway... mowing and shoveling... completely unperturbed by the strenuous nature of the work and the inhospitable weather.

Sometimes I would stroll over to see him, to try to offer some assistance. But Jack would have no part of it. "Go mow your own grass," he would say with a smile, or "Go shovel your own driveway." There was a friendly, teasing quality to his responses. But he really didn't want my help.

I had no desire to undermine Jack's sense of independence or his ability to enjoy his freedom, so I would back off and leave him to his work. But I would often sit in my house, looking out the window at Jack puttering around his yard, realizing that one day he might push himself too hard, and I might look out and see that he had fallen down on the lawn or on the pavement. I would have to call 911 and then rush out to see if I could help him.

Amazingly, that day never came.

But one day, when Jack was ninety-two, I saw an ambulance in his driveway. I went over to see what was happening and to ask if there was anything I might do to help. His daughter, who was visiting, told me that a few days earlier, Jack had been dealing with a water leak in his basement. Instead of calling a plumber, he had attempted to fix it himself. He had spent several hours sloshing around in cold water up to his hips and now had developed pneumonia. He was taken to the hospital.

A few days later he died.

When I got the news, I immediately went next door to offer support to Jack's wonderful wife, Mary, and his lovely daughter, Julie, who had stayed on for a few days to be with her mother.

As I held Julie in my arms, she began to sob. When she finally calmed down enough to be able to speak, she simply said, "I can't imagine life without my Dad. I feel so unprepared for this. I never thought this would happen."

In our culture's relentless quest for happy endings and corresponding denial of illness, aging, death, and disappointment, many of us have spent our lives turning away whenever reminders of life's uncertainty crop up in our field of vision or in our awareness.

Many of us grew up in homes where we were shamed for crying, for feeling vulnerable, for experiencing fear and depression, for raising questions about the inherent uncertainties in life. Many of us grew up in homes where certain subjects were forbidden, especially at the dinner table, and the most forbidden subject was death.

"Don't bring that up at the dinner table, dear."

"We don't talk about that."

"Don't say that. You'll cause something *terrible* to happen."

"If you want to cry, go to your room."

"If you want to cry, I'll give you something to cry about."

At the same time, many of us were surrounded by bizarre superstitions and irrational fears. In my house, whenever salt was spilled at the dinner table, my mother would order whoever spilled it to take a pinch or two of the spilled salt and throw it backward over their shoulder. When I asked her why, she said, "Because if we spill salt, something bad will happen before the day is over. But if we throw what we spilled over our shoulder, we break the curse."

Everyone at the dinner table would stop eating until the "perpetrator" threw a pinch of spilled salt over her or his shoulder. Then the rest of us could breathe a sigh of relief and go on with our dinner in peace, secure in the knowledge that we had skillfully avoided whatever mysterious catastrophe spilled salt might otherwise have caused. That strange custom became so much a part of my consciousness that still — some fifty years later — I find myself automatically tempted to reenact the ritual whenever I spill salt.

Several friends have told me that in their childhood, their mothers would order them to lift their feet and arms into the air whenever they were driving past a cemetery. If they asked why, their mothers would say, "Because the spirits from the cemetery linger close to the ground outside the cemetery, and they're always trying to grab the spirits of people who pass by. They won't be able to grab your spirit if you lift your feet and hands into the air."

How many strange beliefs, customs, and superstitions like that were passed down to you? How many bizarre rituals and thought patterns? How many completely irrational fears? How often did otherwise rational adults act in an inexplicable, somewhat insane manner?

While many of us were taught useless behaviors to respond to frightening, irrational notions generated by inexplicable fantasies, few of us were ever taught how to think or behave or act in the face of life's real challenges and inevitable times of difficulty.

When my friend Jack's daughter said, "I never thought this would happen," I silently wondered how it is possible for our culture to raise us in an atmosphere of such absolute denial. How is it possible that we might — in our mid-fifties — have a parent who, miraculously, has reached the age of ninety-two, and yet, in all those years we might never consider the fact that our parent could die at any moment? Most of us have never consciously acknowledged that we should be preparing ourselves, psychologically and emotionally, for our parents' deaths.

Despite all of our technological and medical prowess, the "death rate" for human beings has continued to hold steady at 100 percent. In a spiritually healthy culture grounded in truth rather than delusion, we would have recognized that our preparation should have begun the moment we were born. The story about Jack's daughter is just one of hundreds of similar stories I have encountered over the years. The two phrases I have heard most often, from nearly every baby boomer who has come to me after losing a parent, are "I feel so unprepared" and "I never thought about this happening."

Our problems arise from the illogical interpretations we make of the information we receive. For instance, we have consistently misinterpreted our average life expectancy. In the United States, because we have relatively good health care, access to highly nutritious foods, and an abundance of information about how to care for our bodies, we have one of the longest average life expectancies of any major culture on earth. As I am writing this, it is approximately seventy-eight years and six months.

It is an average calculated by adding together the number of infants who die in childbirth and the number of people who live more than one hundred years. The census bureau studies the number of deaths at every age between zero and one hundred plus to calculate the average. So, truly, it is just an average life span, not a guarantee.

But we live and think and act as if it were a guarantee. We live and think and act as if — when we came out of the womb — a representative from God was standing in the delivery room ready to hand us a warranty signed by God. We act as if he said, "This is your guarantee of *at least* seventy-eight years in this body. If you don't get it, you can sue God."

But we don't get that guarantee!

We're not guaranteed seventy-eight minutes, let alone seventy-eight years. There is no great religious text, spiritual teaching, or "holy" book I have ever read that offers us a guarantee of *any* particular life span . . . in these bodies. Of course, it isn't just children losing their parents who suffer from the complex of neuroses and delusions our culture has engendered. Parents who lose children in any culture are absolutely, naturally, and understandably overcome with grief.

But in our culture, that grief is often made worse. It is made worse because our cultural denial has been so absolute. When a child dies in our culture, the grieving parents are not only dealing with the natural grief of the loss, they are also struggling to integrate an occurrence they thought was impossible! They had never even considered it. And now their entire universe has been turned upside down.

Most parents make it a point never to imagine that the death of a child is a possibility. Throughout their lives, most of them have been encouraged not to think about bad things, because thinking about bad things might make them depressed and might actually cause those bad things to happen.

It is entirely possible for people in this culture to go through their life span in a state of complete denial and delusion. This dynamic doesn't necessarily change as we age. Recently, I was working with a seventy-five-year-old mother whose fifty-five-year-old son had just died of pancreatic cancer. The bereaved mother said to me, somewhat angrily, "My Jimmy was so young. He got *cheated*! He was supposed to get another twenty-three years! Why would God do this?!"

The point is, we continually ignore the large truths around us because we don't know how to integrate them into our consciousness and still be happy. Instead, we latch on to a small bit of information and interpret it the way we want to interpret it, in an attempt to comfort ourselves. Even when we discover that our interpretation is incorrect, we often continue to cling tenaciously to our interpretation. Then we get angry because things didn't work out the way we expected them to.

We get angry at God because He didn't keep His end of the bargain.

But it's a bargain God never made.

~

There is a wonderful story about a Buddhist meditation master who had received, as a gift, a beautiful crystal goblet. It was an expensive, intricately designed, superbly crafted piece of art. The master loved his goblet and enjoyed drinking water from it.

Since his teaching was rooted in the recognition of attachment as a cause of suffering, one day one of his students challenged him about his own attachment to his goblet.

"Master," said the student, "you teach us about the suffering caused by attachment to form, and yet you seem very attached to that goblet. Isn't that a contradiction?"

"Well," said the master, "it's very simple. You see, I love this goblet. It was given to me as a gift by a student who is very dear to me." He held the glass up to the ray of sunlight streaming through a nearby window and began rotating the glass between his fingers.

"Look at how skillfully this glass was crafted. Look at the beautifully sculpted geometric patterns in the glass. Look at the beautiful rainbows it creates on the walls. The sun beams through the goblet and breaks into glorious dancing rainbows throughout the room. And it is lovely to drink from this glass. I enjoy it immensely. It gives such a clear, crisp quality to the water.

"But, you see, for me, this glass is *already broken*. I can enjoy it, I can admire its beauty, and I can drink from it. But the truth of the matter is... it is already broken.

"When I accept that the glass is already broken, then someday — when I carelessly hit it with my elbow and knock it off the table, or the glass is a little too wet and it slips from my fingers and shatters into a million tiny pieces — all I have to say is, 'Ah so.'

"Because it was *already* broken. Do you see?

"I don't have to fret and fuss and carry on in shock and anger.

"From the day I first got it, it was *already* broken."

Imagine the freedom we would experience if we lived in that state of awareness. Imagine how free we would feel if we had already "let go," if in our awareness everything we treasure is already broken, everything we are attached to is already lost, and everyone we love is already dead. Imagine the vibrancy we would experience in life if — instead of feeling cheated when we lose something or someone — we felt absolutely blessed each moment we have them.

You see, our minds have been trained to experience fear and revulsion in the face of such a suggestion. We recoil in horror at the mere mention of it. We think that keeping the awareness of inevitable change and loss would be a path to misery and morbidity.

But is that really, absolutely... true?

The irony is that most people who have openly faced the truth of their mortality experience a kind of vibrant joy for living that most of us only dream about. It would not be an exaggeration to say that facing and embracing one's own death leads to the awareness that underlies a life of true happiness. When we face and embrace our own mortality, each moment of life becomes a gift, a blessing. We recognize that we don't have time. That recognition makes us much less vulnerable to the petty slights, resentments, fears, and disappointments we often obsess about. Instead of perpetually feeling cheated or postponing happiness to some future date, we become grateful just to be alive . . . now.

From the earliest years of my work with people who are dying and people who are grieving, I have repeatedly seen an amazing phenomenon. In working with many, many people dealing with a terminal diagnosis, who have been told that their case is hopeless, I have seen a significant number who will — after a period of time to work through their shock, denial, depression, and dismay — come to an astounding recognition that I used to find absolutely mind-boggling. These people will say something like, "I have never felt as *alive* as I do since I found out I have cancer."

I have not heard that from the majority of people who have cancer or some other "terminal" illness. But I have heard it often enough to take notice. I would estimate that about 40 percent of the people I have interacted with have said something like that. Of course, it doesn't matter what the illness or physical condition is. If it somehow inspires a recognition that the individual's ability to inhabit his or her body is drawing to a close, the result is the same.

When I first heard that statement, I was stunned. I was twenty-six years old. I had been raised in the affluent suburbs of New Jersey during a period in our culture of almost absolute denial of death. I could scarcely have imagined anything positive about dying. My first reaction was that the disease must be affecting the patient's brain.

Fortunately, Elisabeth Kübler-Ross taught those who studied

with her how to be tactful and inquisitive. She taught us to ask questions. She taught us to never think of ourselves as experts. She taught us to learn from everyone we worked with.

"Ask them what it feels like for them," Elisabeth would say. "Ask them to teach you what it is like going through what they are going through. Ask them what the world looks like through their eyes . . . and how it seems in their mind . . . and how it feels inside their heart."

~

Shortly after meeting Elisabeth in 1976, I began graduate studies in the Department of Religion at Florida State University. There were no hospices in those days. Few people in the culture had ever heard the word *hospice*. Whenever I mentioned it, most people would look puzzled, thinking that I had mispronounced *hospital*.

I was teaching a section of a remarkably popular course called Death and Dying, which drew about 250 students whenever it was offered. It was 1976, and people of college age weren't supposed to be thinking about death. Yet the class usually had an impressive enrollment.

At the beginning of the semester, I told my students that if they knew anyone who was dying and wanted someone to talk to about it, someone who wasn't totally frightened about dying, someone who would be straight with them, wouldn't lie to them, and wouldn't pretend it wasn't happening, I was available.

A few weeks later, one of my students approached me sheepishly. His eyes kept darting around the classroom to make sure there was no one else within earshot. When he was finally convinced that we were alone, he eked out the following, barely above a whisper: "There's a friend of my brother's who lives here in Tallahassee. He's been diagnosed with acute adult leukemia, and he's not expected to live much longer. I was visiting him the other day and told him about this class, and about you, and he said he'd like to meet you."

The friend's name was Leonard. He was twenty-nine years old and had a lovely wife and a beautiful young daughter. In just a few years he had already achieved a great deal of success as a highly respected young attorney in private practice. He was well known and much beloved throughout the state capital. From the standpoint of what we value as a culture, he was losing a lot. A lot of prestige, a lot of potential, a lot of time with his wife and child.

I was reflecting on all of that as I drove up to his house for our first meeting on that beautifully cool, crisp Tallahassee winter day. That morning I awoke to find that about four inches of unpredicted snow had fallen overnight, something that happened about three or four times each winter in Tallahassee. Leonard and I had talked by phone a few days earlier and had scheduled our meeting for noon. But on the morning of our meeting, it was very cold, and the streets were treacherous.

So I called him to postpone for a few hours while the sun had a chance to melt the snow and ice on the roads. I said, "Leonard, it seems that the 'unexpected' continues to happen."

He laughed. A few days earlier, when I first spoke with him, I told him that his friend's brother had shared the story of what he was going through.

"Good," said Leonard, "then I won't have to go through it all again." He sighed gently. "Suffice it to say it is all very . . ." He was searching for the right word.

"Unexpected."

He and his wife lived in a small, pristinely restored, elegantly decorated "historic" home in one of the charming older neighborhoods of Tallahassee, close to downtown, on a relatively steep hill. Their street was a one-way, with little traffic, lots of live oak trees, and abundant Spanish moss. I parked my car and carefully navigated what remained of the snow and ice on his front walk. The walk led to an elegantly broad, typical southern wooden porch that spanned the entire front of his house.

Gently hanging from the ceiling was a double-sized wooden porch swing. To my astonishment, Leonard was sitting on it, slowly — almost imperceptibly — swinging back and forth, bundled in a navy blue pea coat and a big, brightly colored woolen scarf. Under his pea coat he wore a plaid madras button-down shirt, blue jeans, and penny loafers. He was quite thin and pale. Because of his dramatic weight loss, his clothes looked a few sizes too big to fit properly. His hair had withered away, from the ravages of chemotherapy, to a few fragile, disorganized, wispy clumps.

His bright blue eyes looked at me intensely. He smiled weakly.

"Leonard?" I asked.

"John?" he answered, with a wry smile.

"Isn't it a little cold out here for you?" I asked.

"It feels great," he said. "I'm not sure how many more cold Tallahassee winter afternoons I'm going to get to enjoy. So I'm *really* enjoying this one! Would you like to sit?"

I was already shivering and had little interest in sitting outdoors, especially since inside, through the living room window, I could see a roaring fire in the fireplace. But Leonard's enjoyment was infectious, magnetic, and intriguing. I couldn't imagine interfering with a dying man's appreciation of the moment. So I sat. He put his arm around my shoulder like we were old friends and began to softly pat my upper arm.

"I'm very glad you came," he said. "There aren't many people who can handle what's happening to me. I don't have many relaxed, honest conversations these days. Everyone is on the edge of being hysterical. It causes a very *strained* form of noncommunication." He chuckled softly, almost to himself.

After a moment I said, "What would you like to talk about that you haven't been able to?"

"Hmmm," he said. He closed his eyes tightly, as if he were really thinking deeply about my question.

"I'd like to talk about the fact that I don't think I've ever felt as alive as I do right now! I can't seem to talk to people about that. They're all so frightened and so sad, and whenever I've tried to tell them that in spite of all the illness and discomfort in my body, I just feel so alive... they just look puzzled. Or they start crying. Or they say, 'I don't know what on earth you're talking about!'

"They make me feel like I'm saying something absolutely crazy. And sometimes I *feel* absolutely crazy, because I often have a kind of almost ecstatic joy that I've never felt before, and I think it's because I know I'm dying."

I was speechless. I sat next to Leonard with no idea how to respond. I had come expecting that he would want to talk about how sad and frightened he was. Instead, he was telling me about this inexplicable joy.

He was a young man of twenty-nine. He had a beautiful wife and a beautiful daughter. He had a successful law practice. He had a wonderful home. An expensive car. He had — as we like to say in our culture — so much to live for. His body was being ravaged by this terrible disease, yet he seemed so peaceful... and joyful.

I suddenly remembered Elisabeth's injunction that we should never feel like an expert. I thought, "Well, that's easy. I could scarcely feel less adequate, less knowledgeable, less like an expert than I do at this moment." Then I remembered Elisabeth saying, "Learn from everyone. Ask questions. Try to see what the world looks like through their eyes."

So I turned to Leonard and said, "Why do you think knowing that you are dying helps you to feel more alive?"

He was silently reflective for another moment. "The best way I can explain it is to say that life becomes much more immediate. Happiness isn't something you can hope for in the future when you don't have a future. You have to find happiness each day. And you can. When you know that you only have a finite time on earth... when you know that you are nearing the end... suddenly everything looks different. Your priorities change. Your perceptions change. You begin to recognize what is *truly* important in life. You begin to *really* notice and pay attention to your relationships.

"When you know that each day may be your last, you really begin to appreciate *everything* — every moment with a loved one, every ray of sunshine, every breath of fresh air, every hug, every kiss.

"You see sights you've never seen before. You hear sounds you've never heard before. You smell smells you've never smelled before. You taste tastes you've never tasted before. Everything begins to look like great art... to sound like a great symphony... everything you eat tastes like the most delicious food you've ever eaten!

"The faces of my wife and my little girl look like the most beautiful sculptures God has ever created. The sound of their voices is like the sound of angels. The fragrance of their hair is so sweet. The brownies my daughter baked for me yesterday were so delicious they made me cry.

"You don't want to leave anything unsaid. You don't want to leave anything unexplored. You don't want anyone to doubt how much you love them. You just feel *so alive*!"

As I listened to Leonard's story, I found myself both laughing and crying.

He looked at me with a puzzled grin on his face. "What's the matter with you?" he asked with a giggle.

"Well, Leonard," I said, "I'm feeling a little strange."

"Why?" he asked.

"I realize that I'm feeling envious of a dying man!"

We shared a playful moment of laughter. He hugged my shoulder a little tighter. When our laughter subsided, Leonard again became quietly reflective.

"Yes, I know," he said, somewhat wistfully. "The truth of the matter is I've been longing to feel this way my entire life. Isn't it bizarre that it took this for me to finally wake up?"

In subsequent days, whenever I reflected on Leonard's extraordinary enthusiasm for life, I found myself weeping... in awe and despair.

Weeping in awe at the amazing depth and radiance of the human spirit. Weeping in despair for my own small, tight, petty mind that up to that point in my life had so often failed to see the amazing beauty all around me.

A few years ago I saw a program on television about a tribal community in Africa. What I found most interesting was a unique ceremony this community holds to commemorate the passage from childhood to adulthood. When a child reaches the age of maturity, all of the adults and children in the community gather to offer that child a very important gift. It is a gift the adults consider most significant in helping the child understand his or her new role as an adult.

The gift is the child's burial shroud.

For the children of this community, the shroud performs a very special role. Though it is never to be used for anything other than wrapping their body when they die, they are instructed to wear it each day, for the rest of their lives, until they die. Each morning, as their day begins, they carefully and mindfully drape their burial shroud over their left shoulder and wear it throughout the day. At night, when they retire, they fold it in a ceremonial manner, keeping it close to their bed so they can return it to their shoulder the following morning.

The burial shroud is used as a sacred tool, a reminder of their mortality, a reminder of uncertainty and impermanence, a reminder to be fully alive and fully conscious every day, a reminder to keep their priorities clear, to pay attention to what they are thinking, what they are doing, and how they are acting in every moment. It is a reminder to be fully attentive to their loved ones and fully aware of how they treat other human beings.

It is a reminder that every day of their life could be their last, or the last for someone they love.

It is a reminder to pay attention.

It is a reminder to let go of pettiness.

Our culture has believed that acknowledging our mortality will make us depressed. As a result, we haven't really thought about our mortality. But if acknowledging our mortality made us depressed, we might assume that not acknowledging our mortality would make us pretty happy.

If that were so, why are more than 20 percent of the people in our culture taking antidepressant medication? That's one in five people. And the psychology and psychiatry communities feel that there are millions more people with undiagnosed depression who — in their view — should be taking antidepressants.

When we add in the estimated 15 to 30 percent of people who are addicted to alcohol and narcotics, we wind up with an enormous number of very unhappy people in this culture. As a rule, happy people do not have to take antidepressants. Happy people do not become addicted to alcohol and narcotics.

The simple fact is we have been wrong.

Thinking about our mortality isn't what makes us depressed. Not thinking about our mortality is what makes us depressed. Or, more accurately stated, it is not thinking about our mortality that allows us to live in the illusion that we have time to be depressed. And while depression is not unusual for people diagnosed with a terminal illness, the awareness of their mortality often spurs them to find a way to transcend that depression . . . expeditiously.

I am often asked by parents how they can protect their children from being emotionally and psychologically damaged by an unexpected confrontation with death. Their grandmother is dying, someone was killed in a car accident, a child in their school is dying of leukemia, or the family dog has died.

The simple rule is, the best thing you can do to help someone else is to work on yourself. When you are free from fear about death, your children will sense your inner peace, and they will become peaceful, too. But if you are terrified and uncomfortable about death, your children will sense that, and they will become terrified and uncomfortable, too.

Children are like sponges — emotionally, intellectually, and spiritually. They literally "pick up" the vibrations of the adults who surround them. If you lie to them, in some deep inner place, they know. If you say "everything is fine," but you yourself don't really believe that, they will begin to feel distrusting.

One mother said to me, "Even when my children were very young, if I was with them and we came upon a dead squirrel in the forest, or saw a dead dog or cat or deer along the road, I would just point it out to them. Then I would tell them that everything that is born will eventually die... everything that comes into form will eventually leave that form. That's the way nature works. It isn't terrible. It isn't frightening. It's just the way it is."

She smiled and said, "I don't think my children were damaged by that. They grew up quite healthy and happy, and have always had a very clear, realistic perspective on the cycles of life and death."

The downside to our culture's refusal to deal openly and honestly with these realities is that for several generations we have given our children the sense that death is something so terrible, so unworkable, so far outside our ability to understand, comprehend, or cope, that the "big people" won't even talk about it!

So, of course, our children are frightened. They are frightened because most of the adults around them are frightened. Most of those they look to for wisdom, guidance, insight, and protection are terrified, devoid of any useful emotional, spiritual, and psychological tools to deal with the one thing that every one of us absolutely has to deal with.

~

Giving our children tools to deal with life's inevitable disappointments, uncertainties, unexpected changes, and unpredictable endings is perhaps the greatest gift we can give them. Introducing them to the unlimited resources they already have inside themselves sets them on the path to the greatest awakening a human being can have, the awakening to who they truly are.

I have repeatedly seen that when a child is ill and dealing with their own mortality, they are usually much more calm and much more at peace than their parents. In fact, I have seen many circumstances in which the dying child winds up counseling the parents, soothing the parents' fears and heartache, reminding the parents to trust in the benevolence of the universe.

One little twelve-year-old boy with Hodgkin's disease said to me, "You must never be afraid of dying! It is totally safe!"

Children are inherently wise, compassionate, and loving. They know a great deal. Unfortunately, socialization in this culture usually teaches them to ignore what they instinctively know.

May we act instead to help them remember and trust what they already know.

And may they always know that God has given them everything they need to handle anything that happens to them.

CHAPTER 11

Believing I Can Be Happy Only If I Get What I Want

Even getting what you want contains an element of suffering, because — whatever it is — it is in time... it's going to pass away. You become playmate of the month, and next month you're not playmate of the month anymore.

RAM DASS, "HERE WE ALL ARE"

Many years ago, I called my friend Stephen Levine to tell him about a wonderful new relationship that had come into my life. I had met the partner of my dreams. I was in the midst of that giddy, ecstatic flush of excitement we humans just love to feel. I was floating in bliss. Everything was beautiful. It all seemed perfect. I said, "I've never been happier."

Stephen was silent for a moment. Then, very softly and gently, he said, "Watch out for the *fall* after this one."

My heart sank. I knew exactly what he meant.

A part of my mind said, "Why does he always have to be such a *downer*! Can't he ever just be happy?" But I also realized, in my heart, that his comment was an expression of love and compassion. It came from a much deeper happiness than the kind I was experiencing at that moment. His comment came from years of inner work, years of cultivating insight and balance, years of observing the inevitable cycles in the world of form and the habitual tendencies of the human mind.

Stephen knew that such a high must inevitably be followed by a low. It's a law. He wasn't being a downer. He was alerting a friend to a crack in the pavement just around the next curve.

How many of us have met the partner of our dreams only to have that very same person become the partner of our nightmares within a very short time? Even if that transformation doesn't take place, there is always, inevitably, some change or loss that pulls the rug out from under us, that deflates our high and leaves us bereft.

It may come as the result of discovering the dark corners in the personality of that perfect person. It may come because the relationship forces us to confront our own dark corners — parts of ourselves we have skillfully kept buried because we've never let anyone get close enough to see them. For most of us, the effort to keep those dark corners buried is the source of our aversion to intimacy.

We may also fall from our high because, one day, the partner of our dreams suddenly and unexpectedly runs off with someone else, or gets diagnosed with a life-threatening illness, or suddenly dies in a car accident. Even if the relationship turns out to truly be one of those very precious and rare ones, a true union of souls, a union that lasts through ten, twenty, or fifty years of ecstatic connection . . . one of the partners is going to die.

Unless the survivor has prepared, the devastation of that loss will seem so overwhelming it can appear to obliterate all of the years of love and happiness experienced while the partner was alive. Now there is only sadness and longing. Now there is only dismay and confusion about what it all means and how God could have created such an unjust, heartbreaking universe.

It may come quickly, or it may take decades, but eventually the fall will come.

Jesus said, "Lay not up treasures where moth and rust doth corrupt."[1]

In other words, be aware that everything in form takes birth, changes, decays, and dies. Don't put your faith in things that don't last. Don't tie your happiness to things that will inevitably change.

Buddha offered us the recognition that suffering isn't just related to not getting what we want. He points out that getting what we want can be a prelude to suffering as well.

You get a brand-new car. It's beautiful. It's a pleasure to drive. You feel the exhilarating rush of excitement and fulfillment. But then it's time to make the first monthly payment, and you realize that it may be a little more expensive than you can comfortably afford. You drive down the street, and suddenly there's a weird clunking noise. You stop at a traffic light, and somebody runs into you.

You got what you wanted, but now you realize that it is vulnerable, it comes with complications, and, over time, it's going to change, decay, and die. Someday that beautiful new car will be tossed into a junkyard, broken, dented, rusty, and useless.

You get the house of your dreams. It's beautiful. Then you move in and find out the basement leaks, the roof leaks, and the air conditioning doesn't work.

You go on that dream vacation. It's paradise. You get relaxed and refreshed and renewed. Then you come home. While you were away, the plumbing broke and flooded the upstairs hallway. You've got a new and difficult boss at work. Your mother is more depressed and difficult than ever.

Or you work and work and work to achieve the fame and fortune you believe will bring you happiness, only to find — like the friends I mentioned in chapter 6 — that no matter how much you have, it can all seem rather empty. It can actually complicate your life.

Virtually every study about the relationship between money and happiness has shown that money alleviates suffering only when it lifts an individual out of abject poverty. Beyond that, the positive effects of increased affluence drop dramatically. We have seen, time and again, that affluence can complicate one's life and actually impede the ability to be happy.

That is most true of the children of affluent parents. Study after study has shown that children raised in an atmosphere of conspicuous wealth are significantly less happy than children raised in more meager circumstances. Unless wealthy parents make a concerted effort to help the children discover meaning in life beyond money and possessions, the children tend to grow up with a drastically distorted vision of life, society, and culture, and often — right beneath the surface — suffer from a deeply cynical despair.

~

Just to offer a snapshot of this syndrome, let me share a story about a couple — Alan and Christine — who came to see me because they were experiencing marital and family difficulties.

When Christine first called me, she said, "My husband and I are getting to the point that we just loathe each other. We fight constantly. He often doesn't even come home at night. Our children both hate us, and seem to hate the world. We're afraid that they're using drugs. They're failing in school. They're embittered and surly and hanging around with some very questionable friends."

We made an appointment for the following week.

On the day of my first meeting with Alan and Christine, I had a fifteen-minute break prior to seeing them. I made a cup of tea and got up to stretch a bit. I was looking out the window at nothing in particular when I saw a brand-new shiny, silver Mercedes-Benz pull up in front of my house. A moment later, another brand-new shiny, silver Mercedes-Benz pulled up and parked on the opposite side of the street. I was looking at about $150,000 worth of automobiles. Out of one Mercedes-Benz stepped a very good-looking, well-dressed man, and out of the other, a very good-looking, well-dressed woman. They both exuded a palpable aura of wealth. They had the high-fashion look of expensive cars, expensive clothes, and expensive jewelry. Everything was luxurious, spotless, and pristine.

But they wouldn't look at each other. The woman waited across the street while the man walked up my front path. He rang the doorbell. After I let him in, the woman reluctantly crossed the street and followed him into my house . . . separately.

They stood apart and introduced themselves. I took them inside and suggested they sit — in separate chairs — next to each other. They reluctantly agreed. They seemed to want more distance than I was providing. Their body language and demeanor was reminiscent of two people frightened of catching some deadly disease from each other.

I set the ground rules for our initial meeting. Alan and Christine would each have an equal amount of time to talk. But they couldn't interrupt each other. They couldn't get defensive. I just wanted to hear, quietly and clearly — from each of them individually — what they were feeling, what form the "problems" took from each of their perspectives.

As they began to relate their story — or "stories" — each wove a tale of bitter disdain and disappointment. When they finished presenting their cases we took a moment of silent reflection, an opportunity to listen and intuit.

After a few moments, I asked, "Do either of you remember a time when you were happy together? Do you remember a time when you were *really* in love with each other?"

They both fell silent, seemingly deep in thought. The rigid defensiveness in their bodies spontaneously began to soften. They appeared to let down their guard, to let go of their strident stances against each other. The heated tension in the room began to cool.

Suddenly, simultaneously, they turned to face each other. It was as if — after years of searching — they had just discovered a treasured gem that had been missing. It was the first time they had looked into each other's eyes since they arrived. There was a nostalgic sadness in their eyes.

Their eyes welled up with tears. Alan spoke. "When we were just starting out. That's when we were happy. When we had nothing. We were so happy then." With tears rolling down her cheeks, Christine silently nodded in agreement.

Now they couldn't bear to sit in the same Mercedes-Benz. They needed two — to keep themselves insulated from their disappointment and rage... to keep them isolated in their sadness.

They had sacrificed the only thing that really matters and replaced it with meaningless objects and appearances.

Later that afternoon I had an appointment with Jim and Laura. Their problems were very similar to Alan and Christine's.

Jim and Laura arrived in two separate BMWs.

~

Not only do many of us get sidetracked into thinking that things will bring us happiness, but many of us also place a tremendous importance on our bodies and our health as sources of happiness and unhappiness.

We obsess endlessly about our weight, our looks, our hair, our teeth, our muscles, our wrinkles. We think we will be happy when we lose thirty pounds or we get a new look or we overcome whatever chronic physical problem we are dealing with.

Many people who lose weight find that the loss is only temporary. Many who resolve to go to the gym regularly become tired and bored after a few weeks and realize that they would prefer to stay home and rest in the evening. Many who have expensive plastic surgery are disappointed with the results. In cases such as these, the method soon fails to give the hoped-for happiness it briefly offered. The individuals may become depressed, disappointed, frustrated, and angry.

Or they may switch to an obsessive, fanatical approach, assuming that they haven't done enough. Weight-loss programs sometimes morph into anorexia. Some people who originally went to the gym to lose a few pounds and get some cardiovascular training become obsessive weight lifters and bodybuilders, bulking up with layer upon layer of bulging muscles, setting aside other aspects of their lives to spend hours each day at the gym. People who have plastic surgery can become addicted to procedures, constantly thinking they need more — more nips, more tucks, more reductions.

Quite simply, whenever we search for happiness through external means, no amount of effort or experience can ever be enough to counteract our underlying sense of unworthiness and dissatisfaction.

~

In his wonderful book *What Happy People Know: How the New Science of Happiness Can Change Your Life for the Better*, Dan Baker shares insights gathered through many years as director of the award-winning Life Enhancement Program at Canyon Ranch in Tucson, Arizona. Canyon Ranch is an ultra-upscale spa and wellness facility where affluent people can go to rest, relax, rejuvenate, lose weight, and get healthy. He has spoken with and counseled thousands of wealthy people who are still desperately struggling to find happiness.

He says, "At Canyon Ranch, I often hear people talk about hunting — for diamonds, planes, houses, paintings, and boats — but what I really hear, beneath the surface of their conversation, is people talking about hunting down the one big prize that will finally free them from the two basic, survivalist fears that have haunted people since the Stone Age: the fears of not having enough and of not being enough."[2]

~

There is another interesting aspect to getting what we want. It relates to prayers that *are* answered. A great teacher in India said, "Be careful what you pray for. You may not fully understand the consequences. If God grants what you are asking, are you ready to take the consequences and responsibilities that will follow?"

Obviously, through the work with people who are dying and people who are grieving, I have often encountered people who pray that God might spare the life of a loved one who is dying. Ironically, I have seen that there are some circumstances in which — when those prayers have been answered — the outcomes have been vastly different from what was anticipated. I remember one couple in particular.

Jenny and Richard lived in San Francisco. They had been partners for only a year when Jenny was diagnosed with AIDS. She had contracted it in a previous heterosexual relationship. It was during the late eighties, when AIDS was still thought to be absolutely incurable, a 100 percent fatal disease.

Jenny's physical decline went on for about three years. She was in and out of the hospital. Finally she was admitted to the hospital for what doctors sometimes refer to as "the last visit." Richard, Jenny's family, and dozens of their friends had organized nearly constant prayer vigils and a variety of healing services. In one of the most dramatic physical turnarounds I have ever encountered, Jenny, who had been very near death, began to improve.

After a few more weeks in the hospital, Jenny was able to come home. Everyone who knew the couple, including all of the doctors and nurses who had attended Jenny, was astonished. It was truly a miraculous healing. Jenny had defied all of the medical odds, and she went on to live for four more years.

But those years were not easy, either for Jenny or for Richard. Jenny still needed almost constant care. And for unknown reasons, after her "resurrection" she was quite volatile emotionally. It was almost as if she had surrendered to death and was now confused about why she was still alive. She often said she was in emotional agony. She cried almost constantly. Richard wound up saying, "If I had known that prolonging Jenny's life would bring her so much suffering, I might never have prayed for her to live."

Even an "answered" prayer can result in unwanted, unexpected results.

CHAPTER 12

God Will Give Me What I Want If I Am Good

There is only one question which really matters;
why do bad things happen to good people?
Virtually every meaningful conversation I have ever had
with people on the subject of God and religion
has either started with this question,
or gotten around to it before long.

RABBI HAROLD KUSHNER,
WHEN BAD THINGS HAPPEN TO GOOD PEOPLE

Most of us believe that if we do our best to remember and honor God, if we pray and meditate regularly, if we attend religious services regularly, if we support our spiritual teachers and our spiritual community financially, if we are honest and kind and generous, then God should protect us from anything bad happening in our lives or in the lives of our loved ones.

Unfortunately, that is simply not the case.

The important thing to remember, whenever we feel that God should have protected us from some unwanted change or difficult circumstance, is that God does protect us. God doesn't protect us by preventing bad things from happening to us. *God protects us by giving us everything we need to handle anything that happens to us.* That is, when the primary focus of our lives is spiritual awakening, or unfolding, we begin to tap into the infinite reservoir of peace, love, and joy within our own beings.

Bad things happen in the world of form. That's just the way it is. And good things happen, too. In this world, every action has an equal and opposite reaction. Over time the good and bad eventually balance each other.

As we have seen, it is often the disappointments and difficulties in our lives that spur us on to pursue our spiritual path more intensely. When the things that we want fall away, when we find ourselves in the middle of circumstances that we didn't want, when pettiness falls away, we find ourselves — at last — face-to-face and heart-to-heart with our Creator. There is simply nowhere else to turn and no place else to go. It is the moment when the mind burns itself out.

We are forced to surrender. We are forced to surrender our illusion of control, our desires and expectations. We stand alone and isolated, in the ruins of a shattered ego.

While that shattering may be only temporary, it can pave the way for a new perception of our experiences and a new approach to life. When all the ways we have known ourselves and all the ways we have experienced life are shattered, we are forced to unearth a deeper level of meaning beyond all of our concepts about what we need to be happy. We are forced to move beyond all our concepts about how the universe should conduct itself in order to please us, to entertain us, to fulfill us, and to keep us feeling safe within the rigidly defined boundaries of our ego-based fears and desires.

The simple truth is there is *nothing* — at *this very moment* — that stands in the way of our consciously experiencing the infinite, eternal bliss of God other than our own ego, our own tightly packed duffel bag of "stuff" — the thickly tangled web of our own minds, the astonishingly complex array of identities we hold — the thoughts and ideas about who we are, and the intricately woven fabric of desires, expectations, attachments, prejudices, and fears that form the sum total of our "separate" identity. From that standpoint, we might look at the intrusion of unwanted circumstances into our life, or the frustration of thwarted desire, as opportunities to let go of that which separates us from the immediate, conscious awareness of God.

All that stands between you and God is you, whoever you think you are, whoever and whatever you think you need in order to feel happy and safe. It doesn't matter how beautiful, intelligent, successful, prosperous, or well dressed that "you" looks in the mirror, or in the eyes of the world; that "you" is still blocking your ability to really know God.

Even an attachment to negative identities is a source of entrapment: "I'm not beautiful, I'm not intelligent, I am a failure, nobody likes me." It doesn't matter whether your self-perception is positive or negative, it still represents a hard shell of ego that stands between you and God.

~

When the circumstances of life derail our desires, ideas, and expectations, our ego is often subdued. For a time, we are open to experiencing God rather than just thinking about Him. It is for that reason that many great mystical traditions have referred to suffering as Grace.

When we are forced to let go of the ideas and concepts that keep us separate from God, to let go of the thoughts, desires, and expectations that keep us in a constant state of vigilance and anxiety, we have the opportunity to experience something far greater, far more satisfying, and far more meaningful than the transitory satisfactions of this world.

In a poem that begins my book *Awakening from Grief*, there is a line that says, "When our heart is broken, it is also *wide open*."[1] The heart I was referring to is our human heart, the sometimes fragile emotional heart that gets filtered through our ego and our human mind, the limited heart that offers love primarily with expectation attached to it. If we don't get whatever it is that we want in return for loving others, we gradually diminish our love or even withdraw it completely.

But we have another heart. We might call it our spiritual heart. That heart is our real heart. In India, it is called the *hridayam*. Sometimes our human heart has to be broken open in order for us to find our spiritual heart.

Our spiritual heart — our *hridayam* — is the place within us through which the Divine Light and Infinite Love of God flows. It is the aspect of our being that loves infinitely, eternally, unconditionally, and without limit. For most of us, that place of divine connection is usually occluded, to one degree or another, by our ego mind. But our spiritual heart is eternally with us and within us, intimately woven into the very fabric of our soul. In fact, we could say that our spiritual heart *is* our soul.

It is Love.

Our spiritual heart can never be broken. Our soul can never die. Our connection with God is eternal. No matter how much we lose in this life, our spiritual heart, our soul, and our connection with the Divine can never be lost.

It can seem as if we've lost it if our mind gets swept up in the horror, outrage, and heartbreak of fear, thwarted desire, and frustrated expectation. But, truly, it can never be lost. There is a popular expression that says, "Let go and let God." We might also say, "When you let go fully, you will be one with God."

~

I recently received the following email message:

> Dear John,
>
> I am just reading your book, *Awakening from Grief*, and I am finding it tremendously helpful.

> I am fifty-eight years old. A few years ago, I found myself deep in grief following the sudden death of my twenty-three-year-old daughter.
>
> I was hoping you might shed some light on the following:
>
> Two to eight months after Tina's death, there were times when the grief would subside and I would feel this heightened awareness of everything. It was as if my senses had been "fine-tuned" to be capable of understanding everything I was experiencing at a level I'd never felt before. After about eight months, I could sense this ability fading and I missed it tremendously. I still do.
>
> Have you ever heard of anything like this in your work?

This grieving mother was sharing something I have seen over and over again: that having our world turned upside down and having our heart broken can pave the way to spiritual awakening. Experiences that so violently disrupt our habitual thought patterns and ego identities can catapult us out of the rigid, dreary cage of our day-to-day existence. They can thrust us into altered states of consciousness.

The philosopher William James, in his classic text *The Varieties of Religious Experience*, published in 1902, wrote:

> our normal waking consciousness, rational consciousness as we call it, is but one special type of consciousness, whilst all about it, parted from it by the filmiest of screens, there lie potential forms of consciousness entirely different. We may go through life without suspecting their existence; but apply the requisite stimulus, and at a touch they are there in all their completeness.... No account of the universe in its totality can be final which leaves these other forms of consciousness quite disregarded. How to regard them is the question, because they are so discontinuous with ordinary consciousness.... Looking back on my own experiences, they all converge towards a kind of insight to which I cannot help ascribing some metaphysical significance. The keynote of it is invariably a

> reconciliation. It is as if the opposites of the world, whose contradictoriness and conflict make all our difficulties and troubles, were melted into unity.[2]

In the Buddhist tradition there is a fascinating story about a man named Mogalanna, who was generally regarded as Buddha's most advanced disciple. This story presents another insight into how one life might include both great spiritual advancement and great suffering.

Mogalanna had achieved an amazing array of spiritual powers. He was pure, loving, and absolutely scrupulous. He was able to heal the sick and raise the dead. He could, at will, change the energies and atomic structure of his physical body and go through walls. He could become invisible. He could fly. The rest of Buddha's disciples were in awe of Mogalanna and his powers.

But one day, Mogalanna was murdered, brutally beaten by the ancient Indian equivalent of today's gang members.

The other disciples were stunned. They couldn't imagine how such a pure being, such an advanced teacher, who possessed such extraordinary powers, could possibly suffer such a cruel and ignominious fate. They went to the Buddha to express their horror and confusion. And the Buddha told them a fascinating tale.

In a previous incarnation, Mogalanna had brutally beaten and murdered his parents. His wife had been tired of caring for his elderly parents and had berated Mogalanna constantly because of her frustration. Eventually, his will broke, and he performed the dreadful deed.

The Buddha told the disciples that now, several incarnations later, despite his highly advanced spiritual status, Mogalanna still had to atone for those murders. According to the Buddha, when the highwaymen first confronted Mogalanna, he was able to hold them off with his extraordinary powers and slip away from their attacks. But as a result of the karma surrounding the murder of his parents in a previous life, Mogalanna eventually found that he was held back by his previous karma and could not flee.

The Buddha assured the other disciples that the previous bad deeds in no way diminished Mogalanna's greatness in this life. But Mogalanna did have to atone for his past actions — not because God was punishing him, but because, in this realm, every experience must be balanced by opposite experience.

The great psychiatrist Sigmund Freud was not even remotely disposed to thinking in religious or spiritual terms. Yet he believed that behaviors like lying, stealing, cheating, causing harm to others, and even murder create an essential imbalance in the human mind. He believed that self-centered, inharmonious actions automatically engender a subconscious state of guilt in the "perpetrator," causing her or him to leave a trail — a series of "mistakes" that add up to the clues by which misdeeds can be discovered and prosecuted. Whether the authorities actually find those clues doesn't matter. Freud absolutely believed that there was no such thing as a perfect crime. He insisted that a criminal couldn't help making mistakes that would leave a trail behind, because at some level the perpetrator wants to be caught.

Karma functions in a similar fashion. It is not a mechanism through which God punishes our evil actions but the universal quest for balance in the world of form: every action has an equal and opposite reaction.

Throughout the history of Western culture the collective consciousness has been dramatically affected by the Christian doctrine of original sin. The doctrine actually arose from a misinterpretation of the meaning of the word *sin*. In ancient Greek, the language in which the New Testament was written, *to sin* meant "to miss the target." To sin is to fail to understand the true meaning of human life, to live in ignorance and delusion, to create suffering for oneself and for others. It does not imply behavior that can lead to eternal damnation but behavior that is temporarily unsuccessful, that can be improved with practice.

Instead of looking at the difficult experiences of life as cruel punishment from a wrathful God, we might instead look at them as experiences our own soul needs to have. It really isn't important to understand what the precipitating causes might have been. The question always is, How can I use this experience to get closer to God, to unveil my true nature? How can I use it to find greater peace in the world as it is, not as I think it should be?

The story of Mogalanna, if misunderstood, might entice us to once again conclude that God is a punishing God, and when bad things happen to us in this life we are being punished. What it really implies is that despite our inability to perceive clear and coherent order in the world of form, there is an underlying lawfulness and justice that — in many circumstances — our human minds can neither perceive nor comprehend.

When we seek to do good in the world, it is not because we want to be rewarded but simply because it feels better... it is just more fun. It feels better because it is the clearest route to connection with God, the highest expression of our own soul.

CHAPTER 13

Resenting, Ignoring, or Fearing the Way Things Are

The Great Way is not difficult
for those who have no preferences.
When love and hate are both absent
Everything becomes clear and undisguised.
Make the smallest distinction, however,
and Heaven and Earth are set infinitely apart.
If you wish to see the Truth,
then hold no opinions for — or against — anything.
To set up what you like against what you dislike
is the disease of the mind.

THIRD CHINESE PATRIARCH OF ZEN,
TEACHINGS OF THE BUDDHA

In Western society we are trained to be control freaks. We think we can control anything and everything. If we can't control it, then we automatically assume that someone else can . . . or should . . . or must. And if someone on earth isn't controlling things, seeing to it that the experiences of our life line up the way we want them to, we expect God to intervene.

We have achieved an extraordinary level of scientific and technological prowess. We believe that we can find a way to overcome any danger, discomfort, or inconvenience that the natural world, or other human beings, may hurl at us.

We have developed cures for many life-threatening diseases. We have devised vaccines that have totally eradicated other diseases.

We have created climate-controlled environments that allow many of us to live in places that were previously too hot or too cold to support significant populations. We have methods of transportation that can whisk us to the other side of the planet in less than a day. We even have the know-how to travel to the moon and back. We have extraordinary tools of communication. Cell phones, computers, and satellite television allow us to have instantaneous communication with nearly every corner of the globe.

But there have been many downsides to our unabated progress. We have created weapons capable of destroying our entire planet. While we have preferred to think that we would never use them, as long as they are in existence there is always the possibility that we will. In recent years we have been faced with the concern that rogue nations might procure weapons of mass destruction and use them on large populations.

Despite a plethora of warnings and danger signals from scientists and from the earth itself, we have ignored the delicate balance of natural cycles and forces on our planet. For billions of years those cycles and forces mysteriously worked together to pave the way for the eventual appearance of human life and for its sustenance. The process of creating and preparing to sustain human life was happening on earth long before human life ever appeared.

For the last few centuries, a period in history when we have "taken control" of the earth and the environment, we have been unconsciously and relentlessly doing everything in our power to reverse that process. The unacknowledged side effects of our technological "progress" have been slowly and steadily destroying the very planet we live on.

Isn't it interesting that we seldom, if ever, examine our everyday thoughts and actions in the light of these peculiarly bizarre and self-destructive tendencies? Instead, we completely ignore what is so that we can continue to pursue what we want. We can ignore the fact that our addiction to gasoline is creating pollution, environmental problems, depletion of natural resources, and geopolitical problems simply because we want the gasoline, and the lifestyle and freedom that our automobiles give us. We can't imagine our lives without that freedom.

But can we imagine our planet without us?

We may have to, because it looks as if our planet — itself a living, breathing organism — is beginning to perceive us as a threat to its very existence. It appears that our earth may have begun the process of cleansing itself by clearing us out of its system, just as our physical bodies set our immune systems in motion to cleanse out "intruders": imbalances, infections, and opportunistic malignancies.

Wouldn't it be amazing if our own planet took steps to rid itself of us and our uncaring, predatory tendencies?

Despite the increasing plausibility of that scenario, we blithely drift along, continuing to buy gas-guzzling SUVs, fascinating ourselves with the latest edition of *American Idol* or the newest version of PlayStation, while untold millions of people worldwide are suffering the ravages of war, starvation, genocide, and brutal human cruelty that are often a direct result of our actions as a society or an indirect result of our indifference.

What forces in us have allowed us to so totally disregard the long-term effects of our thoughts and actions on our own health, the health of other human beings, and the health of our planet? What forces have impelled us to seek the ease of simple, immediate, selfish gratifications rather than establish a long-range vision for our own life, our species, and our planet? What spirit of diminishment and separation has allowed us to think that what we do, or don't do, has no effect on the rest of the world... both now and in the future? What ignorance has prevented us from adopting beliefs, activities, and behaviors that might have more expansive, positive effects on our planet and the future of our species?

The two elements that join together to create the seemingly dire state the human race appears to be in are separation and fear. We wouldn't be able to do the things we do if we didn't feel separate from one another, from the world we live in, and from God. Ironically, it is that very sense of separation that engenders our fear. We fear other human beings because we feel separate from them. When we fear them, we think and act in ways that make us feel more separate from them. We fear the uncertainties in the natural world, so we feel separate from it. We try to dominate it rather than work in harmony with it.

And we fear God because we feel separate from Him.

It's all so ironic, because our own scientific research has shown us that we are absolutely not separate... not separate from each other, not separate from our planet, not separate from our universe, and not separate from God.

God is as close as our own breath.

God *is* our own breath.

God is the universe we live in. The tree growing outside the window. The river flowing past your house. The delicate atmosphere that filters the sunlight and gives us air to breathe. The ocean growing food... *and* the ocean in a storm swallowing homes, loved ones, and lands.

God is the person moving slowly in the grocery store, the child making noise, the teenage couple holding hands, the old person crossing the street... the child starving in Darfur, the starving mother heartbroken, the parents in Palestine so distraught and hopeless that they would offer their beautiful young children as suicide bombers, the elderly Holocaust survivors in Israel terrified that they and their children and their grandchildren face the ongoing threat of extermination.

The bald children in cancer wards, the limbless soldiers in veterans' hospitals, the innocent young Iraqi wife whose husband and children have been slaughtered by a roadside bomb... the doctors and nurses who treat the ill and the wounded, desperately trying to save their lives and alleviate their suffering, the millions of confused, barely conscious elders who have been cast aside to die slow, lonely deaths in dark and dreary nursing homes.

God is the moon, revolving around the earth, revolving around the sun.

God is your husband, your wife, your parents, your child.

Your friends. Your adversaries.

Your self.

God is everywhere . . . in everything . . . in everyone.

God is all there is.

And in God we are all connected.

~

But we ignore our connectedness. And we ignore the effects of our actions. We ignore the absolute certainty that we are all going to die. We ignore it because we fear it.

The negative consequences of our fear are vast. It was our fear that drove us to create nuclear bombs. It is our resentment about the way things are that has caused us to place so much importance on our own personal comfort and so little importance on the health and well-being of our environment and other human beings. Many among us feel it is just too inconvenient or too complicated to do anything about the harm being done to our planet. Many would rather pretend that the evidence of global warming is inconclusive or perhaps just a hoax. Many of those same people have wanted us to believe that nuclear weapons aren't nearly as dangerous as we've been told, that perhaps we should consider their use if our global adversaries become too obstreperous.

We have a strangely adversarial stance toward life. We think that everything should always run smoothly, that we must never be slowed down or inconvenienced in any way. We feel that whenever something goes wrong, it's someone else's fault. If you have ever observed the anger that erupts in an airport when bad weather forces the delay or cancellation of airline flights, you have seen just how irrational, impatient, intolerant, and unadaptable human beings have become. It is astounding to watch people berate an airline gate agent simply because the natural world has sent a blizzard our way.

In recent years, when working with people who are grieving, I have noticed many instances in which at some point in our dialogues they begin to blame an individual, a group of individuals, or an institution that they consider to be at least partially responsible for that death. The number of those instances has increased dramatically. Our conversation about grief almost inevitably takes a substantial detour into exploring the potential legal ramifications of some real or imagined neglect, arrogance, or dereliction of duty.

The doctor did or didn't do something. The nurses were inattentive and incompetent. The drug company screwed up. The car manufacturer made a mistake. The cigarette makers caused her death.

On and on it goes. The human mind rarely stops questioning and rarely stops looking for someone to blame. The underlying implication is that surely anything that goes wrong — including death — is a mistake. And our culture has been trained to meet every "mistake" with an angry tirade, a lawsuit, an exposé, or some other legal action.

And so our willingness to disconnect from the natural world, and from each other, forms much of the basis of our cultural grief. To find the ability and the justification to keep moving in the same direction we've been moving in, we have to maintain, even exaggerate, that disconnection. We have to keep disconnecting. We have to keep turning away, pretending, numbing ourselves.

As long as we place the conditions of our happiness in externals, in other people and external circumstances, as long as we look for the sources of happiness and unhappiness outside ourselves, we will remain angry, frustrated, sorrowful, and frightened.

The simple truth is that, in the world of form, things don't always go the way we *want* them to. Every one of us is susceptible to danger. Every one of us is going to die. And we don't usually know when.

That doesn't necessarily mean that someone has made a mistake. That doesn't mean that we are being punished. It just means that life is sometimes unfair.

Let me say it again. *Life is sometimes unfair.*

From the perspective of our human, rational minds, it is unfair. Whether cosmically, metaphysically, and spiritually life is ultimately unfair is a matter for discussion in some other format. What we need *now*, when things are not going the way we want them to, is a different way to look at life.

Whether there are places called "heaven," where the righteous spend a glorious eternity, or "hell," where the unrighteous suffer for their misdeeds . . . or whether there really is something called "the law of karma," which automatically balances the scales of human action and human experience, doesn't really matter in this moment.

For our purposes it is sufficient to note that we have, as a species, become increasingly unprepared for disappointment and unwanted change. We think the world should be the way we think it should be. We are under the delusion that if we can just exert enough control, there is some way to make it be the way we think it should be.

What would be really helpful would be to acknowledge that change happens . . . unexpectedly and inevitably. We would do well to cultivate practices in our spiritual lives that prepare us for the inevitability of change and disappointment. We would do well to incorporate some practices into our lives that help us to take spiritual teaching from every unwanted, unexpected change rather than fuss, fume, and sulk about it all.

CHAPTER 14

It Isn't Supposed to Be This Way

If there were not the misconception that
something wrong *had taken place,*
then it would be seen in its truer nature,
which is simply another blessing, another opportunity.
But there is only suffering when there is
the belief that something is wrong.

EMMANUEL

One of our greatest challenges when we are in the midst of a great loss, great sadness, or difficult life circumstances is how to handle the voice in our mind that says, "This is a mistake. This wasn't supposed to happen. This is *wrong*."

It is especially difficult when events take place that seem random, unjust, or unfair. No matter how nonjudgmental we aspire to be, there are still events that push us beyond what we previously defined as our capacity to let go of judgment: the illness or death of a child; a long-term injury, paralysis, or disability; the loss of our life savings; an unjust war; a brutal murder or unprovoked attack.

Our mind's tendency to judge the rightness or wrongness of these and other events in the physical universe is a major obstacle on the path to freedom and happiness. I am not suggesting that these kinds of heartbreaking, illusion-shattering events are good for us or that we should welcome the sadness and desolation that can follow in their wake.

I am merely saying that these events are a part of the universe of form. They are part of human life. And it is possible that the creative impulse in the universe of form does not operate according to the rules of rationality and justice we like to cling to. From our soul's point of view, from God's point of view, these events are neither right or wrong.

They just are. They are elements of life in form.

But our sadness and desolation are also elements of life in form.

We might even perceive them as gifts the universe has left on our doorstep. Gifts we surely don't want, and didn't ask for, but gifts nonetheless. Sadness can give us the impetus to probe more deeply into the truths embodied in our soul. Desolation can pave the way for a longing that can completely transform our values, priorities, and lifestyle. Violence and injustice can inspire us to dedicate our lives to eradicating the root causes of antisocial and unloving behavior.

Still, the words *should* and *shouldn't* can be used as accurate, reliable arrows that always point toward the places in us where we resist the universe as it is. When we are suffering, feeling violated, betrayed, or angry, we need only look to see if there is a tape loop playing in our mind that says, "this *shouldn't* have happened... they *shouldn't* act this way... they *should* have done something different... this *shouldn't* be the way it is. This is *wrong*."

As long as that tape loop is going, we will remain caught in suffering.

The acceptance of things as they are in this context does not imply complacency. It does not imply that we become callous and indifferent, that we ignore cruelty and injustice. The acceptance of things as they are is merely intended to alleviate the suffering we habitually create in our minds with the desire to change things we simply cannot change.

We always have the freedom to work to make things better, to do what we can to make the world a better place, to bring more compassion, more caring, more kindness, and more generosity into the environment. How often do parents who have lost a child go to work to raise funds and raise public awareness about whatever it was that "took" their child from them? In that case, from the soul's point of view, the child's legacy... her or his gift to the world... was to sacrifice their life in a manner that might pry open hearts that were closed, to enliven minds that were numb.

~

In addition to our sadness, our anger can also be a clear indicator of where we are stuck.

Back in the early eighties, when my father was sick and dying of throat and lung cancer, I was annoyed that he wasn't treating me nicely. I had completely reorganized my life to make it possible for me to take care of him. I had made significant sacrifices and felt I was being very kind and caring toward him, and he was responding with crankiness, nastiness, and insults.

During that period, I went to visit Ram Dass, who at the time was living in San Francisco. I took the first evening of our visit as an opportunity to enumerate my litany of complaints about my father's "unfair" behavior.

Ram Dass listened patiently.

When I finally calmed down and took a breath, Ram Dass leaned forward in his chair and gave me a very penetrating look. He tilted his head sideways in a slightly quizzical gesture, then spoke. "Don't you see that all anger is anger at God?" he asked.

I was a little stunned. It had never occurred to me to reflect on the source of anger. I never thought of it as anything other than justifiable outrage. But there was something very powerful about Ram

Dass's statement. In subsequent days, as I thought about what he said, I began to realize that whenever we get angry, what we're really saying is, "If I were God, I would have made the universe better than this! I would have made a better father than this one. I wouldn't have made obnoxious people who irritate me! I wouldn't have made people who drive recklessly and cut me off on the highway! I wouldn't have made people who disagree with me! I wouldn't have made a world where babies can die!"

But this is the world we live in. Every thought that judges it as right or wrong is a thought that separates us from the direct experience of our lives and, thus, the direct experience of God. The most spiritually beneficial strategy is to breathe deeply and let go of our attachment to things being different than they are, let go of our attachment to the idea that we would have done a better job than God. If we soften our hearts and allow the universe to be exactly as it is, we allow for the possibility that it is perfect just as it is, and we acknowledge that it may have some very profound teachings for us just as it is.

The next thing Ram Dass said to me was, "Why don't you see your father as your guru?"

"My father?!" I said.

"Yes," he said, "your father. After all, who else could he possibly be?"

I was astonished. But I knew Ram Dass was right.

Nevertheless, I struggled for quite a while with what he suggested. But when I finally began to see my father as my guru, my relationship with him was totally transformed. Then I no longer had to judge his words and actions as wrong. Instead, I began to see that each time he said or did something that hurt me, frustrated me, or angered me, he was teaching me important things about myself. He was showing me where my attachments and prejudices were so that I could begin to work on letting go of them.

From that moment forward I slowly, gradually learned to give up my anger, resentment, and judgment toward him. It didn't happen overnight, but each day, over the course of the next few years, I made a little progress. I learned to visualize each insult he hurled at me as an arrow. I would try to catch it before it pierced my heart, set it down on the ground, and send back a flower.

Finally, one evening just before my father died, I was sitting next to his bed when he spontaneously began to shout at me in one of his familiar tirades. This time, I couldn't see an arrow. I could only see that what he was desperately *trying* to say, in his own very confused way, was that he loved me. So I looked deeply into his eyes and said, "I love you too, Dad."

The volley of abuse spontaneously stopped. His body relaxed. He settled back into his pillow and began to gaze up toward the ceiling. A blissful smile spread across his face. Tears welled up in his eyes. Gazing upward toward the heavens, he lifted his right hand up and began affectionately patting me on my left shoulder.

"Good. Good. Good," he kept repeating. "Good."

At that moment, I had the most remarkable feeling. I felt as if I had just "graduated." And I felt as if an enormous weight had been lifted from my father's shoulders. He seemed absolutely relieved. It was as if he were saying to God, "Finally! It took thirty-three years, but the kid finally got it! He finally got the teaching. He finally got that it isn't about how miserable and nasty I can be. It's about how loving *he* can be."

When we said good night that evening, my father and I had such a delicious hug. He died peacefully and gracefully the following afternoon.

~

The two questions Ram Dass asked me, and the lifestyle changes they implied, have formed the groundwork for some of the most important transitions in my life. They can work that way for you, too.

First, recognize that all anger is anger at God. It is anger at the way things are. It is anger at the way people are. It is, as Byron Katie said, "our arguments with reality."[1]

Second, begin to relate to everyone you meet, everyone you deal with, as God in human form. Begin to shift your perception so that your focus is more on observing your reactions and judgments — how you distance yourself from others — than on your fantasies about what changes might make that person better, or more appealing, or easier to deal with. Learn to love them just as they are.

When we take the universe as it is, we can begin to open to the lessons it is constantly offering us. What can we learn about love, peace, compassion, and equanimity in the midst of exactly the circumstance we've been put in, eating exactly the meal the universe has put on our plate? When we begin to look at life that way, our everyday experience becomes our spiritual school, a thrilling, divine romance in which our focus is no longer on how to change the world but on how to change the aspects of ourselves that block our ability to see and experience the One behind all the forms... the Love inherent in each moment... the Divine inherent in everyone we meet.

CHAPTER 15

Not Acknowledging What You Really Want

Anyone born into this dimension is born with a hidden, direct communication with the total divine. The universe is our mother. The events that happen to us in life are trying to mother us into deeper awareness. Our task is to wake up to this relationship, which is our birthright.

ANDREW HARVEY, "BURNING FOR GOD," IN *FOR THE LOVE OF GOD*

In the various traditions that teach affirmative prayer, positive affirmation, creative visualization, prosperity consciousness, the law of attraction, and other methods of using prayer to get what we want, we are often told that if what we are praying for does not come to us, then there must be something in us that is blocking our ability to receive what the universe wants to freely offer. It is suggested that our faith isn't strong enough, that there must be some hidden negativity in our being.

But the fact that something in us is blocking what we are asking for need not necessarily be taken as a negative. Perhaps that blocking effect is coming from a deeper, wiser part of us. Or perhaps it is coming directly from God. It is entirely possible that in certain circumstances, at some deep level, our soul doesn't really want what our mind desires.

Our minds are filled with confusion, judgment, and desire. But in the depths of our soul, we all know Truth. The truth is that our soul wants to know itself... fully. Our soul longs to return home, to its source, to the One. It yearns to experience itself in all its fullness and radiance. It wants to know itself as pure love, unbounded joy, unlimited bliss. What the world of form considers to be desirable and potentially fulfilling might very well be recognized by our soul as a distraction.

If what we really long for is wealth, health, and security, and if our soul recognizes that it is in its own best interests for us to have these things, then they will come. But if what we really long for is God, if what we really long for is awakening and the return to our source, if what we really long for is to know that part of ourselves which transcends form, then we might as well get on with the work of unveiling our inner radiance. Whether we have wealth, health, and security becomes a secondary issue, because our real pursuit is to know that which lies behind form and beyond appearances. We want to know that which is Real, Infinite, and Eternal.

We long to know the infinite bliss within us, the Joy that transcends every apparent joy in the world of form.

There is nothing immoral about pursuing wealth, health, and security. The question is, how do we do it? How much do we have to sacrifice in the way of time, energy, relationship with loved ones, heart connection with other human beings, and basic moral principles to get what we "want"? And even if we are successful in achieving these things, we will inevitably lose them someday.

Most of what is valued in the world of form is totally transitory. We have it, and then it's gone. Or we long for it, but when we get it, it turns out to not be as fulfilling as we had hoped. Many of us recognize these issues at a much deeper level than we are usually inclined to admit.

A few years ago I met a fellow named Tom at a New Thought Church in the Midwest. He was one of the most prominent and passionate members of his church. He was a board member and was involved in many different aspects of church life. He began relating to me a struggle he was having with business and finances.

"I just don't know what the problem is," he said. "I've been struggling financially my whole life. And I am *ready*! I am *ready*! I am *ready* for prosperity! I have been praying, visualizing, affirming, being totally positive. I hired a feng shui master to come and reorganize my home so there would be no negative influences in the environment. I am willing to work for it. I've been knocking myself out, often working sixteen- to eighteen-hour days, for more years than I want to count. But no matter how hard I work, it just doesn't come."

"What do you do?" I asked.

He said that he was a sales representative for a high-end product used in home renovations.

"Do you believe in the product you are selling?" I said.

"Yes!" he said. His answer came almost too quickly, like a reflex. But then he was quiet for a moment. "It *is* overpriced," he finally said. "But we market it primarily to affluent people. They can afford it."

"Is it a good value?" I asked.

"Well, it's good quality merchandise."

"But is it a good value? Are people getting their money's worth when they buy it?"

"Well . . ."

I could hear that he wasn't really convinced.

"Do people really *need* it?"

He thought for a moment. "Well, truthfully, they can get a product from one of our competitors that is almost as good as our product, and it's much cheaper."

Then I asked, "Do you believe that the product you are selling is a good, high-quality product, that people *need* it, and that they are getting a good value when they buy it?"

After a moment he quietly said, "No, not really."

"Then how are you going to get prosperous selling it?" I asked.

~

Tom was caught in a situation his spiritual tradition hadn't really helped him to recognize. By placing all of the emphasis in spiritual life on prosperity, we tend to lose sight of the deeper requirements of our soul — for truth, generosity, and oneness, for integrity, sharing, and connection. The more evolved our spiritual consciousness is, the less we can tolerate even the most rudimentary forms of deceit. As soon as we try to ignore truth and oneness to get something we want, our soul will prohibit it. By saying "We're marketing this product to wealthy people who can afford it" and at the same moment knowing that there are products that are just as good and less expensive, we are acknowledging that we are willing to take advantage of another human being. Why should we charge people more just because they are wealthy? That, in essence, is stealing.

But it is difficult to hear the voice of our soul when we are surrounded by a value system that ignores nearly all of the things that are most important at the soul level. When we live in a culture that so tenaciously emphasizes the importance of things that have no inherent importance, even when our instincts tell us that the culture's values are bizarre, we tend to discount our instincts. The brainwashing is so all-pervasive that we don't trust our own intuitive awareness... we don't trust our own hearts.

Remember the quote from Ram Dass in chapter 4? "Once you ask for God, He isn't going to let you have anything that doesn't bring you closer to Him. It just can't happen. He'll prevent it, no matter how much you protest."

The desire for God is a fierce desire. It is the most powerful desire we have, because it is the only desire we have. It is the longing that supersedes all other longings, the yearning to go *home*. Whatever we think we long for, we are longing for because we believe it will bring us happiness, peace of mind, love, and fulfillment — and the only thing that brings us happiness, peace of mind, love, and fulfillment is God.

So whatever we think we are longing for, we are really longing for God.

When that is the highest intention of our soul, when what we really want is to go home, everything that happens to us in life happens because our soul is trying to use every route, every means it can find to get us there. At that point, our desire is no longer for fame, fortune, possessions, power, or prestige. We just long for God. We only want God.

Every event that happens to us is offering us the shortest route for our soul to take... home.

This place of soul, this connectedness with God that I am calling "home," involves much more than just the qualities we are most familiar with, like all-powerful, all-merciful, and all-loving.

In India there are different names for the many different aspects of God. The aspects of God, like God "itself," are seemingly infinite. It is a characteristic of Indian spiritual traditions that has caused confusion for Westerners, many of whom look at the superficial aspects of Indian spirituality and think they are seeing polytheism.

But all of the gods worshipped in India are just manifestations of different aspects of the *One* God — the Formless. In India, the One God is known as Brahman. When God (Brahman) takes form, He manifests as a holy trinity, which in India is identified by the names Brahma, Vishnu, and Shiva, who represent the three fundamental impulses in the world of form. Those impulses are creation (Brahma), preservation (Vishnu), and destruction (Shiva). For Westerners, the inclusion of destruction as an aspect of God in form can be a little disconcerting. It's an element of God that we seldom discuss or even acknowledge, because, in the West, destruction is a characteristic usually associated with the forces of darkness, or Satan.

In India, spiritual traditions have long acknowledged the all-inclusiveness of God. They acknowledge that every aspect, every element of the world of form is within the One, not separate. In this sense, we might accurately say that Hinduism is even more "monotheistic" than Christianity. Even Christianity believes that the embodiment of evil — Satan — was created by God. Christian theology identifies Satan as the angel Lucifer, who, through lust for personal power, fell from Grace.

In India, Shiva has an identity and a role that are significantly different from the Western concept of Satan. Shiva is seen as equal and opposite to the creative aspect, or Brahma, the Creator. Shiva is not evil. Just different. In fact, Shiva is immensely benevolent. Shiva is an integral aspect of God, as are Brahma and Vishnu. Decay and destruction are integral aspects of life in the world of form, as are creation and preservation. For thousands of years it has been understood in India that everything in the universe follows a clearly defined life cycle. Everything arises, exists for a period of time, changes, and passes away. Everything is created, preserved, and then destroyed. Except God. Except the soul. Everything else changes, decays, and dies.

Everything.

Every *thing.*

This natural cycle is not seen as evil but merely as the characteristic journey of all that comes into form. It is also understood that the resistance to that natural flow, the resistance to the cycle of nature, is a primary cause of suffering. What Shiva destroys is ignorance. He destroys that which stands between us and the conscious awareness of God, the conscious awareness of oneness.

There are sects in India, known as Shaivites, who worship Shiva as the primary manifestation of God. His devotees call upon him to destroy their ignorance, to destroy their illusions, to destroy anything in their minds, their personalities, and their lives that is standing between them and God. They also call upon Shiva to destroy illness, to destroy droughts and famines, to destroy their poverty. So Shiva's destructive capacities have both positive and negative aspects.

It's an interesting way to look at what we have been exploring in this book.

It's also interesting to see a culture that embraces *all* aspects of God. Even the sufferings and disappointments in life are seen as the work of the Divine. For many, this approach offers a much deeper and more profound understanding of God than the superficial spiritual paths that offer only success, riches, comforts, good health, and fame as the route to God and as evidence of God's love. Shiva, instead, offers us a spiritual context for understanding the totality of life, the joys and the sorrows, the pleasures and the pains, the prosperity and the poverty, as equally credible evidence of the bestowal of Divine Grace.

When we long for God, and God alone, we no longer fear or resist the aspects of the universe we previously prayed to be protected from. When we begin to understand that it can all bring us closer to God, we sometimes . . . almost . . . begin to welcome the challenges. While we don't seek suffering, we understand and honor its transformational potential.

Many of the rituals that honor Shiva involve ceremonial fires. The fire symbolizes the Light of Wisdom, the Light of Purity, which consumes our ignorance, our self-centeredness, and our ego attachments. It's a fierce fire. It is a fire that "burns away" our impurities, that "burns out" our mind, that immolates the parts of us that keep us separate from the One. It is interesting to note that people suffering through times of grief, times of fear, and times of disappointment often describe their experience by saying that they feel as if they are "on fire."

Western theologies also make reference to fire, but it is generally looked upon not as an agent of purification but as the torture accorded those who die as sinners. They refer to "the fires of hell," the concept of eternal damnation, and being cast into "the fires of hell for all eternity." What is always astonishing is that these Western concepts portray such a cruel, vindictive God — a punishing, ruthless, unforgiving God. As we have observed from different perspectives, it is difficult to imagine a God who is Love, who is all-forgiving yet who would, for all eternity, punish those who stray from the path.

It is a concept that simply does not hold up to the Light of Truth.

In Eastern theologies, and even in Judaism, there is no concept of eternal damnation. The experience of hell and the fire of suffering is always seen as a transitional experience. After it has taught us what we need to learn, after it has burned away what we need to lose, it passes away like every other experience we've had. Only certain sects of Christianity and Islam hold the concept of eternal damnation as an integral aspect of their theology.

Most of us, in our everyday lives, have had experiences that felt like the fires of hell. But most of us have also realized that these experiences are transitory. Like every other experience in the world of form, we eventually pass through them.

Back into the Light.

Back into the loving arms of God.

That is what we have always wanted . . . and where we have *always* wanted to be.

CHAPTER 16

We Don't Always Do What We Know Will Make Us Happy and Healthy

So you see that you cannot depend upon anybody.
There is no guide, no teacher, no authority.
There is only you — your relationship with others
and with the world — there is nothing else.

KRISHNAMURTI, *FREEDOM FROM THE KNOWN*

We have two fundamental predicaments in the unfolding of our spiritual life.

The first is that for long periods of time many of us don't understand what it's all about. We stumble through life confused and disoriented. We don't know what to do, where to go, what to believe, what to practice. We long for someone to tell us.

Eventually we get a glimmer of insight. Sometimes it comes slowly, gradually, instinctively, intuitively... sneaking up on us like a distant, foggy memory reflected in a very dusty mirror, slowly being cleansed by the events of our life. At other times it comes suddenly, as a moment of clarity that arises primarily in our rational mind. A friend of mine likes to call these moments "a blinding glimpse of the obvious."

But insight can also come in a flash of mystical consciousness, an inexplicable, indescribable divine intervention that emerges not from our rational mind but from a deeper part of us, a previously unknown, transcendent awareness. These experiences of "mystical consciousness" are generally the most authoritative and convincing realizations in our lives. They often precipitate a complete reorganization of our mind, our heart, our relationship with God, and our relationship with the world.

No matter how insight comes, eventually we face our second predicament: How do we incorporate that which we now know into our daily life? How do we radically transform decades of entrenched patterns of thought and behavior into a freer, more expansive, nonjudgmental awareness and lifestyle?

The challenge of making this transformation creates one of the fundamental paradoxes in our spiritual life: most of the time we tend to live as if we knew a great deal less than we actually know. That is, we know spiritual truths but we don't act as if we know them. We have awakened to a higher and deeper awareness, but we don't act in ways consistent with what we have awakened to. The predicament is, we are always attempting to grow into the awareness we already have. We are attempting to become that which we already *are*.

The spiritual path is not just a process of gaining transcendent insight, knowledge, and awareness. It is also a process of learning how to reformulate our thoughts, words, and deeds so that our outer life, our earthly life, becomes a clear reflection of our inner awareness. Eventually these two aspects of our being must begin to work together: what we do in our inner life infuses our outer life with increasing levels of awareness. What we do in our outer life becomes an expression of, and support system for, the unfolding of our inner awareness.

It is a delicate balancing act. It is possible to see so much . . . inwardly. We get glimpses of oneness. We see flashes of the Light. We have moments of overwhelming awareness of the presence of God. In the Light of those transcendent awakenings, we begin to clearly see the deleterious effects of the negative thoughts in our minds. We recognize that our thoughts, emotions, and actions have consequences. We recognize that our habitual anger, hostility, despair, depression, and judgment are divisive and destructive.

Sometimes those moments of recognition are balanced by moments when we feel the reassuring bliss of love and connection; the warmth and lightness of kindness, compassion, and generosity; the nurturing, expansive joy of living in a state of Grace. Living in a state of Grace is, simply, living in harmony with our highest awareness, living a life that is an outward expression of oneness. When we do that, our thoughts, words, and actions express the highest, most divine awareness we are capable of. Our challenge is to translate these fleeting glimpses, these moments, into an all-encompassing lifestyle.

In recent years, the momentum in our culture has been moving us away from being able to make that translation. The demands on our time and energy have become overwhelming. The pressures created by our attempt to keep pace with the intensity of life as we now design it are, quite simply, crushing our spiritual nature like a cluster of wheat being chopped and pulverized in a massive, relentless harvesting machine.

Thirty years ago, when I began teaching meditation, I would usually recommend that students start with fifteen minutes twice a day. After the first few weeks, I would suggest that they gradually work their way up to thirty to forty-five minutes twice a day. Most of them would nod and say, "Fine." Now, if I say "start with fifteen minutes twice a day," most students will completely freak out.

"How would I find an extra *thirty* minutes in my day?! I don't even have time to do what I'm *already* doing!"

Their panic and frustration is profound, palpable, and pervasive. But what is even more profound is that so few among us are questioning the sanity, or lack of sanity, of living such a demanding, exhausting, yet unfulfilling lifestyle. So few people question the rationale, or lack of rationale, behind it all. Hardly anyone is asking, "Why am I doing this?"

The very lifestyle that creates this overarching sense of depression, depletion, and despair will continue to create exactly those same conditions if no changes are made. Unfortunately, it appears — at the moment — that the culture has little interest in making such changes. The commitment to this intense, disconnected, fragmented lifestyle just keeps increasing. It is the very definition of a vicious cycle.

When I travel, I am constantly amazed at how rarely I ever see anyone in an airport, on an airplane, or in a hotel lobby who looks happy. Most are scowling and agitated, constantly in a hurry, and often angry. The lifestyle we have created allows us to fly to several different cities in one day and to be perpetually connected to machines and to a bizarre electronic conglomerate of information known as the Internet. But we are rarely connected to each other... to human beings. We have no time to smile at a stranger, but endless time to communicate electronically. We have become extensions of the machines we have created, a manifestation of the futuristic nightmare scenario foreseen decades ago by people like George Orwell, Aldous Huxley, Marshall McLuhan, and Alan Watts.

Most of us have heard that humorous yet wise definition of *insanity*: "continuing to do the same thing and expecting a different result." Measured by that standard, our entire culture has become a vast insane asylum with three hundred million inmates. When we feel our life is moving too fast, we often respond by finding ways to make it move faster. We rush through our days at a frantic pace. We feel astonishing pressures we can't seem to break free from. Our lives are driven by the economics of insatiable desire, desires we ourselves create. There are so many things we believe we simply have to have, and that our children simply have to have, that our lives are motivated by the lust for stimulation, merchandise, and prestige rather than the love of harmony and connection. We spend hours and hours at work, disconnected from our families, generating income to purchase things, rather than create more opportunities to experience the only thing that will ever bring us happiness... love.

Season after season, people straggle into my meditation classes full of agitation, sadness, and exhaustion, desperate for some deeper experience of life, yearning for some fulfillment and peace of mind. Yet an astonishing number are reluctant to make lifestyle changes that would create space for a new peacefulness and joy to arise in their life.

In a society where most problems are perceived to be someone else's fault, where we pay others to "fix" our problems because we "don't have time" to do anything different, many people come to meditation class thinking that ninety minutes once a week for four weeks is going to completely overhaul a lifetime of accumulated stress. Each week at the beginning of class, I ask if anyone has meditated on their own at home during the past week. The number of hands that rise do not even begin to correspond to the number of sad, haggard, harried faces I see in the group.

Health-care providers, bodyworkers, and yoga teachers notice the same syndrome. Many of their clients and students don't want to make any significant lifestyle changes. They don't want to stop doing the things that are damaging their bodies and undermining their health. They want to keep doing all the same things. They want to keep smoking cigarettes, eating unhealthy foods, drinking alcohol, staying out late, avoiding exercise, doing stressful jobs, and they want the bodyworker or health-care provider to "fix" them.

The truth of the matter is, many of us have often tried to use prayer exactly the same way. We want to pray for what we want, and we want our benevolent Heavenly Father to give it to us. But we don't really want to do anything to help ourselves achieve it. If we want peace of mind, we're going to have to do something to achieve it. If we want the happiness that has eluded us, we're going to have to change something in our lives in order to pave the way for it. If we want good health, we're going to have to do things that encourage and cultivate good health. No one else is going to do it for us. Not even God.

~

The form our daily spiritual work takes can change and evolve over time. It's a delicate balancing act. And even great effort has great pitfalls.

All too often, a rigorous spiritual practice or deeply held theological belief can become a tool of divisiveness, judgment, and, in extreme cases, violence. What started as a glimpse of insight gets processed through our ego mind and becomes a dogmatic bludgeon with which we beat and berate anyone who doesn't believe what we believe, who doesn't practice what we practice.

Sometimes, when we are making great effort to come into the arms of God, we get overly zealous and think that everyone else in the world should be making the same effort. Other times, when our effort has gotten a little shaky, we become even more judgmental of others.

Judgment of others comes directly from the things we fear in ourselves. We only judge in others the things we dislike in ourselves. We become ruthlessly evangelical when our own faith is shaky, when we're not fully convinced that we really believe what we say we believe. Or when we are seething with resentment and envy of those who are doing the things we think we are supposed to be restraining ourselves from doing. A voice in our subconscious says, "I'd feel a *lot* better about this if a *lot* of other people agreed with me . . . if a *lot* of other people were behaving the way I am *attempting* to behave."

The spiritual path is the most intensely personal pursuit in our life. It is an elegantly choreographed, multifaceted, celestial dance between our separate self and our universal Self. Our separate self, which was originally the source of all loneliness, suffering, and isolation, slowly fades away, paving the way for the "rebirth" of the universal Self. This is the true resurrection of the Spirit.

The spiritual path is the process of merging back into the One. It is the journey home. But we have to do it. No one else is going to do it for us. And our ability to traverse this path has nothing to do with what anyone else is or is not doing, nothing to do with what anyone else believes or doesn't believe. The spiritual path is totally personal. And it is work. But it is totally joyous work.

Imagine. All we have to do is love. Just love. What could be more joyous work?

How refreshing, reassuring, and rejuvenating to take a few moments each day to connect with the divine source within us, to touch the one light from which it all emerged, to taste the pure, silent majesty of the ever-present wellspring of creation . . . within our own hearts . . . within our own souls.

In a very real sense, all that it requires is that we love. Ourselves and others. The world around us. The Light that creates and sustains us.

Just love.

CHAPTER 17

God Is Not Distant from Us

God pervades everywhere...
All places on this globe are... His Abodes.
All rivers, lakes, and ponds are sacred...
The many shapes and forms of this world embody
the sound of God's name...
Limitless is His Being!

SWAMI MUKTANANDA, *PLAY OF CONSCIOUSNESS*

Many of us begin our spiritual quest with the understanding that God is far removed from us, that He is the Almighty, the Great Mystery, the Heavenly Father, the Divine Judge reigning over us, casting down judgment and punishment, occasionally bestowing some reward, or delight, or pleasure upon us, only to withdraw it whenever our sinful nature manifests and we incur His wrath.

But God, as manifest in the world of form, is Love... only Love ... pure, undifferentiated, unconditional Love. God has no wrath. And God is not in any sense removed from us.

The difficulties in life are not punishment raining down from a judgmental, wrathful God but the ripples of discord generated by our own inharmonious thoughts, words, and deeds. God is a vast ocean of undifferentiated calmness, peace, oneness, and harmony ... the One Energy... the One Light out of which the entire universe of form arises. It is the intrusion of *our* chaotic thoughts and tenacious expressions of separateness that create the discordant waves of chaos we call "suffering."

Suffering occurs in our egos. In our souls there is no suffering, because in God there is no suffering. God is everywhere, in everything, and in everyone... as close as our own breath. God is all there is. There is nothing but God. Nothing but the One.

So why do we so often feel so separate?

The only thing standing between us and God is us. Through millions of years of evolution we have evolved these extraordinary prefrontal lobes in our brains. We have full consciousness, and we also have fully formed minds. Our problem is, we haven't yet learned to use those minds to their fullest advantage. Our unenlightened mind is the only thing that blocks our ability to be consciously aware of God in every moment.

Most of us are ruled by our minds. So from the spiritual point of view, our task is to begin to take the reins of those minds, to use them as the tools they were meant to be rather than live our lives under their tyranny. In a very real sense, we can say that our own minds are the source of the endless stream of insatiable desire, inconsolable fear, and insistent separateness that keeps us in an almost constant state of discontent.

Learning to take the reins of our minds and our consciousness marks the beginning stages of the next phase of human evolution. The last major evolutionary phase was the transition from instinct to reason. It was the transition from living as slightly more evolved creatures to living as "intelligent," "rational" beings. That transition happened slowly, over thousands and thousands of years, as we gradually learned to develop our intellects. We developed the capacity to think, to reason, to analyze. Because we appeared to be the only creatures on earth who could do that, we began to believe that we were superior.

We began to believe that it was our divinely ordained right to subdue and dominate the rest of the world. As we began to think, reason, and analyze, we began to feel separate.

We ate the fruit of the tree of knowledge.

Now we are witnessing the inevitable end result of a "civilization" that lives primarily in the rational mind rather than in the intuitive heart, that places greater emphasis on thinking than on love. As a result of all the discord and discontent this has engendered, we are slowly beginning to recognize that our long-subdued faculty of intuition might offer a higher means of knowing than rational thought and deductive reasoning.

The only thing that prevents us from cultivating a deeper awareness of our intuition is the primacy we have ascribed to our rational minds. But our intuition is always present, just as our soul is always present. We get so lost in our minds that we can't hear our own intuition. Even when we can hear it, we don't often listen to it because we don't really trust it.

There is always a place within us that knows. We know. We actually do know where to go and what to do. We know what is safe and what is unsafe. We know what is true and what is false. But we haven't learned to listen to that still small voice within, the voice of our own intuitive heart. Intuition is the voice of God. It is the mechanism through which God speaks to us. It is always available to us if we can learn to listen, if we can quiet our minds and open our hearts. Cultivating a regular practice of meditation in our lives can help us greatly to hear and trust our intuition.

It could be said that thought exists apart from nature. We think about things rather than experience our connection to them. Intuition springs from our soul's connection to its source, its recognition of its identity with the One and therefore its connection to everything. Only a rational, separate mind could be deluded enough to ignore that connection, to think that its thoughts and resultant actions do not have an effect on every living thing. Simply stated, only a being lost in her or his own mind could think that throwing garbage out the window of the car won't cause a cascade of rippling negative effects that touch every corner of the earth and ultimately arrive back at their source. Because it will. It absolutely will.

On the other hand, beings who live in their intuitive hearts recognize that every thought they think and every action they take effect every other living being. Every thought and every action effect our entire planet. So the next phase of human evolution will be about learning to use our minds as the tools they are meant to be rather than as the weapons of mass destruction they have become. It will be the transition from reason to intuition.

I had an interesting discussion recently with a psychologist friend. He was frustrated with my assertion that happiness lies in transcending thought. "Why would God give us these extraordinary minds if he didn't want us to think?" he asked.

Even though these brilliant human minds are a part of God's creation, I doubt that the intent was for us to think twenty-four hours a day. After all, if you own a Ferrari, you don't drive it twenty-four hours a day. You put it in the garage and allow it to rest from time to time. You turn off the engine so you can perform maintenance and keep it tuned up. Perhaps God intended us to learn how to "turn off" our minds from time to time so we can experience Him instead of thinking about Him.

~

Just as an exercise, begin to envision that the One Energy that forms the basis of all creation, that infuses every cell, every molecule, every proton, every neutron, and every electron of the physical universe, also infuses every cell, molecule, proton, neutron, and electron of your body and your mind.

There is *no* difference. None.

That same One Energy is flowing in and through and around you in every millisecond of your life.

Your consciousness, your awareness, is fully capable of experiencing that One Energy... and your absolute identity with that One Energy. But your consciousness is encumbered by your mind, your ego, your personality, and all the different elements that make up your separate identity. Those are the only things that prevent you from knowing your oneness with God at this very moment, because you are not separate from Him.

You can *never* be separate from God.

You never *will* be separate from God.

You are *always* connected to the One Light.

CHAPTER 18

God Can Be Known and Felt

Thou seemest, Lord, to give severe tests to those who love Thee,
but only that in the extremity of their trials
they may learn the greater extremity of Thy love.

SAINT TERESA OF AVILA

In the previous chapter, we began to explore the problems that arise from our sense that God is somehow apart from us. We looked at the differences between reason and intuition, the two fundamental forms of knowing. We began to sense that living in our rational minds prohibits us from ever really knowing God. All we can do through reason is think about God. To really know God, we have to cultivate our capacity for intuition.

There is a third mechanism for knowing, a way to know that involves more visceral experience and perception. We have the ability to sense something we might call "Presence," the perception of Holiness or Divinity within and around us.

For many of us, this sense might first arise in a rudimentary form in churches, temples, and mosques — holy places — where we experience the warm, soft hum of sanctity and purity, the Presence of Divinity. By utilizing architectural components that symbolize the intersection of Spirit and form, architects consciously designed many of these structures to engender experiences of holiness. They represent the meeting ground of the sacred and the profane. Towering steeples; vast, enormous, awesome interior spaces with uncommonly high cathedral ceilings; and rounded domes that crest in the center all contribute to a sense of otherworldliness and connection with the Divine. They point toward heaven. The physical structure fosters a welcoming atmosphere, inviting God to descend to a sacred point on earth, to manifest in the receptive form of that sacred space. So churches, temples, and mosques are often referred to as "Houses of God." In the pure forms of sacred architecture, the structure itself is thought to be the nexus where the Creator meets the created.

Some of us are more attuned to feel the presence of the Divine in other places. We find it at the beach, in the ocean, traversing a mountain range, or wandering through a forest. Some of us feel the Presence of Divinity when we gaze at a clear nighttime sky filled with countless stars. The sheer boundlessness instinctively causes us to ponder infinity. For many, these feelings of Presence arise much more freely in natural surroundings. It's as if we spontaneously surrender our separateness and judging mind when we gaze upon the beauty our Creator has created. We also tune to the place of connection in ourselves where we and the Creator are one. In that inner place we are tuning to the part of ourselves that actually created the vast universe upon which we now gaze, that sacred place where all creativity and creation happen spontaneously, eternally springing forth from the one source.

Many astronauts have experienced this sense of Presence in profound ways. Ascending into space, they gaze out on the vastness of the universe. When they look back at our planet, it seems so remarkably insignificant, small, and delicate. Looking at our tiny ball floating through infinite space, many astronauts have recognized the sad, ironic truth that humankind is constantly fighting and dying over comparatively meaningless ideas and prejudices, comparatively tiny parcels of land, and natural resources that could easily be shared by everyone were it not for the fearful greed and possessiveness that permeate the character of so much of humanity. All of this is happening on a minuscule ball floating somewhere in vast, infinite space...

For many astronauts the experience has been absolutely life changing. Even for many of us who have not had that experience, the ability to see an image of our own planet from the vantage point of space has also been life changing. The first photo of our earth taken with the moon in the foreground and the earth in the distance was the beginning of a dramatic shift in our consciousness. It gave rise to the whole-earth concept, the ecology movement, and the many and varied "holistic" philosophies and practices that have arisen in subsequent years. It gave us a clear view of our place in the universe, as tiny, tiny creatures clinging tenuously to our fragile planetary home, whirling together in infinite space, united in ways we can't seem to comprehend but absolutely must embrace.

The point is, we like to have these experiences. We like to hear others tell us about these experiences. We like to feel awe. We like to be reminded of the fundamental paradox: we are quite insignificant in the vastness of creation, yet we are gloriously unique among the creatures of the earth because we possess the ability to be consciously aware of the very impulse that created it.

We are both. We are insignificant *and* we are connected to the source of everything. Each time we feel love, awe, joy, and connection, we are feeling the Divine. These feelings come in many ways. Usually they are just a dim reflection of the vastness that lies at their source. But they are reminders and guideposts, whetting our appetite, gently reassuring us that we are part of something much greater than our minds can comprehend.

There are many beings who have walked this earth, who are

walking this earth, who are bearers of the Light. They are the ones who have traversed the path, who have seen Truth, who are an embodiment of Divinity in form. They vibrate with Presence. When we are near them, we can feel it. We call them saints, gurus, masters, *majzoobs*, avatars. We recognize their wholeness, and their *holiness*. People like Mother Teresa, Pope John Paul II, Mahatma Gandhi, Neem Karoli Baba, Meher Baba, and the Dalai Lama are beings who have awakened to the fullness of their connection to the source of everything. They have diminished the separating power of their ego minds. They have merged into the One. When we are in their presence we feel strangely but beautifully different. We can be transformed merely by being close to them.

With beings in that state of exalted consciousness, even the concept of getting "close" is different. When there is no separation, there is no separation. When a being is fully merged into the One, merely to think of them, to look at their picture, is enough to bring us into their Presence.

One friend of mine was talking about being with the great Hindu saint Neem Karoli Baba in India back in the 1970s. He said, "I don't think any of us were ever as good as we were when we were in Maharaji's presence. It was just astounding. But it wasn't just the fact that *he* loved us so much that astounded me. I mean, he was a saint. It was his job to love everybody, you know? What astounded me was that when I was in his presence, I loved everybody."

In my own life I have felt the experience of *darshan*, or the blessing of the guru, in so many different circumstances. I first felt it in my own being lying in my bed one night when I was eighteen. I felt it in Meher Baba's home. I felt it in the tomb of Saint Francis of Assisi. I felt it in the Sistine Chapel. I felt it in a Lutheran church outside Columbus, Ohio. I felt it standing next to a dear friend in an orthodox synagogue in New York City. I felt it in the Hanuman Temple in Vrindaban, India. I felt it when I met Baba Muktananda. I felt it standing on a ledge in Rocky Mountain National Park.

The list goes on and on. Think about your own list. What places have you visited where you felt Presence... where you felt at peace and connected to the universe? Who are the people you've been with who engendered that feeling in you? If you feel it would be helpful in noticing and remembering moments of Presence you may have been ignoring, make a list.

At this point in my life, I feel these experiences are everywhere, all the time. As one friend shared with me shortly after the death of his wife, "I always knew, whenever I looked into Roberta's eyes, that I was looking into the eyes of God."

Know that whenever you look into *anyone's* eyes you are looking into the eyes of God.

~

When you are feeling abandoned by God, when things haven't gone your way, when God hasn't delivered whatever it is you wanted on a silver platter, don't assume that you are disconnected from God. Seek, rather, to find new ways to see, feel, and experience God. Seek to be in His Presence. Take yourself to places where you might more readily feel His Presence. Put yourself in the company of those whose lives are dedicated to being in His Presence. When your heart is hurting, and your mind is confused, you probably won't find much in the way of transformative experience in the local bar, or watching a football game, or sitting at home alone with the curtains drawn and the lights turned off.

Instead, begin to transform your home into a place of spiritual Presence. If it feels comfortable to you, create an altar in your home. In India, the altar is known as the *puja* table. Fill it with images that open your heart. A picture of Jesus, a statue of Buddha, a dancing Shiva, photos of your loved ones, a candle, a flower vase, a beautiful rock or crystal, some incense — whatever is meaningful to you, whatever inspires in you a feeling of love and harmony. Take a few moments each day to invite the sacred into your home and into your life. Ask for help. Ask to feel His Presence. Ask that your loneliness and fear be consumed in the vast ocean of His love.

Then get up. Go out. Walk, or sit, in beautiful natural surroundings — the beach, a mountain, a river. Go to holy places where you can sit quietly and meditate. Soak up the atmosphere of sanctity. Visit with sincere, respected, genuine teachers of God. Go on retreat. Just because God didn't give you exactly what you were asking for exactly when you were asking for it, don't assume that He is ignoring you or that He has abandoned you.

Continually ask yourself this question: "Do I want what I want, or would I rather have God?"

Sometimes we don't have the luxury of making that decision. Sometimes it is made for us. When it is, the most healing response is to open our hearts to receive that which is freely offered rather than moan and groan that we didn't get exactly what we asked for when we asked for it.

We *always* have God. We don't even have to ask.

PART THREE

Feeling God's Presence No Matter What

Your pain is the breaking of the shell
that encloses your understanding.
Even as the stone of the fruit must break,
that its heart may stand in the Sun,
so must you know pain.

KAHLIL GIBRAN, *THE PROPHET*

CHAPTER 19

You Aren't Being Punished

That thou mayest have pleasure in everything,
seek pleasure in nothing.
That thou mayest know everything,
seek to know nothing.
That thou mayest possess all things,
seek to possess nothing.
That thou mayest be everything,
seek to be nothing.

SAINT JOHN OF THE CROSS

As we have seen, when things don't go our way, our first tendency is often to experience our frustrated desire, our loss, our unanswered prayer as some form of punishment. But we have also seen that to interpret every event as a direct reward or punishment from God becomes both complicated and confounding. To restate the obvious, there are many ruthless, self-absorbed, dishonest people who experience worldly success, and there are many good-hearted, honest people who don't.

One option we sometimes fall back on is the notion that all accounts are settled by God in the afterlife or, if you believe in reincarnation, in some future earthly life. But that doesn't do much to help us understand what is happening to us right now and how we can effectively respond to it.

So let's give up the fairy-tale notion that piety and good deeds are rewarded and selfishness and evil deeds are punished. Let us assume, instead, that no matter what happens to us, our goal in life is to consciously connect with God. That is the ultimate reward. Whether we are getting unfairly punished for something or someone else is getting unfairly rewarded is not our concern. Our only concern is to learn how to merge with God.

When the British imprisoned Mahatma Gandhi in India, he was placed in solitary confinement in a fetid, rat-infested cell. He was given a filthy, lice-infested uniform. He was fed putrid, rotten food. Yet he lovingly looked into the eyes of the prison guard and said, "Thank you."

He wasn't being cheeky. He was acknowledging that even an unjust circumstance of great suffering and discomfort could provide a powerful environment for inner work. He knew that this apparent injustice could offer him an opportunity to go deeper into his spiritual practice.

After all, it's easy to love those who love us. The great challenge is to learn how to love those who don't love us. Gandhi's commitment was to Truth, to Love, and to nonviolence. He gave no thought to obtaining comfort for himself. And he had no interest in punishing those who inflicted injustice on others.

Stopping them, yes. Punishing them, no.

My friend Stephen Levine has often said, "Every bit of fear, suffering, sadness, betrayal, physical illness, and despair in our entire lifetime can be wiped out by one moment of pure Love." As we begin to incorporate what we are learning here, we can learn to refocus our prayers. As we become more spiritually "connected," our prayers will not be so focused on how to get what we want. Instead, we will pray for the wisdom to want that which will bring us real joy, that will guide us toward connection... that will bring us home to God.

Many of the people I have worked with and counseled over the past thirty-five years have had some extraordinarily transformational spiritual experience or insight in the wake of a profound loss or disappointment. To understand this phenomenon we need to reflect on the times of difficulty we all have experienced. Many of us can look back on an event that at the time seemed overwhelmingly painful emotionally. But a few months or a few years later, many of us can say, "That was the worst experience of my life. I wouldn't wish it on anyone. I never want to go through it again. But, *boy* did I grow from it!"

This concept of growth might seem infuriatingly trite. Many of us have had experiences that offer us growth we don't really want, experiences that are so painful, that so derail our ability to enjoy life and our plans for the future that there seems to be no space for growth, no relief from the pain, no way to ease the suffering... no way to understand why or how something so horrendous could happen.

But, as we have seen time and again, it may be our understanding of God, and our assumptions about how God should show us that He loves us, that create the disconnection between our spiritual life and our life in the world of form. Quite simply, we could say that Love itself is the demonstration that God loves us. For God *is* Love. God can't do anything *but* love. Love is the essential nature of the being we are referring to when we talk about God.

If, in our lives, we feel deprived and sense an absence of Love, the problem is not so much that there is an absence of other people who love us. The problem is that we are temporarily unable to access the Love in our own hearts. For Love is there, inside each and every one of us, infinite and unlimited... always.

Whenever we have experienced that ecstatic, wondrous, joyful exuberance we call Love, we have experienced it within ourselves. God placed it there as "standard equipment." It is the most magnificent awakening a human being can have. When we experience Love, our life has meaning — we understand what it is all about. We say, "This is what I was *born* for! This is how I want to feel *always*."

Because we live in a culture that trains us to look outside ourselves for happiness, we usually attribute those rare moments when we do feel Love to whatever we were doing or whomever we were with when we felt it. We forget that the experience is inside us. When we forget the truth of our own spiritual self-reliance, we pursue happiness in unwise, counterproductive ways that often complicate our lives and make it even more difficult to awaken to our inner connection with God.

So let us attempt what is known in psychology as a "figure-ground reversal." Let us take what we have perceived to be of secondary importance (our inner experience) and move it to the foreground. Let us imagine that Love is a state of being inside us and that when we are in contact with that place inside us, we experience bliss, ecstasy, peace, contentment, and a sense of connection with everyone else on earth. From this perspective, whenever we are experiencing Love, it has little to do with what is happening in the world around us or what the people around us are doing or saying.

For instance, have you ever noticed that when you are really in love... when you are vibrating with joy... when you feel really connected... even the people you don't like don't look so bad?!

Conversely, when we are angry, *everyone* triggers our anger. Everyone seems like an enemy. Every event unleashes the snowballing effect of rage. When we are angry, the universe feels hostile. We have the sense that every person and every event is part of a vast conspiracy aimed at making us miserable. When we are sad and depressed, everything that happens seems sad and depressing. Jokes aren't funny. Beauty doesn't seem beautiful. We are distrusting of kindness and generosity, unable to open our hearts sufficiently to receive Love.

From just these few insights, and from the many stories we have shared in this book, we can begin to see that our happiness in life — in fact, our entire experience of life — is much more grounded in our internal state than in the external circumstances of our lives. To return to the supposition that Love is within us, we might say — when we "fall in love" — that the person we have fallen in love with is a stimulus that allows us to feel the love in our own hearts. They awaken us to who we truly are. They are like a doorway through which we are able to see a part of ourselves we may have never seen before. That part is our connection to God, to our soul.

Of course, because our interactions with the universe are so often rooted in fear, most of us immediately become attached. We immediately fear that we are going to lose that blissful experience. We immediately assume that we have to control that person, that we have to be with them, and that they have to behave the way we want them to behave in order for us to feel Love.

The irony is, the minute we place the conditions for our own happiness outside ourselves — in some other person or some external condition — the very second our minds try to sustain the experience of Love by injecting fear into the equation, we lose the ability to fully connect with the source of Love within us...

And that source, our spiritual heart, our *hridayam*, is ever present, infinite, and eternal. It is the spark of Divinity within us, that place of eternal connection with our Creator. It could be said that it is the place where the Creator lives inside us, in the vast, edgeless ocean of Love that exists eternally in our own hearts.

Love does not punish. Love just loves.

But every action has effects. We might just call them consequences. If we put our hand in a hot fire, we will get burned. That doesn't mean that God doesn't love us or that we are being punished. It simply means that this energy we call fire can burn us if we aren't careful. It can also warm us and cook our food. But it has to be respected and understood. We learn how to honor it and work with it through experience.

In the Bible, it is said, "Whatever a man sows, that he will also reap."[1] That is, in essence, a statement of the law of karma. But the law of karma is often misunderstood as a system of rewards and punishments. What it is, rather, is a recognition that every action has an equal and opposite reaction. Good deeds engender good results, and bad deeds engender unpleasant results. The unpleasant results are not punishment. They are much more akin to scientific reactions. If you send hatred and anger out into the universe, hatred and anger will come back to you. If you send out Love, Love will come back. If you send out violence, violence will come back. If you send out generosity, generosity will come back. If you send out greed, you will be surrounded by greed. If your thoughts and actions express oneness, then you will experience peace and joy. If your thoughts and actions express division and separateness, then you will experience agitation and suffering.

All of this exists in a complex system of energies that is much more vast and intricate than we could possibly imagine. The "boomerang" results of action do not always manifest instantaneously. There are many circumstances where callous greed and indifference to the well-being of others seems to be rewarded. People sometimes get wealthy exploiting other people, their community, and the planet. But eventually the painful effects of not honoring our oneness, our interconnectedness, will manifest. It's unavoidable.

Nevertheless, those painful effects are not punishment in the strict sense. In the philosophical and spiritual systems that support the notion of reincarnation, it is understood that the individual soul will keep reincarnating until it has experienced every experience available in the world of form and until it has balanced all of the many and varied experiences it has had. The soul will go through a seemingly infinite number of pleasant experiences and a corresponding number of unpleasant experiences.

What is being sought through this process is balance. The soul itself is one with God. And God is beyond good and evil. Little by little, the soul is learning to experience itself through a process of elimination. Its eternal existence, its identity with infinite Love, its enduring peace, all exist beyond — and in some sense despite — the seemingly endless experiences of opposing or dualistic forces in the world of form.

The concept of eternal damnation is a perversion of Truth. It is a theological weapon created in centuries past by members of the clergy and priesthood. It was designed to manipulate and frighten believers and nonbelievers into subscribing to the officially sanctioned theological dogma and prescribed codes of behavior. It is the greatest contradiction in theology. It has absolutely no validity.

It is impossible for God, who is Absolute Love, to condemn anything in His creation to eternal suffering. It is impossible for the individual soul that is one with God to ever be destroyed. That Absolute Love is *always* available. It is the One Energy that binds the entire physical universe together.

But the law of karma does provide that every experience that has been earned will be experienced. If you murder someone . . . you will be murdered. If you steal . . . you will be stolen from. If you lie . . . you will be lied to. It isn't punishment. It is the balancing of opposites.

So allow yourself to begin to see the spiritual opportunities that might be presenting themselves whenever your prayers appear to be unanswered. Ask yourself how this disappointment, this dramatic change of direction, this unanticipated loss, might help you to dive more deeply into the search for your own soul. Ask yourself — from the point of view of the infinite, formless, eternal soul that you are — if what you were hoping and praying for might have been an expression of fear, or attachment, or desire.

Ask yourself how your desire to control the universe, to have it behave the way you want it to behave, might be standing in the way of finding the oneness that is readily available — the peace, love, and joy that are eternally present — when we just allow things to be as they are.

CHAPTER 20

What Have You Really Been Asking For?

I don't think any sensitive person can be satisfied with having fun, no matter how much of it we may cram into our lives. Our need is not for pleasure, but for joy.... Fun is living for ourselves; joy comes from living for others, giving our time and love to a purpose greater than ourselves.

EKNATH EASWARAN, *THOUSAND NAMES OF VISHNU*

It's amazing how often, when we dive beneath the surface of our emotional pain, we recognize that there is a part of us that *didn't really want* our prayer to be answered in the way we were asking it.

What I am suggesting is that sometimes there is an element of our consciousness that is relieved that we didn't get what we were asking for. This relief often manifests in broken romantic relationships and difficult marriages that have ended in divorce. A part of us is crying out, "Don't leave me! Don't leave me!" Another part of us is saying, "My God, how can I get free of this madness?" When the end comes, if we're listening carefully, we can often hear another part of us saying, "Whew! Thank God that's over!"

The same thing can also be true when someone we love dies after a long illness and great suffering. We miss that person, but we are relieved that the suffering has ended. Sometimes we might also experience relief when we don't get into a college we prayed to get into or we don't get a job or a promotion that we were praying for. Perhaps at some deeper level we knew that that college, or that job, wouldn't make us happy.

This relief can arise even in circumstances when we are praying to be healed from some illness or injury. If we examine our minds and intention carefully, we may see that there was something in us that didn't really want the healing we were praying for. Even when we're in the midst of financial difficulties and the dream of winning the lottery and paying off all our debts just won't come true, there can sometimes be a very subtle sense of relief inside us. Our resistance, our *not wanting* whatever it is, can arise from some subtle fear… or it can come from a higher wisdom.

Perhaps our soul knows something that we do not consciously know.

To understand this, we have to look back at our discussions in chapter 9 about perceiving the many different levels of consciousness existing within us simultaneously. Sometimes we *think* we want something, we *say* we want something, we beg and plead and cajole to *get* something, but there is a deeper or higher part of us that doesn't really want it. Or perhaps that deeper or higher part of us just wants to confront our fear, our attachment, our craving, and finally let go of it.

Whatever the inner motivation, we need to keep acknowledging that we are complex, often contradictory beings. There are many different "parts" of us. We are both human and Divine. And those different parts don't always agree with each other. Understanding the totality of who we are is an important step on the path to spiritual awakening. The part of us that doesn't want what we're asking for might arise from some recognition that what we're asking for isn't really the best thing for us.

Many have experienced this syndrome vividly when struggling with an addiction. At first, you are not addicted. You enjoy whatever it is. It is a choice. Whether it is chocolate or coffee or cigarettes or beer or marijuana or sex or vodka or heroin . . . in the early stages the relationship is one of choice and enjoyment.

But eventually that enjoyment is overtaken by ever-increasing craving and attachment. The desire for the activity or substance becomes so powerful that the original enjoyment has become submerged in a seemingly uncontrollable, all-consuming lust. Every waking moment is filled with the overwhelming urge for whatever it is we are now addicted to. Powerful physical sensations intertwine with obsessive thought patterns, until our entire life is consumed by a desire that desperately demands to be filled.

For many people, the suffering of living in bondage to an insatiable desire can lead to the beginning of spiritual awakening. This awakening involves a recognition that the addiction has become so all-pervasive that there is little space left in life for anything else. Every thought, every action, every moment has become focused on satisfying that insatiable desire and the desperate fear that we might not be able to.

Alongside that faint awakening, a little voice begins to cry out in our soul. Our Inner Light mourns that our outer life is obscuring our radiance. We experience a deepening spiritual despair. Our soul has become shrouded by our desire and attachment. We begin to feel one of the most painful experiences a human being can feel: the magnificence of our own Divinity being dimmed and degraded, its radiant Light getting snuffed out by the excruciating illusions, constricting limitations, and ruthless demands of our desiring minds. Like the malevolent monsters from Morbeus's Id in the classic science fiction movie *Forbidden Planet*, our own minds have generated thought patterns, behavior patterns, and desire patterns that originally were intended to bring us pleasure but have now become the instruments of our own destruction.

It is in those moments that we often experience not wanting what we think we want. Each time the desire of addiction is fulfilled, a little part of us dies. Our self-doubt, self-hatred, self-judgment, and shame all increase, each shutting down a little more of our sacred, holy Inner Light. It becomes a classic love-hate relationship. A part of us loves that which we are addicted to, and a part of us hates it. But what we really hate is the spiritual bondage we are caught in. When our not wanting what we want becomes a kind of quiet desperation, a moment of profound *spiritual* desperation finally forces us to "let go, and let God." At that moment, our Inner Light, our soul, is so desperate to come back into the awareness of its own infinite radiance that we are finally willing to let go of our entrapment, to free ourselves from the torture chamber of desire and limitation.

In less dramatic circumstances, our aversion to what we're asking for might not be as vivid as it is in the inner conflicts that arise from a physical addiction. But it is useful to acknowledge how very complex we are. We are multidimensional beings with many different levels in our minds and many different, competing desires emerging from each of those levels.

In fact, the thought and behavior patterns that block our connection to God usually involve some form of addiction. Such an addiction may not deplete our health and disrupt our daily life the way alcohol and drug addictions do, but it is an addiction nonetheless. We can become addicted to our job, to a relationship, to money, to sex, to friends, to fame, to possessions, to power, to prestige, to clothes, to gambling, to golf, to surfing, to jogging, to weight lifting, to depression, to anger, to arguing, to violence . . . the list is endless. Any one of these patterns of thought, emotion, or behavior can easily draw us into the emotional and behavioral patterns we call addiction.

A few years ago during a workshop in a town on the coast of

Virginia, a young woman came up to me and said, "Is there anything you can do to help me? I am totally addicted to surfing. I can't stop. It's gotten to the point that it's just agonizing. I don't enjoy it anymore."

I was fascinated. I said, "Do you surf every day?"

She said, "Yes. Every day."

I said, "Even in hurricanes?"

"Oh yes!" she said. "Even in hurricanes."

"Even when it's cold and snowy?" I asked.

"Yes! Absolutely! I have to surf every day! I can't stop. Even when it's cold and uncomfortable and dangerous... I can't stop! I don't know what's wrong with me, but it's an incredibly powerful addiction!"

After a short pause, she continued, "You know, it's really strange, but sometimes I hope that I will break my leg, or an arm, or something, just so I'll have to stop for a while."

This young woman's admission offers us a remarkable insight into the tenacious intensity of desire and addiction. Our attachment to forms and behavior patterns can become so strong that we might even long for some kind of physical injury to interrupt the injury we are doing to our soul.

~

Back in the 1970s one spiritual teacher shared a profound insight about the ambivalence of our spiritual quest. She said, "Most of us don't want God. Most of us *want* to want God."

Isn't that painfully true?

When we want to want God, our path is a little lukewarm, a little half-hearted. We *sort of* want to do things to change. We *sort of* want to bring more peace and Light into our lives. But a more potent or magnetic desire can easily distract us.

Most of us find that we don't fully commit to our spiritual path until we really want God. Because at the deepest level, at the soul level, *all* we want is God. Our desire for God is our soul wanting to know itself.

The awakening of the soul is the greatest threat to the ongoing existence of the ego mind. So our ego mind tends to either resist spiritual awakening or attempt to co-opt it in any way it can. The seemingly unquenchable thirst for experiences and possessions, and all of the appetites and longings that constantly divert us from a life grounded in connection with God, are the desperate grasping of our ego mind attempting to find happiness in something external, something that we can call "I," "my," "me," or "mine." Swami Satchidananda used to jokingly say that we are all caught in a very seductive but dangerous "mine" field. It would be equally accurate to call it a "mind" field.

Another great teacher said, "When you long for God the way a drowning man longs for air... then you will find God."

~

We can see that our quest is fraught with endless layers of paradox and contradiction. So many conflicting and competing desires and impulses, some of which are quite adept at masquerading as intuition and spiritual longing. Whenever our prayers seem to be unanswered, we might just make it a practice to ask, "Is there a part of me that really didn't want what I was asking for?"

If you were praying for a sick child to be healed you might think it unlikely that you would find a part of yourself that didn't want the healing to occur. It may be that you really wanted what you were asking for with every fiber of your being. But it is interesting to look inside to see.

Don't judge yourself for what you find. Don't judge yourself if you find a trace of something in you that really didn't want what you were asking for. Judging yourself would only be destructive and counterproductive. Just observe what you find in order to learn more about who you are and what your path is in this life.

Recognize that there are times when we judge ourselves for something we do want. In circumstances where a relationship has involved the ongoing, long-term care of a sick relative or loved one, if we are totally honest with ourselves we will usually find a part of ourselves that would find relief if the person we are caring for were to die. We are tired. That person is tired. Her or his life may appear to be consumed with suffering. Our freedom has been drastically curtailed by the ongoing responsibility. *Of course* there is a part of us that would feel relieved. And the relief isn't just for our own ability to be "free" but also for our loved one's "freedom" from suffering. That doesn't mean we don't love that person. And it doesn't negate the fact that another part of us will miss her or him terribly. It just means that a part of us will feel relief. Getting caught in guilt and shame about feeling that relief is just one more way to cause *ourselves* suffering.

A few years ago, I experienced an amazing moment of honesty and insight from a mother whose beloved six-year-old daughter had died of leukemia. After months and months and months of emotional agony and spiritual despair, this beautiful young mother turned to me and said, "You know, if I'm honest, I have to say that there was always a very subtle part of me that felt afraid for my daughter if she were to survive her illness. I am very concerned about the future of our society and the future of the world. I almost didn't want her to have to grow up with all the suffering I feel is on the horizon. She was such a pure, innocent angel. I'm almost ashamed to admit it, but a part of me felt relief. A part of me thought, 'Thank God, she can go back to heaven, where she belongs.' "

While we may feel relief, we can also feel confused and disoriented. A long-term care relationship can become such a strong identity for the caregiver that, for a period after the relationship ends, the caregiver often feels lost and empty. Not only have we lost the relationship, but we have lost our everyday routine as well. For a while, we don't know who we are or what our role is in life.

Every identity we have and every role we fulfill can become an addiction. It can become such an all-consuming means of defining your self-image that you can scarcely imagine yourself *not* being whatever it is. One of the most frequent statements uttered by a mother who has lost an only child is, "I'm not a mommy anymore." When marriage partners separate, they often spend a long time thinking and saying, "I'm not a husband anymore" or "I'm not a wife anymore." When people retire, they often have to face the fact that without their professional identity, they don't know who they are. They don't know what to do. They had learned to define themselves in terms of what they did rather than who they are. When we become addicted to any relationship or activity, it can begin to have a kind of obsessive quality to it. We can actually develop an inability to conceive of who we are or what our life might be without that other person, that role, or that identity in it.

Our soul, in contrast, doesn't want to be addicted to anything other than its own Light, and that is not an addiction but a yearning to know Truth. The struggle to break free of addiction can be grueling. Sometimes the struggle is forced on us through circumstances seemingly beyond our control — death, divorce, job layoff, financial problems — whatever it might be. But it is a struggle that eventually brings us into the fullness of our own being . . . into a recognition of the place within where we are eternally whole.

Sometimes, when I work with people who are dealing with chronic illness, I have seen some very interesting correlations. There are a number of "diseases," behavior patterns, and psycho-emotional syndromes frequently diagnosed in today's culture that were all but unknown twenty or thirty years ago. ADD (attention deficit disorder), chronic fatigue syndrome, and fibromyalgia are three that are frequently diagnosed but seldom understood.

I am not a medical doctor. But I will share some tendencies I have observed among individuals who are dealing with chronic fatigue syndrome and fibromyalgia. There is *almost always* an underlying spiritual weariness that preceded the onset of the syndrome. When people relate to me that they are experiencing a crippling fatigue and a constricting pain throughout their bodies, I often explore with them what the conditions of their life and consciousness were prior to the appearance of their symptoms.

In case after case, these individuals have reported lives that had in some way become dreary, frustrating, frightening, or unfulfilling. Their primary relationship had become burdensome and emotionally empty. Their job had become meaningless and spiritually debilitating. Or some family discord was causing them to feel groundless and uncertain.

Sometimes, at the outset, they will say something like, "I don't know why this would happen. I had everything anyone could hope for. I had a great job. I was successful. I had a great partnership, a great marriage..." But when we probe a little deeper, there were strong feelings of discontent simmering just beneath the surface. Something in their life was constricting their ability to know their own soul. Something in their soul was crying out for freedom, even if that meant getting sick.

One woman named Katherine had been a university professor in the Pacific Northwest for more than thirty years. When she began teaching in the late sixties, she absolutely loved her profession. The university was filled with enthusiastic, open-minded students and brilliant professors with widely diverse interests and broadly ranging points of view. It was a rich, fertile environment full of wonder and opportunities for intellectual and spiritual growth.

In recent years, however, she had begun to see what she considered to be an unhealthy transformation that was slowly spreading throughout the institution. The administrative philosophy and structure were being transformed into something that Katherine felt would lead to a stifling educational bankruptcy. Over time, what had originally been an uplifting and nurturing environment came to feel hostile and alien. A new generation of faculty and administrators seemed to perceive Katherine as a threat to their more rigid, conservative philosophy of education. Over the years they instituted policies that seemed specifically designed to make Katherine's professional life difficult. Eventually, it became impossible for her to teach the courses she had always taught, courses that her students consistently referred to as the finest courses offered at the university.

One September, just after the school year began, Katherine fell ill with a mysterious, undiagnosable illness.

"I'm just *so* exhausted!" she would say. "I have no energy. I have no appetite. I can't seem to do anything but lie on my couch and sleep all day. I'm frightened. I'm afraid I'm dying. In the brief periods when I am awake, I pray and meditate and visualize. I'm taking tons of vitamins and herbs, and I'm going to see all kinds of healers, but nothing seems to help. I have to get back to work. I can't afford to live without the income."

I reflected on what she had been saying to me for the past several years about her work environment and her discomfort with the changes that were happening. "Katherine," I said, "do you really want to go back to work at the university?"

"I have to," she said.

"But do you really *want* to?" I asked.

"It doesn't matter," she said. "I have to!"

We sat in silence for a moment.

I tried again. "Katherine, my dear, do you really, in your heart of hearts, in the deepest levels of your soul, in the most clear, intuitive awareness you possess... do you *really* want to go back to the university?"

"No!" she said. "Absolutely not!"

Suddenly there was energy in her voice and vitality in her limbs.

Suddenly, her lifelessness abated, and I began to feel my friend returning.

~

Katherine ultimately realized that she couldn't return to her old job. It was clear that no matter how much she tried to push herself, she wasn't going to find the energy to do it. So she resolved to figure out how to live on the income that was available to her... and how to let go of her attachment to her identity as a university professor. In the years that have followed, I have watched Katherine slowly and steadily flower. The longer she has been away from her old job, the stronger, healthier, happier, and more energetic she has become.

"At the time, I thought it was the end of the world," she now says. "What I didn't realize was that the illness was coming from a deeper part of me, a deeper wisdom. In my heart, I really wanted to stop working at the university. Earlier in my life it was totally nourishing and fulfilling. But by the end, it was just crushing my spirit, and I guess there was no way for me to stop other than to just get so sick I simply couldn't go back there anymore.

"And, you know, I think if I had continued to try to push myself to go back, I would have just kept getting sicker. I might have actually died. Because somewhere in my soul, I knew that the job was killing me, spiritually.

"And I think that ultimately I would rather die physically than die spiritually."

If we honor the fact that our soul's longing to know itself is the primary motivation behind everything we want and everything we do, we can begin to see our lives differently. Sometimes being denied the things we *think* we are yearning for might actually be a blessing. Breaking free of our addictions — to substances, roles, identities, and behaviors — can pave the way for realizing that which we *truly* long for, that which we truly are.

CHAPTER 21

From the Soul's Point of View

When you enter into a human life
you enter into a perceptual falsehood.
This is what the Eastern traditions call illusion.
If you treat the illusion as truth
you may become embittered, fearful and ill.

EMMANUEL, *EMMANUEL'S BOOK*

If there is one insight that is most essential in understanding the confusing complex of experiences that come our way in human life, it is that *we are not human beings having spiritual experiences, but spiritual beings having human experiences.*

That may sound trite, or confusing, but just allow for the possibility...

We are habituated to processing every bit of information and every experience we have through our limited ego minds. We evaluate our lives through the lens of our cultural training. We see it all through the fog of our sometimes limited religious traditions. We judge it all against the backdrop of our narrow psychological desire systems. We measure it all against our insatiable complex of voracious emotional needs.

Am I getting what I want? Are my desires being fulfilled? Am I finding what I need? Am I succeeding the way I aspire to? Are you behaving the way I want you to? Are you meeting my needs? Is the universe lining up the way I think it should?

For most of us, most of the time, the answer to these questions is an emphatic "no!" But all of these questions are generated primarily by our ego minds. What we have forgotten to ask is, "What does my soul want?"

~

Reshaping our awareness so that we begin to look at life from the soul's point of view is the most revolutionary, audacious, and transformational process a human being can undertake. We have spent our entire life looking at the world from one vantage point. Now we are asking ourselves to look at it all from an entirely different vantage point, a vantage point that is often 180 degrees removed from our "normal" perceptual awareness.

So what does life look like from the soul's point of view?

Our soul is our Divine essence. It is the One Light manifest within us, the place within where we are eternally connected with God. We might look at it as the reflection of God in every aspect of His creation. Or we might look at it as the actual presence of God in every aspect of His creation.

Our individual soul is one and the same with God... God in His totality, in His infinite, formless existence. There is no difference between our soul and God. None. They are one and the same. In the One Light, the One Energy out of which all form is born, there is no differentiation... no separation.

It's all One.

If our individual soul is actually God "itself," then what would the experience of being squashed into these tight little bodies, these tight little minds, and these rigid personalities feel like to a formless, eternal being of infinite Love and Light?

Pretty constricting. Pretty uncomfortable, sometimes. We can actually interpret most of our discomfort and suffering as the manifestation of that constricting relationship between our infinite soul and our limited human identity. But we are the vehicles through which God *experiences* Himself. We are the bearers of the Divine plan. In our seemingly small and simple human existence, we play out the entire Divine melodrama... the manifestation of infinite existence, unlimited energy, and unbounded light in finite form.

God, the One, simply wants to know itself. And since it is formless, it has to create form in order to know itself. As soon as it creates, there *seems* to be something other than the One. Now there are two: "Creator" and "created." Two implies duality, and duality creates opposites.

Remember Newton? Every action has an equal and opposite reaction.

And so we have form and not form. We have light and darkness. We have pleasure and pain... good and evil. But all of these opposites are only apparent. Behind it all, there is still only the One. In some sense, God comes to know itself through a process of approximation, or elimination. As the source of all, how does it experience itself most clearly?

Through Love. Through finding its way, in the midst of all of the dualities of form, back into its only *real* identity as the One. In some sense, we might say that God creates unloving forms, unconscious forms, forms that appear lost in darkness, to know what He is not. It's paradoxical, because everything is a part of God. The closer we are to expressing pure Love and Light, the closer we are to the original oneness.

How amazing to experience that oneness in the midst of the many-ness.

Everything in creation is an aspect of God. The Infinite spins off a seemingly infinite number of forms. Forms in all shapes, sizes, and permutations. Forms seemingly lost in darkness and forms that become perfect reflections of the One Light. Odd forms, ugly forms, beautiful forms, scary forms, malicious forms, benevolent forms... all kinds of forms. Each one masquerading as something other than the One.

From the soul's point of view, our work in human life, our work in the world of form, is to transcend all barriers, to find our way back into the oneness by acknowledging and ultimately embracing all of the forms we find aversive, all of the people and things we fear, all of the elements of the world of form that we dislike. From that perspective, every person, and every circumstance that causes us to react with fear, anger, and judgment, is teaching us, showing us the places in ourselves where we are closing off our awareness of the One.

Healing this fragmented awareness, this illusory sense of separation, can only happen in the individual human heart. Each individual heart can become the instrument for healing the entire universe. We do it by bringing everything and everyone we dislike back into the sanctuary of our own heart. We surround that which we disapprove of with Love. We reincorporate all that our minds have made separate back into the oneness of our own soul. Like Carl Jung's concept of embracing our own shadow, we embrace everything in the universe, both beautiful and ugly, back into ourselves.

In recent years I have been fascinated by the number of otherwise "spiritual" people who feel justified in sending out hatred where they have concluded it is warranted, often toward our government leaders. Nothing is ever helped by hatred. Nothing is ever healed with hatred. No improvement is ever made with hatred.

Nothing in the world gets better when our commitment is to hatred rather than Love. It only gets worse. Hatred only feeds the very thing we seek to get rid of. Yet many among us who profess that we want to make the world a better place still feel justified in directing hatred and anger toward those with whom they disagree. Sometimes there is even a degree of delight experienced in fostering separation.

I am not suggesting that we turn a blind eye or become complacent and apathetic when injustice and violence are perpetrated around us or on our behalf. I am simply saying that there is nothing to be gained by hating *anyone*. In fact, those who can stir up anger and hatred in us might well be seen as our most potent spiritual teachers. We should thank them. Because, from our soul's point of view, we came into the world at this time, in this place, specifically because the events of our individual and collective lives offer us the optimum conditions for awakening out of our slumber of unconsciousness. Our soul *wants* to awaken so that we might return to our true nature, to Love. So it keeps showing us the places where we are asleep, where we are *un*-loving.

It doesn't matter whether we are talking about the president of the United States; the president of some other country; a "terrorist" leader; a corrupt congressman; a dishonest corporate executive; an arrogant, self-absorbed athlete; a rude, obnoxious celebrity; a cold-hearted serial killer; a person driving wildly and recklessly on the highway; or a noisy and inconsiderate neighbor... *anyone* who can throw us off center, who can trigger the chain reaction of hatred and fear in our minds, whose words and actions can inspire outrage in us and cause us to close our hearts, can be seen as a great spiritual teacher. They are showing us where we need to work on ourselves.

Until we can love all of it, we won't be free.

Again, loving all of it doesn't imply allowing cruelty and injustice to continue. It simply means finding the place of oneness in ourselves, the place that actually *created* all of it, and recognizing the steps we can take from that vantage point to make the world a better place.

Through love. Not through fear.

~

A number of years ago I was working with Pat Rodegast and Judith Stanton, setting up lectures and workshops titled "Emmanuel and

Friends." Emmanuel "speaks" through Pat through the process known as channeling. His words are unfailingly soothing, uplifting, inspirational, and healing.

One cold winter evening in January of 1983, we were in Boston at Arlington Street Church, a wonderful historic sanctuary just across the street from the Boston Public Garden. We had settled into our meeting room in the church's basement. A crowd of about seventy people had gathered, and everyone who had preregistered had already arrived.

About twenty minutes into the workshop, the door to the meeting room suddenly swung open, and a slightly disheveled-looking man, probably in his mid- to late thirties, came straggling in. He didn't look like someone who would be coming to our workshop. His clothes were a bit ragged, and his hair was uncombed and slightly dirty. I was a little edgy because there were some questionable-looking people hanging around the neighborhood. Just that afternoon, Pat's purse had been stolen from her on the sidewalk in front of the church.

But this fellow seemed relatively benign. He surveyed the room and then gently, intentionally, walked over to an empty chair and sat down. The chair he chose was close to the one I was sitting on. As soon as he sat, a pungent fog of noxious alcohol fumes permeated the space. My heart sank. "Oh no," I thought. "He's not supposed to be here, and he's drunk! What on earth will I do? What if he becomes a problem? Will he disrupt the workshop? Is he a threat to our safety?"

But he just sat very quietly, listening intently.

In a few moments, Pat asked the group if anyone had questions. The drunk fellow raised his hand, and before I could get her attention to let her know he wasn't one of us, Pat called on him.

He stood up and spoke. "How does a person forgive himself, and others, while trying to recover from alcoholism?"

Such a sincere and honest question, I thought.

Emmanuel, our spirit guide and friend, answered through Pat. "Bless yourself," he said, "for you have chosen a path of great courage. Your entire life, even the portions wherein you feel you cannot forgive yourself, are the choice of a spirit, the soul that you are, that has come to tackle a tremendous growth step.

"How can you forgive? I might ask you, how can you blame? Who are you to place a judgment on yourself? Judgment belongs to God. You feel you have hurt others. I say to you that there is choice in all things, and though certainly the responsibility for your acts is commendable, the guilt is destructive.

"Responsibility and guilt are two different things. Guilt is negative. It is unrealistic. Responsibility is mature and will take you out of the forest and into the Light. You are a most blessed, blessed being. Others may take a gentler way. You have chosen to see all of the negativities, or most of them, that you possess in this lifetime. Isn't it remarkable? And now as you have seen your darkness, and have recognized it, have owned it, you can bring it into the Light.

"This is a time of celebration, not of self-chastisement."

It felt as if the entire group had been transported to another realm . . . a realm of pure, unconditional love. Our visitor sat back down and began to sob, quietly, almost silently, rivers of tears streaming down his cheeks.

For the rest of the session, as other people asked their questions, he sat very quietly. Most of the time he kept his eyes closed. His face looked both serene and radiant. He seemed to be experiencing some sort of private, inner dialogue.

At the break, he slowly stood up and gently walked over to Pat. "Thank you," he said. "I've never felt so loved and so forgiven."

Before he left, he told us that when he walked into our meeting room earlier that evening, he *thought* he was at the AA meeting down the hall.

Sometimes a wrong turn can lead us to exactly the right place.

I have always been deeply moved by the unexpected reversal of perspective Emmanuel offered in that moment. It was an opportunity to see that, from the soul's point of view, life might look entirely different than it looks from the point of view of our mind and personality. How astonishing that living out a lifestyle pattern we might judge as weakness and failure could be seen, from the soul's point of view, as an act of courage.

It is certainly clear that living with addiction is a source of extraordinary suffering. But the idea that our soul might *choose* to take on such an assignment to explore our own darkness — or, in Jungian terms, our "shadow" — seemed absolutely revolutionary to me. Perhaps even more important was the suggestion that once we recognize our own darkness, we can bring it back into the Light. From that moment on, my understanding of our individual human lives and the collective lives of couples, families, communities, and nations has been radically different.

We often hear the suggestion that whatever the circumstances of our lives are, at some level we chose them. Some of us might be inclined to say, "I couldn't possibly hate myself enough to have chosen these circumstances." But when we look at it all from the soul's point of view... if we see it all as a process of exploring and experiencing everything in order to discover the oneness behind the forms... it looks entirely different, doesn't it?

CHAPTER 22

The Blessings You Have Been Given

Humility and gratitude go hand in hand...
Awareness increases so that we become grateful
for everything we are given. We have to learn, literally learn,
to be grateful for what we receive day by day, simply to balance
the criticism that day by day we voice because of powerful emotions.

SWAMI SIVANANDA RADHA,
KUNDALINI YOGA FOR THE WEST

As we have seen, there are certain critical turning points when grief and despair begin to transform into acceptance, contentment, and Love. In my own life, and in the stories people have shared with me over the years, I have seen three common ingredients that seem to signal the moment when the weight of depression and disappointment starts to lift:

1. When we begin to find a way to *give* to others again.
2. When we begin to find a way to *connect* with and love others again.
3. When we begin to find a way to feel *gratitude* again.

Our cultural tendency is to experience life from a standpoint of lack. We are the wealthiest country in the world, yet much of our lifestyle is fueled by a desperate sense that we don't have *enough*... we don't have enough money, we don't have enough possessions, we don't *know* enough, we haven't *achieved* enough, we aren't *safe* enough, we don't have enough time... we haven't received enough approval... we aren't getting enough *love*.

We seldom stop to reflect on the irrational, insatiable quality of that sense of not-enough-ness. It carries over dramatically into the situations when we find ourselves despairing over a disappointment, a loss, an unwanted change, or an unanswered prayer.

In the experience of grief, for instance, we generally find ourselves caught in despair and outrage that a loved one has been "taken" from us. In those moments, we find it difficult to be *thankful* that we had them for whatever period of time we did. We forget to be thankful that they were a part of our life and that they made extraordinary contributions to shaping our character and our life experience. We are lost in loss. In those moments we tend to forget all we had, and still have.

Finding our way into that remembering and gratefulness can be a delicate dance.

I was recently doing a workshop during which a woman raised her hand and began sharing the story of multiple losses she had experienced in a short period of time.

"I am a minister in a New Thought church," she said. "I know all there is to know about creative visualization, affirmative prayer, and the Power of Attraction. But I am puzzled about a few things.

"For the past eight years, I have been the primary caregiver for both of my parents. They both developed Alzheimer's. I had them living with me. I'm not sure how I did it, but I took care of them twenty-four hours a day.

"About a year ago, my mother died. A few months after that, my father died. Then my best friend died. Then I was diagnosed with MS. The three people I was closest to, with whom I spent most of my time, have all died. And my body is now betraying me. The MS is limiting my ability to work, and my financial situation is pretty dire.

"I've spent most of my life trying to give to others and trying to be an expression of God's Love in the world. And now, frankly, I feel like I've gotten screwed. I am exhausted, depressed, sick, and angry. And it doesn't help to tell me that lots of people are worse off than I am. So please don't do that!"

Her last comment was offered in an ironic, humorous tone. The group laughed. But we honored her request.

What we were able to give her in that moment was our attention. All of the forty people in the room just focused on her. We all listened with open hearts and nonjudgmental minds. Eventually, having been given the opportunity to express what was in her heart, she softened. As she was concluding her story, she said, "Of course, I do have to admit that there really are lots of people who are worse off than I am. I have a lot to be grateful for. But thank you for not reminding me of that."

Many of us have a tendency to ignore the blessings that do come our way. Perhaps we were asking for something else, hoping for something else, thinking that God should be giving us something else. A wonderfully humorous story graphically illustrates this tendency. Many of you have probably heard it, but it so perfectly illustrates our predicament that it deserves repeating here.

The story concerns a certain Mrs. Jones. She is a devout and devoted member of her church, a practitioner of positive and affirmative prayer. In all aspects of her life she trusts God fully to take care of her and to protect her.

One day the weather service alerts Mrs. Jones's community that a terrible storm is on the horizon. The river will rise and overflow its banks. The entire town will flood. A police car arrives at Mrs. Jones's house. Two officers come to her front door and ask her to come with them. Everyone in the town is being asked to evacuate before the flood comes.

Mrs. Jones smiles and says, "Thank you, but no. I'm going to stay here in my home. I have a personal relationship with the Lord, and I know He will take care of me." The policemen reluctantly leave.

The next day, after twenty-four hours of torrential rain, the river has indeed overflowed its banks. The water has completely submerged the first floor of Mrs. Jones's house. She has had to seek safety on the second floor. The police come again in a boat. They stop outside her second-floor window and beg her to come with them.

Mrs. Jones just smiles and says, "No, thank you. I'm going to stay here in my home. I have been praying and praying, and I know the Lord is going to take care of me." Again, the police reluctantly leave.

On the third day, the floodwaters have continued to rise, now submerging both the first and second floors of Mrs. Jones's house. She is sitting on the roof, hanging on to her chimney. A police helicopter hovers above. Using a bullhorn to communicate against the roar of the engine, an officer calls out, "Mrs. Jones, please come with us! We'll lower a basket down to you. You can get into it, and we'll lift you up and take you to safety."

Mrs. Jones just smiles up at them from her perch on the roof. "No, thank you. I'm still praying and I just know that God is going to take care of me."

A few hours later, the swirling torrents of water rise up and completely submerge Mrs. Jones's house. She drowns.

When she gets to heaven, she's extremely upset. "I want to see the man in charge!" she screams.

"Well, He doesn't usually greet newcomers."

"I don't care!" she shouts. "Bring him here now! I want to talk with him!"

So, after a few phone calls, God appears to talk with Mrs. Jones.

She's furious. "What kind of God are you?! I've been praying and praying for you to take care of me. I had faith in you and you let me *drown*! How could you do that?!"

God pauses for a moment, and smiles softly. "Mrs. Jones, I don't know what you expect from me. I did everything I could. I sent you a police car, I sent you a boat, and I sent you a helicopter! You turned them all down!"

~

On December 13, 2006, as I was nearing the completion of this book, one of my closest and dearest friends died suddenly at the age of forty-five.

Richard Carlson, author of the fabulously successful *Don't Sweat the Small Stuff* book series, was on an airplane flying from San Francisco to New York City. We had been looking forward to an opportunity to spend some time together. We were planning to spend the following day visiting in New York City. The night he was scheduled to arrive, I was out to dinner with some friends. When I left the restaurant, I checked my cell phone for messages.

Rather than the usual cheerful message from Richard announcing that he had arrived safely in New York, there was an urgent message from his assistant, Susan. When I returned her call, she took a deep breath and said, "John, Richard died on the plane today."

I felt as if my heart had stopped.

After a moment, Susan asked if I would be able to drive over to the hospital near Kennedy Airport in Jamaica, Queens, where the ambulance had taken Richard's body after his flight landed. "John, would you be able to retrieve Richard's personal effects and to identify his body?"

The assignment was one I did not relish, but there was never a thought that I wouldn't do it. At some point in life, most of us will have the opportunity to experience a moment when reality changes so quickly and so dramatically that it feels as if the entire universe has screeched to a halt and abruptly reversed course. We are left confused, numb, and disoriented. Having to struggle to see and hear through the fog of shattered expectation and disbelief, to focus on questions, details, and information while our heart is broken and our mind is reeling, is nearly an impossible task.

I've been teaching people for years to be prepared for anything. Yet I was reminded, through Richard's beneficent grace, that the greatest teachings often come from the things we aren't prepared for. Richard was an apparently healthy, energetic forty-five-year-old man, nearly twelve years younger than me. We had been making plans to teach together, to write together, and to travel to Hawaii and India together.

After two trips out to Jamaica, Queens, on subsequent days, all of the logistics with the hospital, the medical examiner's office, and Richard's family back in California were taken care of. I returned to my home in New Jersey, walked through the front door, kicked off my sandals, and stretched out on my living room sofa. I stayed there for two full days, allowing myself to feel absolutely miserable. I let my sadness have free expression. I wallowed in it.

In those moments there is no way to understand, no way to make sense or order out of the chaos of ever-changing emotion and unfathomable reality. I realized, with great interest, that a part of me found a kind of reassuring vital energy in the sadness. It was such an intensely human, exquisitely excruciating experience. I would almost call it "delicious suffering." I kept reflecting on what it was that was so compelling and so strangely pleasant about the emotional pain.

I realized that I was experiencing a magnificent internal dance — the interplay of deep and abiding love intersecting with attachment, expectation, and a temporary inability to comprehend the events of my life. I was in terrible pain, but something beautiful was happening. My heart was being torn open. It was as if my love for Richard and my despair over his death were combining to perform a kind of spiritual open-heart surgery on me. When I closed my eyes and quieted, I had an overwhelming sense of Richard's presence. I saw him in ethereal form, standing over me like a skilled surgeon hovering above a patient on an operating table. He was smiling and gently laughing. I could almost feel his skilled, compassionate hands burrowing deep into my chest, into my heart, into the core of my being, deftly removing layer upon layer of the "rational" thought forms and emotional armoring that so often enshroud our Love.

Richard was an extraordinary friend. What I found, as I lay on my sofa, was that all of the things I missed, and anticipated missing, about Richard were also pointing the way to the places in me that were so very grateful to have had such a friend. I just kept allowing the sadness to surface. Each turbulent wave of sorrow would envelop my body and mind, heaving it this way and that, emotionally knocking the wind out of me. I felt breathless, as if a twenty-ton elephant were sitting on my chest. But I knew that if I just relaxed . . . if I just kept breathing . . . if I just kept allowing everything to be exactly as it was . . . all of the confusion, despair, disappointment, lack of understanding, and debilitating sadness . . . if I just let it all be, I would float back up again.

By early evening on the second day, I began to feel the weight starting to lift. Slowly it was supplanted by a deep and inspiring joy. Not a giddy joy, just a serene, reverent joy. I began to let go of the slightly self-indulgent suffering I had been enjoying so much and began to think about Richard. I began to think about what an extraordinary human being he was.

Because of his example, because of the way he lived his life, there has been much more joy than sadness surrounding his death. While we are all profoundly sad that we won't have his radiant warmth and the inexpressible delight of his physical presence anymore, it is impossible not to feel joy about having had the opportunity to know him.

It was fascinating to watch my own emotional and physical energy patterns shift as the thoughts in my mind began to move from shock, sadness, and disbelief to appreciation, gratitude, and love. I could see, quite clearly, the magnetic attraction and compelling fascination the darker feelings contained. They offer such a palpable sense of connection with the person we've lost. Our minds resist letting go of those thoughts and feelings because they are so strong, so heavy and thick. They give us a powerful, though somewhat illusory, sense of connection to the person who has died.

Feelings of joy have such a soft, ethereal lightness to them. For a mind compelled to taste life in all its thickness and robustness, joy sometimes seems oddly boring. Like many of the other tricks our mind plays on us, the fearful clinging to sadness keeps us stuck in a place of isolation and disconnection. Grief is much more often about our lack of connection during someone's life than it is about our sadness that they are now physically gone. We get stuck in replaying our guilt and remorse over lost opportunities. When we do that, we become caught in the hollow emptiness of that place in us that, for whatever reason, resisted opportunities to be together, to come closer, to develop more intimacy.

Our mind's attempt to cling to the sadness results in our staying caught in our sense of disconnection from that person. It keeps us emotionally paralyzed and incapable of beginning the transition to a *new* relationship, a new connection with their "new" form. One of the major problems with the way we manage sadness in this culture is that we tend to keep the sadness frozen rather than allowing it to freely flow through its entire life cycle. We get to a certain point and we get frightened. The river of emotion is flowing near flood stage, like a raging torrent of turbulent water. It seems that the pain just keeps getting worse. So we run to a doctor and get a prescription for an antidepressant, or we grab a drink, or we take some other drug . . . to numb ourselves.

What we are doing, in effect, is causing the emotional body to calcify. We stop the flow of emotion and freeze the stream of sadness where it is. When emotions are frozen, like frozen water they begin to expand. They become hardened and immovable, taking up more space than when they were liquid and flowing, causing their container to stretch and expand beyond its limits until it cracks and breaks. Like ice, frozen emotions contain the rigid, lifeless remains of ancient life forms, forms that look like they did when they were alive but that are actually preserved in a kind of freakish rigor mortis, morbid, motionless carcasses of dead, immovable emotions.

When our emotions are frozen, we can't find our way back to joy.

It turns out that one of the most potent antidotes to frozen emotion is gratitude. Just feeling thankful.

We don't have to ignore the things that are causing our sadness; we just have to cultivate alongside them the awareness of all of the blessings in our life. Every human life is a combination of joy and sorrow, success and failure, progress and retreat. We get stuck when we see, or *try* to see, only one side of the ledger. When we are in deep despair, or profound regret, we often feel as if there is nothing good at all in our lives. Simply stated, when we're not getting what we want, we don't see what we've got. But if we are totally honest, most of us can find an abundance of gifts and blessings that the universe has bestowed on us.

For one thing, we are alive. We have life. We have consciousness. We are aware. That is a miracle. Our parents may not have been perfect, but they made it possible for us to be born, something for which we can cultivate gratitude every day.

We can breathe. We can see. We can touch. We can hear. We can taste. We can feel. We can laugh. We can love.

Even if one or more of our basic senses is compromised as a result of illness or injury, we can still feel... we can still laugh... we can still love. If you doubt that, just study the lives of people like Helen Keller, Stephen Hawking, Stevie Wonder, Mattie Stepanek, Christopher Reeve — great souls who lived, or are living, in bodies that are not "normal," who learned how to dive deep into their beings to unearth presence, creativity, joy...and love.

So make a list — right now — of all that you are thankful for. If your mind wants to focus on all that you have lost, or all that you feel you have been denied, just keep gently guiding it back to what you have been given.

If you have lost a loved one, focus on the blessing of having had their presence in your life for whatever time they were with you. Focus on the love their presence in your life awakened in you. Notice that the love is still 100 percent alive within you.

If you have lost your money, focus on the blessing of having experienced what it was like to have it. If you feel you have never achieved the affluence you want, focus on the ways you have been provided for. Notice how your circumstances make you more mindful about spending and more compassionate toward others who experience financial difficulties.

If you experience health problems, focus on how they have given you compassion and understanding for others with similar problems. Look for the blessings. Perhaps your physical situation has brought you into contact with beautiful, caring people. Perhaps it has given you the time, solitude, and impetus to focus on your spiritual search.

If others have treated you unkindly or unfairly, focus on the place within you that feels compassion for their predicament. Focus on the awareness their unconscious behavior has generated in you: how being treated unkindly can inspire you to be kinder and fairer toward others. You have experienced the pain of feeling disconnected. Make your life about creating *less* disconnection in the world.

In the song "Constant Craving," K. D. Lang sang, "Maybe a great magnet pulls all souls towards truth." Our difficult experiences, our disappointments, our unanswered prayers can be the fulcrums that counteract our resistance to that magnet. The experiences of life can either turn us inward toward greater disconnection or inspire us to go toward the Light with clearer focus and greater determination. The choice is ours.

We are, indeed, the creators of our lives. That does not mean that we are in control of all the events that happen to us, but we *are* in control of how we respond to those events. Cultivating gratitude for what we have — and what we have had — is a major route to taking control of our responses, and one of the primary routes *out* of suffering... into joy.

CHAPTER 23

How This Experience Can Deepen Your Spirituality

Life is not a perpetual honeymoon. This earth is a school. Spiritual growth does not come without effort, and effort and change often mean pain. I think it is meant to be that way: if there were no difficulties, we wouldn't look for anything higher. And that would be hell because it would keep us from the infinite bliss which is our birthright.

BROTHER ANANDAMOY, "THE PSYCHOLOGY OF THE SOUL: AN INTERVIEW WITH BROTHER ANANDAMOY"

Throughout our exploration, we have repeatedly considered the many ways in which the trials and tribulations of life might actually bring us closer to God. Herein lies the challenge of understanding the concept that "suffering is Grace." Sometimes when we first hear that, we are inclined to react with annoyance and anger, thinking that what it means is that God is punitive and sadistic.

But, as Brother Anandamoy points out in the above quote, perhaps if we didn't experience difficulties in life we might not be motivated to look for a higher truth, a deeper peace, a more abiding joy. The recognition that hell would be living in a state in which we are forever cut off from the "infinite bliss which is our birthright" is immensely important. It bears repeating that our culture's vision of heaven — a state in which we would have all the wealth, health, beauty, power, and fame we *think* we want — has not, over the entire course of human history, often delivered the happiness it seemed to promise.

In his landmark book *Emotional Intelligence*, Daniel Goleman points out that one of the key indicators of emotional maturity is the ability to delay gratification.[1] Study after study has shown that children who learn at an early age to forestall immediate fulfillment of desire are the children who grow up to be the happiest, most well-adjusted, most successful adults. In other words, if given the choice to have one cookie now or two cookies in thirty minutes, the children who demonstrate the ability to analyze the situation and to *wait* for the better reward are the children who will most likely experience success and happiness in life. Mastering that simple childhood skill is an almost unfailingly reliable predictor of a much more successful future not only socially but also intellectually and professionally.

Children who do not learn to delay the fulfillment of desire are much more likely to be poorly adjusted later in life. They perform at a much lower level academically and socially, and they are much more likely to exhibit "delinquent" behavior in adolescence and adulthood. We might reasonably conclude, then, that parents who resolve to help their children cultivate the ability to delay gratification are giving them one of the most important life skills a human being can have.

Now think of how often our interactions with God have involved offering up a list of requests, or even demands, and expecting that God or the universe should just deliver what we want right now. We are often seduced by new methods and new formulas for fulfilling our desires immediately. Rather than seek the happiness that would spontaneously arise from a higher vision of human life and a deeper connection with our own soul, we turn to teachings and practices that function in service of what the culture values. Many of us are drawn to spiritual paths that offer us wealth and possessions rather than those that emphasize love, peace, contentment, and kind-heartedness. We have been so totally brainwashed by our cultural value system that we assume love, peace, and contentment will come from wealth and possessions, despite a profusion of evidence to the contrary.

Unfortunately, our culture has so completely indoctrinated us with its deluded model of happiness that we don't fully recognize just how deluded it is or how very easily it can infiltrate our "spiritual" beliefs. When we feel unhappy we most often, unwisely, conclude that it is because our lives are not yet filled with enough of the *things* our culture values. Even in our spiritual lives, we are susceptible to confusing greed with enlightened action. It doesn't matter whether the greed is for money, or sex, or power, or more relationships. It doesn't matter whether the greed is for continuing something that has ended or the desperate longing for something that has never begun. Greed is greed. It isn't a route to happiness.

The simple truth is, there is no reason that you cannot be totally fulfilled, totally at peace, and totally in love — *right now* — no matter what the circumstances of your life are. I intentionally did not include "totally happy" in that list. It would be cruel to suggest to ourselves or to each other that we should be totally happy when we are going through heartbreaking, heart-wrenching losses and disappointments. The expectation that we should be happy, happy, happy all the time is one of the fundamental problems in our cultural psychosis. It often plays out vividly in the spiritual teachings that our culture most readily embraces. But while total happiness is an unrealistic expectation, we can still be peaceful, fulfilled, loving, and, yes, joyful.

Remember Meher Baba's suggestion that being spiritual means "being 100 percent human and 100 percent Divine." It means becoming a living embodiment of both form *and* formless, matter and spirit, being capable of unbounded love, infinite peace, and undisturbed joy, and — paradoxically — also being capable of feeling deep sadness and boundless compassion when the conditions of life call those emotions into play.

Despite all the benefits that positive thinking, creative visualization, spiritual healing, and the Power of Attraction (like attracts like) have offered to us throughout the ages, the simple fact is that these paths only work for certain people in certain circumstances. Sometimes, the unrealistic expectations they foster result in a kind of boomerang effect. It is absolutely true that our thoughts exert a tremendous influence over our life experience. It is also true that the Power of Attraction is a fundamental law in the world of form and widely recognized in the field of physics. But jumping to the conclusion that all our problems are caused by negative thoughts and all our joys and successes are caused by positive thoughts can create unforeseen complications and suffering when not viewed in the wider scope of human experience. Our thoughts in this moment are by no means the only determinants of our experience. They certainly have an effect. But there may be much larger and more complicated forces at work. In other words, many of our experiences are determined by karmic forces set in motion long before we were born.

To suggest to those who are dealing with cancer that they *caused* their own illness with negative thoughts is both ill informed and cruel. To suggest to a mother whose child was murdered that her child's death was *caused* by her negative thoughts is coldhearted, presumptuous, and preposterous. To suggest to someone that his spouse's sudden heart attack was *caused* by his negative thoughts is both callous and unenlightened.

Twenty years ago, my friend Scott Chesney was a healthy, handsome, popular, athletic sixteen-year-old. One night while sleeping in his bedroom, he had an extremely rare spontaneous spinal cord stroke. There had been no injury and no warning. He woke up the next morning ready to go to school, only to find that he was now paralyzed from the waist down. He has been in a wheelchair ever since.

Would anyone be so cruel as to suggest that his own negative thoughts — or his parents' negative thoughts — attracted this event into his life?

It is absolutely possible that in certain circumstances the eradication of "negative" thought patterns can result in physical healing. But it is also possible that it won't. I have seen far too many people wind up in increased despair if their efforts to reformulate their thought patterns haven't resulted in their disease going into remission, or their loved one's disease going into remission, or the manifestation of some other change they are longing and praying for. If the effort to change their thought patterns doesn't result in the healing they were working toward, many people are left with even deeper feelings of loss, betrayal, and failure. My friend Stephen Levine used to say, "I have an entire library of books on healing that were given to me by people who have died."

While cultivating a more positive, joyful outlook on life is *always* helpful, the downside to spiritual teachings that focus solely on creating positive effects is that they tend to deny the realms of experience in which all the positive thinking in the world doesn't appear to change circumstances at all. Simply stated, there is no amount of positive thinking that will remove all suffering from life. Even the greatest positive thinkers of our time have not been able to achieve lives devoid of suffering. Their facility for looking at things in a positive light has often assisted them in traversing life's troubled waters more quickly and easily, but it hasn't eliminated those troubled waters from their life experience.

Every great spiritual teacher, every enlightened being, every God-realized soul eventually dies. Some die of cancer. Some die of heart attacks. Some have been assassinated. Would anyone suggest that enlightened beings are attracting their own illness and death with negative thought forms?

The cultivation of *real* happiness is one of the great challenges and primary goals of all spiritual endeavor. Though our life circumstances may cause us to go through periods of intense sadness, there is no loss, no disappointment, no catastrophe that can arise in our lives which in and of itself deprives us of the ability to be happy. Happiness is always within us. It resides within us eternally. It isn't a state of knowing, it is a state of being. It arises when we awaken to our eternal connection with our Creator, with God, with the source of all that is. There is simply no way to ever be disconnected from that. If we were disconnected from it, we wouldn't exist. It is the very source of our existence.

If you are feeling miserable at this moment, rest assured that nothing written here is meant in any way to denigrate the excruciating agony of emotional misery. But you have everything you need at this very moment — within you — to find your way back to joy. You can begin now.

~

So we come back to the fundamental question, how can this experience bring me closer to God? If God is within us, if Love is within us, if Joy is within us, then we might consider something revolutionary: we might consider being grateful when God takes away, or prevents us from attaining, those people and things that might distract us from our intention to consciously know God.

If our sadness involves the loss or death of someone we love, it would be outrageous to suggest that we cultivate gratitude to God for the loss. Instead, in those circumstances we might cultivate gratitude to God for all the time we *did* have together. And gratitude for all that we continue to have. We might thank God for His eternal presence within us. We might cultivate gratitude that He has given us the boundless spiritual resources to handle life in all its sometimes horrific manifestations. We might cultivate gratitude that this extraordinary person came into our lives to help us in the process of opening our hearts.

Our anger and despair are often fueled by the misguided belief that

God somehow promised us that we would be protected from difficult and heartbreaking circumstances. He didn't. He only promised us that He would *always* love us, *always* forgive us, and *always* be with us.

So we might begin to look at all of life as a training program, a skillfully designed process of coming into the fullness of who we are, the infinite radiant Light of our formless, eternal soul rubbing up against the restricting, constricting delusions and attachments that stand in the way of our ability to see our Light clearly. The sufferings of life become the sand wearing away the dross surrounding the pearl of awareness, polishing it until its inherent perfection shines in all its brilliance. The process can, at times, feel excruciating. But if we have a clear vision of the end result, the intermediate stages may not seem nearly as overwhelming.

~

Thirty-five years ago when I first studied Zen, there was a student in my class who kept challenging the teacher about the fundamental principles of Zen philosophy. It was the seventies, and our culture was just tasting the early phases of the Me generation, a period in our cultural history that has sometimes been seen as the underbelly, or "shadow" side, of the peace, love, and happiness generation of the sixties. The Me generation was characterized by a quest to achieve a lifestyle unfettered by social norms, conventions, and mores. We thought we were searching for freedom. But what emerged was a generation often entrapped in self-absorption, self-centeredness, and disconnection, tendencies that continue to affect our culture to this day.

In the midst of that confused and disjointed social milieu, this obstreperous student would upbraid the teacher daily. "What's up with this Zen stuff?" he would ask. "I thought we were going after freedom here. But this is the most overly disciplined, uptight bunch of senseless, arbitrary rules and regulations I've ever seen. They don't make any sense! I mean, you can't even spit in this program! I think it's a crock!"

The teacher sat quietly, serene and poised, unperturbed by the student's rude outburst. He had grown accustomed to this student's confrontational nature. He closed his eyes as he reflected on the question. A calm peace began to pervade the atmosphere, so recently jarred by anger and judgment. We all looked on, expectant and anxious.

When the teacher finally opened his eyes, he looked directly at the student and spoke in a voice that was soft, calm... and *powerfully* resonant.

"My dear friend, Zen gives you the *discipline* you need to be free. You feel free to speak out whenever the impulse strikes you, but you aren't free at all. And you won't ever be free until you stop needing to be right all the time and recognize that your obnoxiousness affects other people adversely."

The student fell silent. The class was silent.

In that moment I began to realize that real inner freedom requires discipline, restraint, and patience. The Me generation had misidentified "freedom" as the ability to do whatever we wanted, whenever we wanted, with whomever we wanted, with no consequences. In this Zen class I first began to recognize that in order to find *real* freedom, it was necessary to cultivate the ability to control one's thoughts, words, and actions. We do not exist in isolation. We are part of a whole. And the treasure we are seeking is uncovered through a process we might call "spiritual mining." It requires probing, digging, drilling — and sometimes blasting — through layers and layers of rigid, entrenched ego identity, until at last we begin to get a glimmer of our inner treasure.

In subsequent weeks the cranky student's angry tirades became much less frequent, as he began to experiment with humility and open-mindedness.

~

Working with a disappointment, a shattered dream, an unfulfilled expectation, or an unanswered prayer can offer exactly that same process of spiritual mining. We might look at all of these experiences as "spiritual surgery," a loving and compassionate unveiling that can feel bloody and painful, and often requires a period of healing and convalescence.

Just keep asking, "Dear God, if I can't have what I want, then help me to know what it is that You *want* me to have. Help me to receive whatever it is that You are trying to give me." Know, in your heart, that somewhere inside you there is a treasure much greater than the one you have been asking for. Know also that when you find that treasure, wrapped within it you will find the love of all of the people you think you have lost and the satisfaction of all of the things you thought you needed.

But the fulfillment you seek is *inside* of you.

Now.

CHAPTER 24

Allow for the Possibility That the Universe Is Perfect

Who wants to see God?
People shed jugs of tears for money, and wife,
and children. But if they would weep for God
for only one day, they would surely see Him.

RAMAKRISHNA, *THE GOSPEL OF SRI RAMAKRISHNA*

One of the most startling teachings offered by Neem Karoli Baba was conveyed in his oft-repeated question, "Can't you see it's all perfect?"

Many of us first heard that in the early 1970s. At the time, the United States was engaged in a brutal, unpopular war in a tiny, far-off country. Our president seemed to have gotten ensnared in a web of lies, deceits, and flagrantly illegal, unprincipled actions. It was all starting to come to light. Our country had never been through such a divisive period.

On the international scene, there was terrible flooding and famine in Bangladesh, right next door to India. There was horrible starvation and genocide on the continent of Africa. We were just becoming aware that all of our technological progress was causing serious disruptions in the delicate balance of nature. If we failed to change course, our earth might well become uninhabitable as a result of our uncaring, unconscious, unrestrained greed and consumption. We were engaged in an ongoing arms race with the Soviet Union, and the specter of a potential nuclear war was never far from our consciousness.

"Perfect?"

Yes. "Perfect."

It is one of the most difficult aspects of spiritual truth for us to comprehend. Even if we *do* comprehend it, it is not intended to suggest that we adopt an attitude of complacency toward life. It doesn't require that we turn a blind eye to injustice, unkindness, dishonesty, and cruelty. It merely invites us to let go of our internal conflict with the way of the world. It invites us to stop arguing with reality. It invites us to let go of our expectation that things should be different than they are at this moment.

From a purely practical point of view, cultivating the ability to allow things to be just as they are is an important step on the road to joy. The mind keeps replaying the past. It seems to believe that merely thinking and obsessing about what has already happened, resenting and regretting things and events that are over, will somehow change history. It won't. The pursuit of answers, the need to understand and affix blame somewhere, only stands in the way of moving on... moving toward joy and contentment.

The world is as it is. What has happened had to happen. There is no way to change it. The way things are in this moment is a direct result of all of the factors and events that have led up to this moment. Things are as they are today as a result of what happened yesterday, and the day before that, and so on. We can learn from the past, but we can't change it. We can grow. We can cultivate understanding so that we are more attuned to the effects of our own thoughts and actions. We can resolve to make the world a better place, despite the fact that it is already perfect.

Making the world a better place happens when we ourselves become an embodiment of a higher truth, a greater realization. Mahatma Gandhi said, "We must be the change we wish to see in the world." It's a simple, straightforward concept. In fact, it is the *only* way to effect real change in the world. As long as we are caught in an endless expectant wait for others to change, we are stuck. As long as we believe that some external condition has to change or someone's behavior has to change so that we can be happy, we will be spinning our wheels in the mud of frustration and dissatisfaction.

The minute we resolve to "be the change we wish to see in the world," real transformation takes place. When we no longer *expect* others to be sweet and kind and generous to us before we are willing to reciprocate, we can be sweet, and kind, and generous to them . . . no matter what. In so doing, we naturally become happy. We no longer need a response, a thank you, an expression of recognition or gratitude. We do what we do, simply because it is just *more fun* to be loving. Whether people receive it or acknowledge it or appreciate it doesn't matter. Our reward comes from the joy inherent in being a living expression of the highest part of ourselves. We act from our *hridayam* rather than from our minds. Pure and unconditional, Divine Love — itself — is perfect.

~

In recent years, we can't help but notice how very isolated, disconnected, and self-centered our culture has become. So many people are living as if they are the only person in the world, thinking that their happiness and safety are all that matters, acting as if no one else exists. My British mother was very concerned with good manners and etiquette. She taught us a protocol for nearly every situation. When I was a rebellious teenager, I thought her codes of behavior were just meaningless, uptight rigidity. But now, when I reflect on the effects of good manners, I realize that manners are really about paying attention, being alert, acknowledging that there is someone in the world besides you, and being kind, thoughtful, and considerate to them.

Consciously cultivating manners can be a superb spiritual exercise. They can offer a profound tool for cultivating a state of perpetual meditation in everyday life. After all, meditation is largely about *paying attention*. And manners are about *paying attention*. Meditation can be about learning to see God everywhere, in everything. Manners can be about treating others, even absolute strangers, as God in human form. As Christ said, "Just as you did it to one of the least of these who are members of my family, you did it to me."[1]

When we attempt to live in our own isolated little cocoon of consciousness, we are doing so with a desire to *protect* ourselves. But the end result is that we *isolate* ourselves. Living instead with a heightened, intentional awareness of the other people in our environment is a major step on the path to joy. Stop. Look. Wait. Recognize that *everyone* you encounter is God in human form. No matter how bizarre they look, or how bizarre they act, they are God in human form.

Do as Brother Lawrence suggested, "Practice the presence of God."[2] Let God go first. Smile. Greet God with a warm hello. Hold the door for the next incarnation of God, and the next incarnation after that. Let God pull out of the side street. Let God merge in front of you. Let God have that coveted parking space. Say please and thank you to God. Most incarnations of God won't notice or acknowledge. Some incarnations of God will act numb. Some will seem confused and suspicious. Occasionally, a particularly interesting incarnation of God will respond with hostility. You offer God kindness, and He reacts as if you just spat on Him. Like a great Zen teacher.

But every now and then some form of God will lift Her or His face and look you directly in the eyes, smile broadly, and say thank you. And you know — in that instant — that you just changed God's life a little bit.

There is no denying the fact that when we look at the world around us, much of it seems totally *imperfect*. Our friend Emmanuel has sometimes referred to it as "perfect imperfection." The One Energy behind it all is perfect. As it manifests in form, it is also perfect. But our judging minds look at it all and conclude that it isn't perfect. We think God has made huge blunders, huge errors. We could have done it so much better. We could have created a much better universe.

Whenever I perceive my mind getting cantankerous and judgmental of other human beings and the conditions of the world, I find it useful to remember the Five Hindrances as delineated by Buddha. They are lust and greed, hatred and ill will, agitation, sloth and torpor, and doubt. In essence, those are the primary issues we come to earth to work on. We might see earth as a school where we incarnate because we have at least *one* of the five hindrances, if not *all* of them.

If we relate to the Five Hindrances as the "selection criteria" for all those who are admitted to live on planet earth, we might not be so surprised that our encounters with other human beings can be so difficult at times. We have enrolled in a school where we and our fellow students are full of lust, greed, hatred, ill will, agitation, sloth, torpor, and doubt.

So it isn't that the earth is full of mistakes but that we are enrolled in a kind of reform school where the other students are as corrupt and delinquent as we are. But we can't get caught in thinking it is *the others* who should change.

The only one we can change is ourself.

That is what we came here for. And God, the Creator, the universe, is always holding out His hand, always offering to lead us to peace and joy if only we can surrender our attachment to thinking we have a better idea of how to get it.

CHAPTER 25

Cultivate Meditation and Contemplative Prayer

As you become absorbed in meditation,
you will realize that the Self is separate from the body
and for this reason will not be affected by
disease, old age, or death.

SVETASVATARA UPANISHAD

We have seen that many if not most of the frustrations connected with unanswered prayer arise from the mind-set generated by our cultural values. When we use those cultural values to measure our spiritual success, the result is often a profound misunderstanding of spiritual values. Our cultural values, by their very nature, foster self-interest and separation. Spiritual values cultivate oneness and connection.

To live in a perception rooted in spiritual values, we need to cultivate a completely different *means* of perception. We need a mechanism for breaking free of the tyranny of our "rational," discursive minds in order to awaken to a higher consciousness, a higher perception, a higher awareness. There is simply no way to think our way to happiness. We need a way to quiet our minds so we can simply be happy and peaceful, by awakening to our true nature that, itself, *is* happiness.

The most efficient vehicle for cultivating that awakening is meditation.

There are many, many different forms of meditation. Not all of them are useful, but many are. You can discover the forms that work best for you through some conscientious exploration and a sincere effort to try. The willingness to try is essential. There simply is no pill, no CD, no magic bullet that will cultivate inner peace and understanding as effectively as a regular practice of meditation. If we characterize the spiritual path as "spiritual mining," meditation is the effort to dig the mine shaft and to probe for the diamonds. The diamonds don't just pop up to the surface and deposit themselves on the ground for easy picking. Significant effort and persistence are required to produce a bountiful harvest of jewels. So we just begin by mining on a daily basis. We keep sitting in meditation, listening to God . . . listening to the universe . . . listening to our inner wisdom.

As pointed out at the very beginning of this book, meditation might simply be defined as "listening to God." It is a simple, straightforward practice that will, over time, create both physical *and* psychological balance. Many clinical studies have shown that a regular practice of meditation results in lower blood pressure, lower heart rate, lower respiration, better sleep patterns, increased energy, and a general overall sense of well-being. There are even studies that indicate that a regular practice of meditation enhances the immune system, giving the meditator greater resistance to illness and disease.

Buddha generally used the term *nirvana* to identify the state of enlightened awareness, beyond thought, beyond suffering. Nirvana has also been identified as "the space between thoughts." When our thoughts are running at full steam, they might be compared to a speeding freight train. If you have ever stood next to railroad tracks when a freight train is speeding past, the train appears to be a solid blur. But as the train slows down, you can begin to see the spaces between the freight cars.

Meditation functions to slow down the train of thought. The spaces between the thoughts are pure awareness, pure consciousness... nirvana. Buddha pointed out, however, that the untrained human mind generates about seventeen thousand thoughts per second. At that pace, understandably, perceiving the spaces between them is exceedingly difficult. But by retraining the mind with meditation, learning to slowly, steadily take the reins, we can begin to perceive those spaces, that pure awareness, that inner realm of peace, equanimity, and contentment.

One of the most frequent misunderstandings about the practice of meditation is that it requires the ability to stop thinking. People often say, "I can't meditate because I can't stop my thoughts." That's like saying, "I can't do yoga because I'm too stiff." Yoga is intended to help you transcend your stiffness so that you become flexible. It was originally intended to prepare the body to sit for long periods in meditation. Meditation is intended to help you slow down your thought process so that your mind becomes peaceful.

Meditation takes many forms. In traditional Buddhist *vipassana* (mindfulness) we learn a practice called *anapanasati*, or "mindfulness of breathing." We learn how to use breathing as a focal point of awareness. We learn to *pay attention* to something that is always happening, the softly repetitive, natural process of breathing in and breathing out. We observe the breath as sensation. We learn to pay attention to exactly what's happening... in this moment.

In the Vedas, the most ancient spiritual texts in the Hindu tradition, it is said that if you can bring your attention to *exactly* what's happening in this moment, *you will see God*. But that's a tall order. Most of us can't pay attention to this moment. Our minds are all over the place — thinking about yesterday, planning for tomorrow, disliking and judging, longing for something different, fantasizing and worrying. Nirvana, enlightenment, freedom are all always available... in this moment... and this moment... and this moment... all we have to do is learn to *pay attention* to this moment. That is what meditation training is intended to do.

One of the nice things about Buddhist meditation is that it doesn't require that we subscribe to any theological dogma, story line, or belief system. It merely involves paying attention. It doesn't conflict with any belief system. Nor does it require that one ascribe to any particular belief system.

In addition to traditional Buddhist meditation, there are countless other forms of meditation: Zen training, Hindu and yogic forms of mantra meditation, Christian forms of contemplative prayer and meditation, and Jewish forms. There are forms like hatha yoga, tai chi, and Sufi dance, which combine physical movements with techniques for training the mind — essentially prayer in motion. These practices create a state of heightened awareness through dance and movement, propelling the physical body through patterns designed to produce balance, tranquillity, and mental clarity.

What we sometimes call contemplative prayer is a form of prayer closely akin to meditation. It is a quiet, devotional, inner approach that doesn't ask for anything but seeks to create a constant state of awareness of God — the practice of the presence of God. It is a form of prayer that praises God, offers thanks and gratitude, and is grounded in constant reflection on the qualities and attributes of God, qualities like infinite, eternal, all-loving, all-forgiving, pure light, and so on. Contemplative prayer seeks no result other than the cultivation of constant remembrance and constant awareness of His presence.

Meditation and contemplative prayer are practices that can absolutely transform your life. If you are frustrated because you haven't gotten what you wanted, what you hoped for, what you prayed for, what you fantasized that God had promised to you, these two paths offer an opportunity to begin to unfold that which God *has freely offered* to you . . . the ability to know, recognize, and feel His presence within and around you . . . eternally . . . supporting you and sustaining you through every moment of your life.

CHAPTER 26

Learn to See as God Sees, to Love as God Loves

Something within you dies when you bear the unbearable,
and it is only in that dark night of the soul
that you are prepared to see as God sees,
and to love as God loves.

RAM DASS

The notion of the dark night of the soul was first explored by Saint John of the Cross in his extraordinary spiritual manifesto of the same title. It refers to those moments when we feel all is lost, that there is nothing but despair, that all hope for joy and connection with God is gone. We are left totally bereft, abandoned, and distraught with no hope and no will to go on.

It is exactly in those moments when *real* transformation can occur. It is exactly in those moments when our separative ego mind has been completely exhausted, confounded, and derailed so that we can finally let go and transcend into another reality. It is in those moments when we can really begin to "let go and let God."

Thomas Merton said, "Prayer and love are really learned in the hour when prayer becomes impossible and your heart turns to stone."[1] In other words, we might never know the extraordinary bliss of God if we hadn't experienced the most devastating disappointments and losses life can offer.

Saint John of the Cross and Thomas Merton are just two voices in a huge choir of seekers who, throughout the ages, have understood this concept clearly. It is not in getting what we want that we find true joy. We find true joy when we give up wanting. Then we can discover the beauty and joy inherent in what is. Immaculée Ilibagiza, author of the extraordinary book *Left to Tell: Discovering God amidst the Rwandan Holocaust*, is another, more recent member of this choir. Having watched her entire family and most of her friends brutally beaten, raped, tortured, and murdered, Ilibagiza shares a story of survival that is an astounding portrayal of miracles and forgiveness. The greatest miracle of all is her ability to both love and forgive those who tortured and murdered her family. Through witnessing humanity at its worst, she was catapulted into a pure, unconditional Love beyond all human concepts, values, and limitations.

The point is, God is within us. Always within us. But we have forgotten. We don't notice. We mechanically stumble through life thinking that we know what we need to be happy, and we know where we can find it. Yet we keep looking in all the wrong places. We look in places that are familiar, the places where we think we *should* be able to find happiness, even though we have never really found happiness there.

We're like the drunk who is out on the sidewalk stumbling around under a streetlight, hunched over, staring at the pavement. He sees someone coming.

"Can you help me?" the drunk says. "I've lost my watch." So the good Samaritan says, "Sure," and begins to help the drunk. He, too, starts visually combing the sidewalk, bending over, looking all around, trying to help this poor desperate drunk find his missing watch. Finally, convinced that they have both scanned the entire area several times over, the man looks at the drunk and says, "It doesn't seem to be here. Are you sure this is where you lost it?"

"Oh, no!" says the drunk. "I lost it over in the alley."

The helper becomes exasperated. "Why are we wasting our time looking here when you lost your watch in the alley?"

"Because there's a streetlight here," the drunk says matter-of-factly. "It's dark over in the alley."

Just like the drunk, we keep looking for happiness in places where we can't find it. We look for happiness in the places and things our culture values rather than in the subtle purity and depth of our own heart, our own soul. The storms of life break through our arrogance and confusion and force us to look within, simply because there is no other place left to look. When our hopes are dashed, when our greatest desires have been denied and our greatest fears have been realized, when the world has fallen down around us, if we let go and look within, we find pure, unconditional, unbounded Love.

If you doubt that, just look at what happened in New York City in the minutes, hours, and days immediately following the attack on the World Trade Center on September 11, 2001. While the attack itself might be seen as an example of humanity at its worst, the response of the people of New York was nothing short of angelic. When our minds were completely blown, when we didn't know what to do, where to go, or what was going to happen next, hundreds of thousands — if not millions — of us spontaneously reacted with gestures of love, kindness, generosity, friendliness, and bravery that in all probability had never been seen on such a widespread scale in New York City. The crime rate dropped to zero for several days. Total strangers who had never spoken to each other before were suddenly interacting like old friends. People invited strangers who were displaced from their hotel rooms and unable to leave the city into their homes.

When our minds were completely blown, our hearts spontaneously opened. Love and kindness poured out in abundance. We can only conclude that in that dark night of the soul, we had, at least temporarily, learned to see as God sees and to love as God loves.

Unfortunately, this blissful feeling did not last. As the shock and fear began to subside in subsequent weeks, we slowly, gradually reverted to our old disconnected, separate ways. Sometimes it seems as if the disconnection and separation are *worse* now than they were before September 11.

But in those hours, days, and weeks, we got a taste of heaven. It was a precious and rare opportunity — one that, as a culture, we shouldn't so easily have squandered.

As we read and reflect on the issues covered in this book, we can choose to "be the change we wish to see in the world." We can choose to do all we can do to bring that amazing Light of love and peace into the world again... to keep the flame of Love alive.

Dramatic, all-encompassing spiritual transformations don't just happen on their own. Have we been sitting back, just waiting for God to turn a switch and make everything on earth lovely and wonderful? Are we so lazy and complacent that we feel everything should be done *for* us? Perhaps we actually have to *do* something. Perhaps each and every one of us actually has to take responsibility for making the world a better place.

Even if the rest of the world didn't respond, if you or I turned out to be the only ones on earth whose hearts longed to see as God sees and to love as God loves, still, life would be infinitely more beautiful than if we stayed attached to anger, judgment, and divisiveness.

Imagine... just loving everyone... just being in love all the time ... incapable of hatred or fear... only love... floating in God. What else have you got to do? It's worth a try.

Don't you think?

CHAPTER 27

The Infinite Nature of Truth; the Infinite Nature of You!

Only through a clear and tranquil mind
is the true nature of spiritual infinity grasped . . .
When every moment is rich with eternal significance
there is neither the lingering clinging to the dead past,
nor a longing expectation for the future,
but an integral living in the eternal Now.

MEHER BABA, *DISCOURSES*

During our journey together, we have taken various approaches to explore one simple truth. And this truth, though simple, may well be the most difficult aspect of spiritual life to grasp. Because this truth is, in essence, *impossible* to comprehend with our human mind.

It is the truth of Infinity.

To gain some sense of the difficulty you have comprehending Infinity, just go out and look at the sky. Look at it during the day. Look at it at night. Just look and ponder the vastness of the sky. Lie down in the grass, or on a lounge chair, and just gaze up at the sky until you can feel your own soul begin to merge with it. Recognize that what you are looking at has no end . . . no walls . . . no borders . . . no boundaries.

It is *infinite...* and you are a part of it. Do this exercise frequently as one way to embark on the path of meditation. Just use the sky as the object of your focus and recognize that the boundless space at which you are gazing exists within you, too: every bit as vast, every bit as spacious, every bit as incomprehensible.

The infinite universe has sometimes been referred to as "God's shadow." Obviously, only an infinite Being could cast an infinite shadow. How can we possibly comprehend that with our minds?

We can't. And we are completely habituated to experiencing life through our minds. We can scarcely imagine another way to perceive reality. That is our essential spiritual problem, because, as we have discussed repeatedly, our minds just aren't capable of actually *experiencing* life or spiritual experience; they are capable only of *thinking* about life. The effect of living in our minds is that we remain separate from experience. We are always evaluating and categorizing, analyzing and judging. Experience, and enlightenment, come through faculties other than rational thought.

Spiritual awakening does not come through deductive reasoning or analytic thought. It isn't a conclusion we suddenly arrive at. It comes through breaking free from the bondage of our minds. Spiritual awakening comes from transcending thought and moving into a different realm of consciousness, a realm of being rather than knowing.

Our minds can, at best, attempt to order, define, and analyze data. But from the spiritual point of view, when our minds order, define, and analyze the data connected to our existence, they often wind up creating a structure for something that — in a very real sense — has no structure. Most of our religions have grown up around the teachings of visionaries who had no choice other than to use human words and concepts to attempt to describe the indescribable, to explain the unexplainable. We have lost the essence of their teachings when we have gotten attached to their words and stories rather than to the formless essence *behind* the words.

The great Hindu master Ramakrishna achieved enlightenment through three different paths — Hinduism, Christianity, and Islam. He would often attempt to describe God to his devotees. But whenever he began, he would spontaneously slip into *sahaj samadhi*, the highest state of God-realization. Suddenly he would fall silent. A radiant smile would spread across his face. Tears of joy would stream down his cheeks. His body would go limp. If he was standing, he would spontaneously topple over. His devotees would try to catch his body before it crashed to the ground. When he returned to "normal" consciousness, he would again try to explain what he was experiencing in that inner state of ecstatic, transcendent awareness. But every time he tried, he would get to a certain point and then he would slip right back into *samadhi* and fall over again.

Finally, he would say, "I want so much to tell you what it's like, but the Divine Mother won't let me."

The mystical experience of God is the classic experience about which it is said, "For one who has experienced it, no explanation is necessary, and for one who hasn't, no explanation is possible." William James called this aspect of mystical experience "ineffability": "The subject of [a mystical experience] immediately says that it defies expression, that no adequate report of it can be given in words. It follows from this that its quality must be directly experienced."[1]

Yet despite all of the mystery and paradox that surrounds the direct encounter with God, it is the most familiar experience a human being can have. It is the stripping away of all illusory identities and all pretense. It is the return home, back to our true nature, our true identity, the direct awareness of our soul. When we encounter God, we immediately recognize our true nature, so long forgotten in the daily humdrum of worldly thoughts and exhausting, self-absorbed concerns.

From the vantage point of our highest awareness, the dreamlike nature of everything else is vividly brought into focus. Our human melodramas seem trivial, almost comical. A clear and vivid realization arises that the only thing required for us to feel successful in our human life is Love . . . just Love . . . only Love.

Love is all that matters. Nothing else does.

Love is God. Love is Eternal. And Love is Infinite. When we love purely, without thought of self, without expectation of reward, we are connecting directly with God. But every little hint of wanting will squeeze out another degree of that precious, holy communion.

All souls are eternal, because all souls are God. Every apparent individual soul is a part of the One. The closest approximation of God we can attain in our human forms is to become as loving, as forgiving, and as inclusive as possible, to recognize that we are all One . . . that every being on earth is a brother or a sister . . . that no amount of suffering or disappointment can rob us of the infinite nature of our souls and our infinite capacity to love.

Quite simply, the holiest souls on earth are the most loving souls. It doesn't really matter what we think, believe, or profess. The real question is, how much love have we brought into the world, how much healing, how much alleviation of suffering, how much diminution of separation?

Meher Baba suggested that in many circumstances a responsible, loving atheist is far more "blessed" than someone who *presumes* to be a devout believer.[2] He said, "A jolly, devil-may-care fellow may have a better heart than a dry-as-dust ascetic."[3]

Every religious path has led individuals to God, to the Light, to the One. And every religious path has been used to spread hatred, judgment, division, and separation. No spiritual path has the exclusive route to God. The issue always comes down to whether one is using one's chosen path as a series of guideposts pointing toward the Light *or* as a vehicle to justify feeling superior to everyone in the world who doesn't believe the same thing.

Ultimately, God is equally approachable through all religions, and through no religion. There are many points along the path where discipline, structure, and dedication are immensely useful. But finally, like all other structures, they can become obstacles to true spiritual freedom. Hugh Prather once created a church he named "The Dispensable Church," because he believed that any spiritual path worth its salt should be dispensed with when the essence of the teaching has been realized. Throughout history, human beings have looked to others who appear knowledgeable to tell them what to do, how to behave, how to make sense of this strange, chaotic universe, how to make meaning out of an otherwise confusing human existence. When those we turn to are sincere and evolved lovers of God, their help can be immensely useful. Unfortunately, most spiritual teachers are subject to the very same human foibles the rest of humanity is subject to, and sometimes disappointment and disillusionment follow in the wake of their teaching.

There is a wonderful story of a Buddhist teacher who was challenged by one of his students for being hypocritical. He would instruct his students to eat slowly and mindfully. Then this student would observe him eating quickly and sloppily. Finally, the student decided to confront the teacher.

"Master, I have noticed that you don't seem to be able to follow your own teachings. What's going on here?"

The teacher leaned back in his seat and smiled. "You should be thankful for the imperfections in your teachers," he said. "They are there to remind you that the Buddha is nowhere to be found but inside yourself."

That is the overarching message of this book.

The Buddha, the Christ, the godhead, your true nature, your true self, nirvana, *samadhi*. . . are all inside you. You don't find them in the fulfillment of desire. You don't find them in the expansion of needs. You don't find them in the pursuit of the perpetually elusive dream of intellectual understanding. You don't even find them in "answered" prayers.

You find them in your own heart, your own soul, your own consciousness. You find them by expanding your capacity for love and forgiveness. Whenever the things you have prayed for have not been forthcoming, don't assume that the Creator is ignoring you or punishing you. Ask what it is — *right now* — that the Creator is offering you instead.

We are never left alone. We are never ignored. We are never abandoned. Our connection to God is closer than our own breath. No matter what.

For ages and ages we have sought happiness, peace of mind, and security in all the places we can never find them. Now we can finally turn toward the Light and resolve to *pray* — constantly — to feel closer to God, to be a pure vessel for His infinite Love . . . to know that He exists and to know that we are One.

When we do, we are offering the one prayer that our Creator eternally answers,

"Yes! I *am* with you, in you, and around you . . . always."

In Love there is no separation. No fear. No doubt.

In Love there is no you, no me . . . just "we."

Just One.

Notes

Chapter 1: A Look at Our Human Predicament

1. Matt. 6:19 (Revised Standard Version).
2. Matt. 18:20 (Revised Standard Version).
3. Edward M. Hallowell, *Connect: Twelve Vital Ties That Open Your Heart, Lengthen Your Life, and Deepen Your Soul* (New York: Pantheon, 1999), xv.
4. Meher Baba, quoted in *Sai Baba, the Perfect Master* (Pune, India: Meher Era Publications, 1991), 115–16.

Chapter 2: The Treasure Once Found...

1. *The Complete Works of Swami Vivekananda* (Hollywood, CA: Vedanta Press, 2003), vol. 1, chap. 6.

2. Byron Katie, *Loving What Is: Four Questions That Can Change Your Life* (New York: Harmony, 2002), 1.
3. Foundation for Inner Peace, *A Course in Miracles* (Mill Valley, CA: Foundation for Inner Peace, 1992).

Chapter 3: Understanding That Which Is beyond Understanding

1. Saint Anselm, *The Proslogion*, chap. 2.
2. Matt. 19:24 (Revised Standard Version).
3. Mary Baker Eddy, *Science and Health with Key to the Scriptures* (Boston: First Church of Christ Scientist, 1971), chap. 6.

Chapter 5: When Expectations Turn Upside Down

1. Mohandas K. Gandhi, *Prayer* (Berkeley, CA: Berkeley Hills Books, 2000), 24.

Chapter 6: When Fear Inhibits Love

1. John 4:18 (Revised Standard Version).

Chapter 7: When the World Turns Upside Down

1. Harold S. Kushner, *When Bad Things Happen to Good People* (New York: Anchor, 1981), 50–51.
2. Albert Einstein, quoted in Ram Dass, *Paths to God* (New York: Harmony, 2004), 75.
3. Pope Benedict XVI, Christmas Eve homily, Vatican Basilica, December 24, 2005. Available at http://www.vatican.va/holy_father/benedict_xvi/homilies/2005/documents/hf_ben-xvi_hom_20051224_christmas_en.html (accessed July 2007).
4. Meher Baba, *God Speaks* (Walnut Creek, CA: Sufism Reoriented, 1973), chap. 2.

Chapter 9: We Have a Limited View of Life and of Ourselves

1. Robert Kastenbaum, "Gerontology's Search for Understanding," *Gerontologist* 18 (February 1978): 59–63.

Chapter 11: Believing I Can Be Happy Only If I Get What I Want

1. Matt. 6:19 (Revised Standard Version).
2. Dan Baker and Cameron Stauth, *What Happy People Know: How the New Science of Happiness Can Change Your Life for the Better* (New York: St. Martin's/Griffin, 2003), 43.

Chapter 12: God Will Give Me What I Want If I Am Good

1. John Welshons, *Awakening from Grief: Finding the Way Back to Joy* (Maui: Inner Ocean, 2003), xxiii.
2. William James, *The Varieties of Religious Experience* (New York: Modern Library, 1902), 378–79.

Chapter 14: It Isn't Supposed to Be This Way

1. Katie, *Loving What Is*, 1.

Chapter 19: You Aren't Being Punished

1. Gal. 6:7 (Revised Standard Version).

Chapter 23: How This Experience Can Deepen Your Spirituality

1. Daniel Goleman, *Emotional Intelligence* (New York: Bantam, 1995), chap. 6.

Chapter 24: Allow for the Possibility That the Universe Is Perfect

1. Matt. 25:40 (Revised Standard Version).
2. Brother Lawrence, *The Practice of the Presence of God* (Garden City, NY: Image, 1977).

Chapter 26: Learn to See as God Sees, to Love as God Loves

1. Thomas Merton, *New Seeds of Contemplation* (New York: New Directions, 1961), 221.

Chapter 27: The Infinite Nature of Truth; the Infinite Nature of You!

1. James, *Varieties of Religious Experience*, 371.
2. Meher Baba, quoted in C. B. Purdom, *The God Man* (Myrtle Beach, SC: Sheriar Press, 1971), 213.
3. Meher Baba, *Sparks of the Truth* (Myrtle Beach, SC: Sheriar Press, 1971), 94.

Recommended Reading

Baker, Dan. *What Happy People Know: How the New Science of Happiness Can Change Your Life for the Better*. New York: St. Martin's/Griffin, 2003.

Carlson, Richard. *What About the Big Stuff?: Finding Strength and Moving Forward When the Stakes Are High*. New York: Hyperion, 2002.

———. *You Can Be Happy No Matter What: Five Principles for Keeping Life in Perspective*. Novato, CA: New World Library, 1992.

Carlson, Richard, and Benjamin Shield. *For the Love of God: A Handbook for the Spirit*. Novato, CA: New World Library, 1997.

Chödrön, Pema. *The Places That Scare You: A Guide to Fearlessness in Difficult Times*. Boston: Shambhala, 2001.

———. *When Things Fall Apart: Heart Advice for Difficult Times.* Boston: Shambhala, 2000.

Chopra, Deepak. *How to Know God: The Soul's Journey into the Mystery of Mysteries.* New York: Harmony, 2000.

Cope, Stephen. *The Wisdom of Yoga: A Seeker's Guide to Extraordinary Living.* New York: Bantam, 2007.

———. *Yoga and the Quest for the True Self.* New York: Bantam, 2000.

Dalai Lama, the. *The Art of Happiness: A Handbook for Living.* New York: Riverhead, 1998.

———. *How to Expand Love: Widening the Circle of Loving Relationships.* New York: Atria, 2005.

Dossey, Larry. *Prayer Is Good Medicine: How to Reap the Healing Benefits of Prayer.* San Francisco: HarperSanFrancisco, 1996.

Dyer, Wayne W. *Inspiration: Your Ultimate Calling.* Carlsbad, CA: Hay House, 2007.

———. *The Power of Intention: Learning to Co-create Your World Your Way.* Carlsbad, CA: Hay House, 2005.

———. *There's a Spiritual Solution to Every Problem.* New York: Harper, 2001.

Foundation for Inner Peace. *A Course in Miracles.* Mill Valley, CA: Foundation for Inner Peace, 1992.

Fox, Emmet. *The Sermon on the Mount: The Key to Success in Life.* San Francisco, HarperSanFrancisco, 1989.

Goldstein, Joseph. *The Experience of Insight: A Simple and Direct Guide to Buddhist Meditation.* Boston: Shambhala, 1987.

Grollman, Earl A. *Living When a Loved One Has Died.* Boston: Beacon Press, 1987.

Hallowell, Edward M. *Connect: 12 Vital Ties That Open Your Heart, Lengthen Your Life, and Deepen Your Soul.* New York: Pantheon, 1999.

Harvey, Andrew. *The Direct Path: Creating a Personal Journey to the Divine Using the World's Spiritual Traditions.* New York: Broadway, 2000.

Ilibagiza, Immaculée. *Left to Tell: Discovering God Amidst the Rwandan Holocaust*. Carlsbad, CA: Hay House, 2007.

Katie, Byron. *Loving What Is: Four Questions That Can Change Your Life*. New York: Three Rivers, 2003.

Keith, Kent M. *Anyway: The Paradoxical Commandments*. New York: Putnam, 2001.

Klein, Allen. *The Courage to Laugh: Humor, Hope, and Healing in the Face of Death and Dying*. New York: Tarcher, 1998.

———. *The Healing Power of Humor: Techniques for Getting through Loss, Setbacks, Upsets, Disappointments, Difficulties, Trials, Tribulations, and All That Not-So-Funny Stuff*. New York: Tarcher, 1989.

Krishnamurti, J. *Freedom From the Known*. New York: Harper & Row, 1969.

Kushner, Harold S. *When Bad Things Happen to Good People*. New York: Anchor, 2004.

Lama Surya Das. *Awakening the Buddha Within: Tibetan Wisdom for the Western World*. New York: Broadway, 1997.

———. *Awakening to the Sacred: Creating a Personal Spiritual Life*. New York: Broadway, 2000.

———. *Letting Go of the Person You Used to Be: Lessons on Change, Loss, and Spiritual Transformation*. New York: Broadway, 2004.

Lesser, Elizabeth. *Broken Open: How Difficult Times Can Help Us Grow*. New York: Villard, 2005.

———. *The Seeker's Guide: Making Your Life a Spiritual Adventure*. New York: Villard, 2000.

Levine, Stephen. *Who Dies?: An Investigation of Conscious Living and Conscious Dying*. New York: Doubleday, 1982.

———. *A Year to Live: How to Live This Year as If It Were Your Last*. New York: Bell Tower, 1997.

Mascaro, Juan, trans. *The Bhagavad Gita*. New York: Penguin Classics, 2003.

Meher Baba. *Discourses*. Myrtle Beach, SC: Sheriar Press, 1987.

———. *God Speaks*. Walnut Creek, CA: Sufism Reoriented, 1973.

Ram Dass. *Journey of Awakening: A Meditator's Guidebook*. New York: Bantam, 1990.

———. *Paths to God: Living the Bhagavad Gita*. New York: Harmony, 2004.

———. *Still Here: Embracing Aging, Changing, and Dying*. New York: Riverhead, 2000.

Rodegast, Pat, and Judith Stanton. *Emmanuel's Book: A Manual for Living Comfortably in the Cosmos*. New York: Bantam, 1985.

———. *Emmanuel's Book II: The Choice for Love*. New York: Bantam, 1989.

———. *Emmanuel's Book III: What Is an Angel Doing Here?* New York: Bantam, 1994.

Rosenberg, Larry. *Living in the Light of Death: On the Art of Being Truly Alive*. Boston: Shambhala, 2001.

Sogyal Rimpoche. *The Tibetan Book of Living and Dying*. San Francisco: HarperSanFrancisco, 1994.

Swami Prabhavananda. *The Sermon on the Mount According to Vedanta*. Hollywood, CA: Vedanta Press, 1991.

Tolle, Eckhart. *A New Earth: Awakening to Your Life's Purpose*. New York: Dutton, 2005.

———. *The Power of Now: A Guide to Spiritual Enlightenment*. Novato, CA: New World Library, 1999.

Williamson, Marianne. *A Return to Love: Reflections on the Principles of* A Course in Miracles. New York: HarperCollins, 1992.

Index

A

D

E

F

H

I

J

K

L

M

T

U

V

W

Y

About the Author

John E. Welshons is a speaker, workshop leader, and meditation teacher. He is the author of *Awakening from Grief: Finding the Way Back to Joy*, a book that came from his thirty-five years of helping people deal with dramatic life change and loss. John has studied world religions throughout his life. Beginning in 1976, he trained with Dr. Elisabeth Kübler-Ross, and he has also worked extensively with Ram Dass and Stephen Levine.

His workshops and lectures are offered in hospitals, hospices, corporations, colleges, universities, yoga schools, and personal growth centers. He is also available for one-on-one consultations. John lives in northeastern New Jersey, twelve miles west of New York City. John's speaking schedule and more about him and his work can be found at his website, www.johnwelshons.com.

New World Library is dedicated to publishing books and other media that inspire and challenge us to improve the quality of our lives and the world.

We are a socially and environmentally aware company, and we strive to embody the ideals presented in our publications. We recognize that we have an ethical responsibility to our customers, our staff members, and our planet.

We serve our customers by creating the finest publications possible on personal growth, creativity, spirituality, wellness, and other areas of emerging importance. We serve New World Library employees with generous benefits, significant profit sharing, and constant encouragement to pursue their most expansive dreams.

As a member of the Green Press Initiative, we print an increasing number of books with soy-based ink on 100 percent postconsumer-waste recycled paper. Also, we power our offices with solar energy and contribute to nonprofit organizations working to make the world a better place for us all.

Our products are available
in bookstores everywhere.
For our catalog, please contact:

New World Library
14 Pamaron Way
Novato, California 94949

Phone: 415-884-2100 or 800-972-6657
Catalog requests: Ext. 50
Orders: Ext. 52
Fax: 415-884-2199
Email: escort@newworldlibrary.com

To subscribe to our electronic newsletter, visit
www.newworldlibrary.com